VOICES
Singers & Critics

To QUITA
who was there

VOICES
Singers & Critics

J.B. Steane

Amadeus Press
Reinhard G. Pauly, General Editor
Portland, Oregon

Reprinted 1993
First published in 1992 by
Gerald Duckworth & Co. Ltd.
The Old Piano Factory
48 Hoxton Square, London N1 6PB

© 1992 by J.B. Steane

First published in North America in 1992 by
Amadeus Press (an imprint of Timber Press, Inc.)
9999 S.W. Wilshire, Suite 124
Portland, Oregon 97225, USA

ISBN 0-931340-54-3

Acknowledgements

The articles in this book were first published as follows (references to the pages of this book are given in *italics*). The author and publisher wish to thank all the editors involved for giving permission to reprint.

Part I. *Opera Now*: *3-8*, June 1990; *8-16*, May 1989; *16-22*, Aug. 1989; *22-8*, Oct. 1990; *29-34*, Nov. 1990; *35-40*, Oct. 1989; *40-6*, Dec. 1989; *47-55*, Mar. 1990; *56-60*, July 1989; *61-5*, July 1990; *65-71*, Aug./Sept. 1990; *71-81*, June & Sept. 1989; *82-7*, Apr. 1990; *87-93*, May 1990; *94-9*, Jan. 1990; *99-106*, Feb. 1990; *107-11*, Apr. 1989; *111-16*, Dec. 1980.

Part II. *Opera News*: *119-24*, Dec. 1988; *167-72*, Aug. 1989; *Recorded Sound*: *125-35*, Apr.-July 1977; *Musical Times*: Feb. 1989; EMI Records: *151-9*, CDS7 47308 8; CDS7 49344 2; CDS7 47304 8; CDS7 47959 8; *179-85*, RLS7700; *186-96*, EX290790 3; BBC Radio 3: *136-44*, 29 Aug. 1983; *173-4*, 26 Oct. 1980; Lecture to the Dante Alighieri Society, University of Birmingham: *174-8*

Part III. *Opera*: *199-208*, June 1981; *209-19*, Sept. 1981; *220-7*, Feb. 1982; *227-34*, Apr. 1982; *234-40*, June 1982; *241-7*, Oct. 1982; *247-53*, June 1983; *254-62*, June 1985; *263-9*, Feb. 1987; *270-6*, Nov. 1983; *276-84*, Aug. 1984.

Photo credits

Decca: 1 (Barry Glass); 3 (Barda); 6 (John Swannell); 17 (J. Henry Fair); 12, 16.
EMI: 8, 36 (Bibliothèque Nationale/Roger Pic); 9 (Fayer); 10, 29 (Christiane Steiner); 11, 27 (Angus McBean); 20 (Siegfried Lauterwasser); 21 (Trevor Leighton); 23 (Walter Bird); 37 (Luxardo); 38 (Reg Wilson); 61 (Douglas Glass); 32, 35.
Opera: 13, 15, 19, 22, 24, 44-7, 53-5, 57-60, 62-6.
Marc Ricaldone: 18, 51.

Other photographs are from the author's collection.

Photoset in North Wales by
Derek Doyle & Associates, Mold, Clwyd
Printed in Great Britain by
Redwood Books, Trowbridge

Contents

Contents

Part II. Ten Singers

Part III. Critics at the Opera

Preface

My earlier book on singing, *The Grand Tradition* (1974), confined itself almost entirely to its proposed subject, '70 Years of Singing on Record'. In doing so it relegated for the time being a question which was always at the back of the mind and sometimes claimed immediate attention. Basically, it was a question about truth: how far can we *believe* our records?

No doubt in some form and degree the thought has occurred to everybody who has ever bought from a record shop. Of the very old recordings it used to be objected that the technical processes then in use were so primitive that they were bound to have done much less than justice, while with the advent of electrical recording voices could be so amplified that justice or truth was evaded by flattery. Then came the long-playing record, made up of tapes which everybody knew could be put together in all sorts of clever ways, and which again called into question the credibility of the finished product. Even with 'live' recordings it was not always possible to be sure that the best of one version had not been added to the best of another, with both 'cleaned up' later in the studio.

These are familiar misgivings and pertinent enough, but it was a different kind of anomaly, or of relationship between record and truth, that bothered me. This concerned the differences between two *kinds* of record: the aural and the written. To some extent it was simply a matter of a discrepancy of judgment or impressions. The soprano who, to her contemporaries, was 'cold' ('there was skating on the Nile last night', they reported when Emma Eames sang Aida) seems disarmingly warm on records. The Carmen whose vibrato as represented by her recordings rattles like shaken dice was the subject of extensive commentary 'in the flesh' but rarely (or ever) in respect of this particular characteristic. Within one's own experience, Peter Pears as recorded sounds like a caricature of the living voice as remembered. In many instances records give a misleading view of the relative 'size' or fullness of singers' voices (leading to an expectancy, for instance, that Callas might have sounded more powerful than Sutherland, whereas memory puts it the other way round); and commonly they may leave one unprepared for the beauty of

vii

a voice (Leonie Rysanek is an example here) or for the extent to which a performance (for instance, Gwyneth Jones as Elektra) may be stunningly effective as singing in the theatre and yet have its worst features disturbingly highlighted if recorded.

Cumulatively, such observations may shake any faith in the gramophone record as history. The point is underlined by accounts in the musical papers and periodicals which repeatedly show that the important and valuable event of any particular month lay in the appearance not of some artist who ranks high in the record catalogues but of one who may scarcely show up in them at all. Thinking of Covent Garden in the 1930s, for instance, and asked who it was to whom Ernest Newman attributed 'truly great singing of the kind to which one instantly calls upon one's memory of Chaliapin to supply the parallel', one might eagerly name a score of artists before Rosa Pauly. Our map of the singing world has been drawn very largely with the record catalogues in mind. One might assume that when *Winterreise* was performed in London by two singers within a month of each other in 1926 it would be Elena Gerhardt's interpretation rather than John Coates's that would have caught the attention of the critics: not so in the *Musical Times*, however. Moreover, there could be recitals by Lehmann, Schumann, McCormack and even Chaliapin, all in the same season, and the written accounts could still leave the strong impression that for musical satisfaction you would have done far better to go and hear Miss Dorothy Silk.

It was this line of thought that prompted the studies of critics and their comments on the English opera scene of the interwar years which now comprise the third part of this present book. In only a few of them, most notably that on Herman Klein, who wrote for the *Gramophone* magazine, is the point made explicitly, but all have it to some extent as an intended reference. Equally, in the essays on individual singers in Part II, the relationship between the 'live' and the recorded art is a main theme. In the discussion of voice-types, the subject of Part I, illustrations are drawn sometimes from 'live' experience, sometimes from records, and often from both, or the one in relation to the other. In fact, records play throughout most of these pages, but many simultaneously admit another presence: rather as when the pictures in a photograph album are overlaid by memories that have an independent life, sometimes telling the camera that it has lied.

Meanwhile, a little more should perhaps be said about the origins of these essays, particularly of those in Part I. They were commissioned by the editors of *Opera Now*, and the first in the series (the section on the basso cantante) appeared in the magazine's first number, in April 1989. My brief was to take a type of voice as the subject of each article, describing it, discussing some representative items in the repertoire and explaining why it was appropriate, illustrating it also with examples of singers, past and present, who fall within the category. All this in 2,500 words. I hope I may be forgiven for pointing out one of the problems, which was that the magazine's likely readership ranged from those who knew very little but might want to find out more, to those who knew it all already, or considered that they did. Ideally, one hoped to entertain the connoisseurs while informing the novices who in turn might find something to intrigue them in points which were presumptuously aimed at the more knowledgeable. All that I can say about the success is that at least the series survived the numerous changes of editorship and policy, and was allowed to complete its run in the twentieth issue with basso profondo, subject to editorial pruning and no doubt all the better for it.

Throughout the series I resolved not to use the German word 'Fach', even though it is the obvious and the right one. It simply seemed (and seems) to me that the English tongue does not take to it, so I had recourse to terms such as 'voice-type', scarcely more elegant than the German but easier in the utterance. Of the many writings consulted from time to time I must mention Richard Miller's *English, French, German and Italian Techniques of Singing* (1977) which is a most enlightened and enlightening study of the voice-types as differentiated in these national schools. The subject arises in most of these chapters, and the interested reader will find them more systematically and fully dealt with in Dr Miller's admirable thesis, my own contribution being essentially to provide illustrations by reference to particular singers and their recordings.

The reader may also detect a certain misgiving on the writer's part concerning the whole proposed system of differentiating between the voice-types (or 'Fächer') largely by reference to factors such as power, range and repertoire. Repertoires overlap, range may be misleading, and power is not such a straightforward proposition as it may seem (think of those performances of *Siegfried* with their Wotan world-famous for his massively powerful voice which, however, we hear less well than the squeaky and insignificant tenor of Mime, which comes over loud and clear). At several points I felt a strong desire to cut across the recognised types (lyric, dramatic, spinto and so forth) and recategorise by *timbre*. Vocabulary would then have been a difficulty. The 'thin' and the 'fat', the 'dark' and the 'light', the 'straight', the 'ripe', the 'lush' and the 'loose': such not very satisfactory terms would be the ones we would have to use till somebody devises better. It must have been some such problem of nomenclature that led the French to commemorate their Marie Cornélie Falcon (1812-1897) and Jean-Blaise Martin (1769-1837) by naming voice-types after them. The trouble is that their precise timbre is now lost to memory: if a number of singers whose records served for reference could be set up as archetypes of the essential timbres, there might be something in it.

Of the essays on individual singers in Part II I need only remark that some were occasional pieces, written (as with Schumann and Schipa) as centenary tributes or (Rethberg) shortly after their death; others (Schwarzkopf, Callas, Tauber, Battistini) were for record albums, where critical discussion was sometimes subordinated to the provision of biographical information; and two (Ponselle, Martinelli) come from broadcasts or, in the case of Martinelli, part-broadcast, part-lecture.

The critics in Part III speak for themselves. They were all characterful and highly articulate writers. My principal regret here is that some who on their own merits deserve to be there are not included: Percy Scholes, Richard Capell, Francis Toye, W.J. Turner, for example. There comes a point, however, where the ground has been gone over often enough, and the very names become wearisome. An extremist then gains an undeserved welcome because of his difference, and since extremism can hardly go further than Kaikhosru Sorabji's, with his denunciations of the execrable, the detestable and the crapulous, even that ground is cut away.

The point about these writers, of course, is that though they were men of their own time and journalists concerned with the events of the now distant 1920s and 30s, their problems and endeavours are those of critics in any age. In many ways, modern critical practice has improved a good deal on theirs. Even so, their writings as represented here may prompt one bit of self-searching among their successors. In this query of mine, this search for another form of 'record' to put against the 'gramophone-history' that might otherwise be misleadingly enshrined as 'truth', there were at least these often vivid and detailed written accounts to consult. They were compiled by critics who were interested in singing and singers, and who were not (in their reporting on opera) so monopolised by the stage-producer and his work, or by the conductor and his, that they had no more than a line or two to bestow on the singers at the end of their account. Under modern conditions it may be too much to hope that in half a century from now a searcher into the voices and singers of the present day will find critics whose perceptions of the truth as they hear it in live performances are as fully accessible as those of Newman, Cardus and the rest in the interwar years. It will be easy enough to check up on contemporary views of Götz Friedrich, Patrice Chéreau and Peter Sellars, or of James Levine, Riccardo Muti and Sir Colin Davis. But for the impression made by the singing in opera (not the acting) of Julia Varady, Thomas Allen and even Placido Domingo, truth is likely to be sought almost exclusively in the disc, and the disc will tell only part.

June 1992   J.B.S.

Part I

An Assortment of Voices

1. Soprano

ᓚ Leggiero and soubrette ᔕ

On eighteenth-century canvas in a fine gilt frame there stands and smiles a pretty girl, sweet seventeen if she's a day, and not a care in the world. A pink-embroidered apron tied with ribbons, ribbons also in her curly hair: these adorn a figure lithe and supple, the slender waist inviting the encircling arm while even then preparing to slip still more provocatively out of reach. The lips are lightly parted and there is mischief in the smile. The left forefinger rests upon the cheek while the middle finger and thumb thoughtfully support the dimpled chin. She is, of course, a little charmer, and, as she has often been told, a little minx. There is no great harm in her, but she likes to have her own way.

Transported to the operatic stage, she is the light soprano, the leggiero or soubrette. She will not often turn up in tragedy, though that is not unknown. She sometimes takes the leading part in comedy, but quite often shares honours with, or is secondary to, the principal lyric soprano. Socially, she is rarely a member of the aristocracy; more frequently a lady's maid who is on familiar terms with her employers and more than a match for any vexatious relation or meddlesome visitor. She takes a full part in ensembles, and her solos are prime favourites with the audience.

The trouble is that she is so eternally typecast. That smile of hers beams across the centuries, from Monteverdi to Tippett, and though it is very engaging it has also become a little fixed. The ease with which she can be defined, as with the imaginary portrait described above, is proportionate to the limitations of the stereotype. She can smile, she can pout, may look winsome or demure, may put a hand on hip or both hands on hips, wag her finger or stamp her foot, flick her feather duster at a stage cobweb or an importunate suitor; but the possibilities are limited, and there is a certain sameness in all of them. She is the prisoner of her prettiness. Playful and knowing, coy and pert, she takes hearts on the first encounter and her little ways do not necessarily prove more winning on repetition. In fact she can become just a trifle vexatious herself, and the suspicion begins to arise that she is really a spoilt child

3

for whose wilfulness the old-fashioned remedy would perhaps not come amiss.

There are vocal limitations as well. She is a light soprano in two senses: that is, she has no great reserves of power, and her voice will be bright in tone-colour. What this really means in practice is that a small voice, of a type that would otherwise not be associated with grand opera, is trained to develop a penetrative capacity sufficient to compete with the orchestra and to carry in a large auditorium. This often means that the natural tone will be given a sharper point, and in this process the brightness will also be intensified (because a mellower, softer tone will be less likely to project). This bright edge to the voice becomes very like the fixed smile: it is part of the character, the very condition of performance. It can be more limiting still, for while the smile is an external feature that can be dropped, the brightness is *in* the voice, has become the voice's character. Much of the art of the light soprano involves the transcending of these limitations: slipping out of the portrait-frame, giving the character an independent life without affronting the conventions for which she was created, and extending the colour-range of the voice (and hence its emotional possibilities) without weakening the qualities which make up its individuality and its special usefulness.

The usefulness has been proven from opera's earliest days. Monteverdi, for instance, quickly found the dramatic value of contrast, and while the main business of Nero and Poppea or Ulysses and Penelope is unfolding, a lighter element is introduced both to give relief from high seriousness and to raise its status. Thus in *Il ritorno d'Ulisse in patria* after Penelope's long solos telling of her unhappiness there follows an enchanting scene between the maidservant, Melantho, and her sweetheart Eurymachus. The music has a benign melodic flow and a light-hearted rhythmic ease about it, while the relatively lowly characters enjoy freedom from the heroic trials and responsibilities of the great ones. Though this scene forms an interlude, Melantho later becomes instrumental in the plot as she adds to the influences upon Penelope to marry one of the suitors. She then brings the same nonchalant charm to her solo 'Ama dunque', contrasting with Penelope's languishing recitative. In *L'incoronazione di Poppea* there is a similar role, simply given the generic description 'damigella' or maidservant, who has a short scene of delicious lightness and grace with a page ('valetto'). They flirt together with completely happy success while the very next scene brings the death of Seneca, the moving tragedy at the heart of the opera. Here in Monteverdi the essential soubrette characteristics are already defined – the smiling charmer with the playful tongue ('What an observant young man … as naughty as Cupid') and, after a little coyness, bestowing the appropriate reward.

1. Soprano

The line goes on, with occasional bypaths. In *Dido and Aeneas*, for instance, Belinda, though an attendant spirit rather than a mere maidservant, has a partly similar function and the role is very much the light soprano's preserve. Whenever the pastoral convention comes into play, as when a shepherdess appears to sing the song of the nightingales ('Rossignols amoureux') in the final *divertissement* of Rameau's *Hippolyte et Aricie*, the light soprano is again in request. She is then the scheming little heroine of Pergolesi's *La serva padrona*, the well-named Serpina who tricks her master into marriage by pretending to run away with a soldier. In Cimarosa's *Il matrimonio segreto* she is there as the second daughter, Carolina, a lighter character than her elder sister, who is the prima donna. In Grétry's *Zémire et Azor* she is herself the heroine, the Cinderella-sister whose good nature saves the family and gives the Beast back his beauty. Haydn's operas abound in suitable roles, delightful ones too, such as the shepherdess Eurilla in *Orlando Paladino*, Nerina in *La fedeltà premiata*, the servant Lisetta in *Il mondo della luna*, a sparkling character, free in her ways but good at heart so that if (as she explains) she says 'yes' it is not at the expense of her virtue.

During this time the roles have grown more challenging to the singer. The Haydn operas call for some virtuosity, though the vocal range is kept within moderate limits. Mozart extends it in the single instance of Blonde in *Die Entführung aus dem Serail* but generally does not ask too much of his Susanna, Zerlina, Despina and Papagena. These, however, are roles at the heart of the repertoire (with Papagena probably to be exchanged at a later date for the heroine, Pamina). If Blonde is technically the most demanding, Zerlina is perhaps the most rewarding, Susanna the subtlest and Despina the most archetypal. Despina is exactly the little girl of the portrait.

Milder, less scheming and minxish, but still parts for this same singer are Marzelline in *Fidelio* and Aennchen in *Der Freischütz*. These are both secondary roles, but the light soprano takes over as heroine in the Italian comedies, most notably *Don Pasquale* and *L'elisir d'amore*. She now needs to watch her step – or rather, to watch this essential brightness of hers, for both in voice and manner it can become distinctly irritating. Norina's laughter over the romance she is reading on her entrance in *Don Pasquale* just needs to be of that piercing, highly professional kind to set one against this breezy, complacent young woman for the rest of the opera. Adina in *L'elisir*, too, needs a little warmth in her voice as well as the bright edge, and a little gentleness in her manner as well as the teach-him-a-lesson-for-his-own-good pertness. This will be still more imperative if she essays, as she well may, some of the French heroine roles such as Manon, Leila in *Les pêcheurs de perles*, perhaps Juliette, possibly Louise, even Mélisande. But in fact it always has to be borne in mind. Whatever the part – the maid Adele in *Die Fledermaus*, the Snow Maiden of Rimsky-Korsakov, the pretty daughters in *Falstaff* and *Gianni Schicchi*, the pretty secretary Bella in *Midsummer Marriage* – they all do well not to be *too* pretty and coy and bright-as-a-button: men don't always like it, and other women (would it be true to say?) never do.

Having said that, one also has to acknowledge that there appear to be different levels of tolerance among the European nations. As with other voices, the Latin races have tended towards a degree of brightness in their light sopranos which to ourselves, the Germans and Scandinavians is next thing to shrillness. Italian exponents tend to be edgy, strident at the top, 'white' in the lower middle register. The French also favour a young-sounding brightness even if it is thin and (to our ears) tweety. German light sopranos usually have more daintiness, the maidenly charm of the lyric soprano but less full-bodied and warm. The Slav races, often showing an affinity with the French in such matters, have produced a brighter, more piping type of voice. The English have their Gilbert and Sullivan soprano: 'She's very s-weet', as Anna Russell frigidly observes.

That, of course, is not fair. Not fair, for one thing, to Gilbert and Sullivan, or (for another) to the British light soprano. It does, however, raise another matter, that of the transfer of singers to and from the world of light entertainment – musicals, musical comedy, light opera. A good Gilbert and Sullivan soprano, for instance, is eminently transferable to many of the operatic roles under discussion. Elsie Griffin, who died in 1989 at the age of ninety-four, sings Mabel in *The Pirates of Penzance* with great accomplishment on records, as she did for years with the D'Oyly Carte Company; but she was also for a while a member of the Carl Rosa, singing such parts as Rosina in *The Barber of Seville* and Adele in *Die Fledermaus*. Valerie Masterson was principal soprano for D'Oyly Carte; she made us all take notice when, on records, she sang as the daughter of Mary Stuart opposite Caballé in Rossini's *Elisabetta, regina d'Inghilterra* and suffered not a bit in the inevitable comparison. Since then she has become a widely admired Marguerite, Juliette, Louise and (in *Julius Caesar*) Cleopatra. Irene Eisinger, a Glyndebourne Despina in the interwar years, sang in musical comedy and films; Adele Leigh, the original Bella of Tippett's *Midsummer Marriage*, spent much time in operetta. Equally there are those who, one supposes, could have had an operatic career specialising in these light roles but who chose not to: pre-eminent among them, Yvonne Printemps. And this in turn raises the question of – what are we to call it? – status.

All voice-types are equal, but some … Some are represented by the Jessye Normans or Adelina Pattis, the Luciano Pavarottis or Enrico Carusos of this world. Others are less glamorous, and the light soprano may even sometimes be a trifle apologetic. 'Oh, it was a light voice only', the retired Susanna will say. And then: 'I was ... well, you might almost say a soubrette.' Now here is an interesting word, and an interesting fate has befallen it. Old Provençal in origin, it is defined somewhat differently in different dictionaries, but 'coy', 'cunning', 'shrewd' and (less helpfully) 'reserved' are variously offered; in the early nineteenth century it appears also to have been in use in England to mean a maidservant or a lady's maid. I rather fancy that it has now lost these specific connotations and acquired instead a sense of denoting a singer somewhere betwixt opera house, musical comedy and the Folies Bergères. Singers themselves are usually not too keen on being described as 'soubrette' even if the kind of role they generally sing comes within the category. I suppose that one could quite justly object that, 'properly understood', it defines a character rather than a voice, and that it has for long contributed to the process of type-casting from which light sopranos in general would much prefer to be free.

Among modern singers who might not object to the description 'light soprano' but perhaps would draw the line at 'soubrette' are Kathleen Battle and Barbara Hendricks. As heard in Covent Garden, both have light voices, Hendricks sounding rather more slender than the voice heard on records, Battle coming over in the large house rather more effectively than one might suppose from hearing her in the concert hall. Of the two, Hendricks appears to be the more determined to distance herself from the soubrette, or the voice-image which that term calls up. She has mastered the art of making the most of her resources. By careful scaling of tone and volume she can give an impression of considerable power, and by preserving a concentrated, vibrant quality she achieves what might be described in social terms; from the lady's maid (the soubrette, the *damigella*) she ascends to the aristocracy. To take an example from her recordings, she sings Leila in *Les pêcheurs de perles* with the slender tone and bright quality of the light soprano, but also investing her singing with unusual warmth of feeling and a tone which confers dignity upon the girl she is portraying.

Battle is sweeter, less intense, less subtle as an interpreter: if the voice wears a face at all, it is a sunny one, uncalculating and uncomplicated. She too is not the soubrette in the sense of 'cunning, shrewd', as the dictionary has it, or in the vocal tradition of keen-edged brightness. A recording of her concert with Domingo in Tokyo during 1988 includes the *Don Pasquale* aria ('Quel guardo il cavaliere') and provides a good illustration of spirited (and often exquisite) soubrette-work kept within the bounds of a gentle tone and a gentle nature. For the brighter type of light soprano voice, also capable of a mellower softness, a fair representative would be another American soprano, Barbara Bonney.

Between them, these three have adapted much of the best of the various national schools, each of them giving performances of charm and distinction. For the charm of earlier years, two names come unbidden to mind, one still affectionately and widely remembered, the other fondly too but probably by only a small band of record enthusiasts – and that is Lotte Schoene. We must petition some enterprising company to bring out a compact disc, reviving lovely things from the roles of Liù, Pamina, Gilda, Manon and Frau Fluth. The other, of course, is Elisabeth Schumann, to play one of whose records is like opening the curtains on a brisk and beautiful spring morning.

∾ Coloratura ∾

'Wrong!' cry a hundred indignant voices. 'No such person! Misnomer! Leggiero perhaps. Soubrette maybe. Why not just "high soprano"? "Coloratura"! Humbug!'

Put more reasonably, the case against 'coloratura' goes as follows: 'Coloratura' in Italian must have something to do with colour: that is the root meaning of the word. What we understand by 'coloratura soprano' has no connection with what we normally think of as 'colouring' in singing: we talk about the colouration of a voice, or the art of colouring a phrase, both of these being interpretative acts, whereas very often the 'coloratura soprano' is the voice-type least concerned with that sort of thing. In fact the term comes from the German 'Koloratur', and the 'colouring' implied has quite a different meaning. In the mediaeval study of Rhetoric, 'colours' were figurative expressions, or stylistic ornaments along the main line of argument. So, with music, a melody goes its straightforward, unadorned way until, for variety's sake perhaps, it is embellished or, as it used to be called, 'figured'. So there came into being a type of virtuoso singer who specialised in such 'figuring' or 'colouring' of the melodic line, and it is in this sense that he or more frequently she is denoted by the oddly misleading term 'coloratura'.

The word is certainly a curiosity, and so at one time was the thing itself. Early in this century both the word and the 'thing' (the type of singer and the nature of the art) were popular; you asked Auntie Ruby or Uncle Harry what a 'coloratura soprano' was and though you considered them to be totally ignorant in musical matters they could not only give an answer but probably provide an illuminating imitation into the bargain. 'Of course we know what a coloratura soprano is. It's Amelita Galli-Curci singing "Lo, here the gentle lark". Trills and scales and twiddly bits. Higher and higher she goes, up and up, following the flute. That's real singing, that is. Not like your modern ones.'

The 'modern ones' thus alluded to were probably the crooners or jazz

8

singers of the pre-rock age, who had taken over from the music-hall and musical-comedy artists as popular vocalists. But still recognisably 'popular' at that time were what we would call 'classical' singers, most of whom would appear in 'ballad' concerts, a sort of middle ground between the highbrow world of opus numbers and the rougher, more plebeian comic-song or music-hall turn. On a special platform, elevated in social tone as well as musical pitch, stood the great madames: Patti, Melba, Tetrazzini, Galli-Curci. In some strange way they represented the higher realms of art. The *Daily Mail*, announcing a Melba concert, would dub it 'The musical event of the year', when the high spots were the 'Jewel Song' from *Faust*, 'By the Waters of Minnetonka', and 'Home, Sweet Home'. Of these, the 'Jewel Song' exhibited the arts of the coloratura and so validated the artistic pretensions (which used to infuriate the *Musical Times*). Similarly Madame Tetrazzini, a carpet laid for her at the railway station, a military band signalling a welcome, would arrive (looking like everybody's Auntie Ruby), astonish her hearers with the 'Polonaise' from *Mignon* or the Mad Scene from *Lucia di Lammermoor*, collect an outsize fee and depart. To the serious musician there was no more loathed term in the whole musical glossary than 'coloratura soprano'. I can recall a verdict passed by the local music critic of our evening paper in the mid-1940s, after an orchestral concert with a soprano soloist who offered two 'coloratura' arias: 'I have always wondered,' he wrote, 'what the pyrotechnics, shrill and soulless, of "Caro nome" and "Ah, fors è lui" have to do with the art of music. Now I know: absolutely nothing.'

In those years it seemed that the coloratura was a threatened species about whose loss there were very few to care. Simultaneously, the operas of Donizetti and Bellini (with a few exceptions) were generally considered irremediably old-fashioned. Of course there was always Mozart, and *Die Zauberflöte* could not be put on without a soprano to reach the F in alt and sing the triplets and staccatos on the way up. If the colleges of music occasionally turned out somebody who could manage all this, that was quite sufficient. The coloratura was still something of a freak.

In this country she returned through an unexpectedly opened door, the revival of interest in the operas of Handel. The elaborate runs for which English sopranos had kept in training so as to sing 'Rejoice greatly' in *Messiah* required expert flexibility, and the embellishments which scholars held to be part of the authentic style of performance required a free and extensive upper range. Shortly afterwards Maria Callas demonstrated that those despised operas of Donizetti and Bellini had some depth to them after all, and the eagerness with which the operatic public received the news showed that all along there had been a

1. Joan Sutherland as Lucia di Lammermoor

thirst for what the old-timers had designated as 'real singing'. The coloratura was back in business.

In our time it has been Joan Sutherland who has most conspicuously and enduringly represented the voice-type and given new life to the repertoire. Her success, like Callas's, also revived the old excitement of opera-going. Occasionally, in a biography or book of memoirs, we read of an evening when the opera house glowed or blazed with enthusiasm; sometimes it was caused by the opera itself, but usually it was a singer, and the furore was most intense when greeting a new coloratura soprano. Covent Garden saw one such night on 17 February 1959, when *Lucia di Lammermoor* returned to the house after 34 years. Zeffirelli produced, Serafin conducted, Sutherland sang, and of the whole experience one could say that it was the complete fulfilment of the hope most people carry with them when they go to the box office to buy their tickets. I would not say that another kind of soprano could not have had such an effect: De los Angeles produced something like it with her *Butterfly*, Te Kanawa in her early days as the Countess in *Figaro*, Nilsson in Strauss and Wagner. But in fact I have never known another occasion when a singer aroused exactly that kind of enthusiasm, though the annals of opera in this century certainly do record others, as (for

10

example) Tetrazzini in Buenos Aires, Galli-Curci in Chicago, Callas in Mexico. There is something heady about the triumph of the coloratura, an instinctive communal rejoicing in a relatively primitive kind of beauty, the hailing of an artistic achievement which is invigoratingly athletic. It is not surprising that 'serious' musicians look askance; or that the box office thrives.

Both Sutherland and Callas were exceptional not only in quality but also in kind. By comparison with them, the average coloratura soprano was a vocal midget. Probably the first whom I heard and who had an international reputation was the Viennese, Wilma Lipp; on records she impresses as having sufficient power, but in the theatre (I heard her as the Queen of Night and the doll Olympia in *Les Contes d'Hoffmann*) the sound was tiny. Mattiwilda Dobbs was another who sang delightfully as the Queen in *Coq d'Or* and Gilda in *Rigoletto*: a pure, bell-like tone, but distant as well as delicate. Mado Robin of the Paris Opéra had perhaps the most extensive upper range of all (in EMI's new *Record of Singing*, volume 4, she whistles up to the B flat above top C), but the volume was slight and in the usual working range not much more than just audible. A representative of the German school was Rita Streich, whose Zerbinetta in *Ariadne auf Naxos* is so totally satisfying on records; yet I remember her as sounding slight and tonally undernourished even at Glyndebourne. Later, after Sutherland, Beverly Sills took over the role of Lucia at Covent Garden for a season, the tone small and shallow except in notes above the stave where there was a sweeter quality, though still not much volume. With all of these, one could well have said that the term leggiero or soubrette would indeed be appropriate, the 'coloratura' element being merely an additional expertise within the general category of the light soprano. Nor is this just a feature of our times: in the past the same would have been true of many, among them exquisite artists such as Maria Ivogün, Lotte Schoene and Fritzi Jokl. They have taken light roles such as Norina in *Don Pasquale*, or others such as Amina in *La sonnambula* which, though requiring stamina in the theatre, make no great demands upon sheer volume. To this general picture of the coloratura soprano Sutherland, like Callas, presented a stupendous contrast.

Callas had come to the coloratura and bel canto school from Wagner – an extraordinary progression to go from Isolde and Brünnhilde to Bellini's Elvira in *I puritani* or Donizetti's Lucia. Her coloratura was astonishing: in the same volume of *Record of Singing* referred to above she is heard in a variations-aria from Rossini's *Armida*, and the technical mastery leaves one gasping. Moreover, even this music she was able to present in dramatic terms: it was a miraculous moment in the history of the voice. But it *was* only a moment. The prodigious is not far removed from the unnatural, and Callas's career taxed nature too far. Sutherland similarly discovered unsuspected resources, but she had always sung well within her powers and continued to do so. In sheer volume she could certainly compare with Callas: these things are difficult to assess, but people who sang with both have been known to say that if anything Sutherland's was the more ample voice, and that was my own impression. Whatever the truth about the comparison, there is no doubt that Sutherland was very unlike the others mentioned. Where their tone was sharp hers was rounded; where their voices were relatively small points of sound on the stage, hers filled the house. In her prime, the voice was completely steady and, a greater rarity, completely pure, without breathiness or surface-scratch. The ease and fullness of her high notes were beyond anything of the kind that her own generation was likely to have heard; the brilliance of her technique in scalework and trills retained its mastery even in her sixties.

This coloratura, then, has been no 'soprano leggiero' and no soubrette either. Nor will those terms apply to Tetrazzini, from the past, or Gruberova in the present. In common with Sutherland we find in them a good house-filling strength along with dazzling agility. A

2. Luisa Tetrazzini

MME. LUISA TETRAZZINI

12

difference lies partly in style and personality (which are not really our concern here) but also in the tonal quality, which is more sharply edged.

If we place singing voices in a bright-to-dark range, all coloratura sopranos are likely to be seen at the upper end of the spectrum with the basso profondo at the bottom. But within each group are different degrees of light, sometimes following a national pattern. The Germans have generally preferred their sopranos to moderate the brightness; the tone should be sweet and gentle rather than hard and assertive, and the high notes have sometimes been cultivated in a special head-voice where the highest have an almost other-worldly quality. The French have generally liked the voice to be as brightly lit as possible: it may be *petite* and *jolie*, but even if it is no more than a pinpoint the sound must shine out. Italian taste has been closer to the French than to the German, but it is less satisfied by the *little* sound, and mere prettiness does not excite. So a narrowly concentrated brightness is exchanged for light over a wider area. In this international spectrum Sutherland's place would be near the centre, which is no doubt another reason for her wide appeal.

In the upper range, Tetrazzini's voice had by all accounts quite exceptional power and brilliance, very close to the Italian ideal. It can be sensed in her recordings, primitive as they are. In 'Una voce poco fa,' (1911) you can also catch the staccatos in their trajectory to the back wall

3. Edita Gruberova

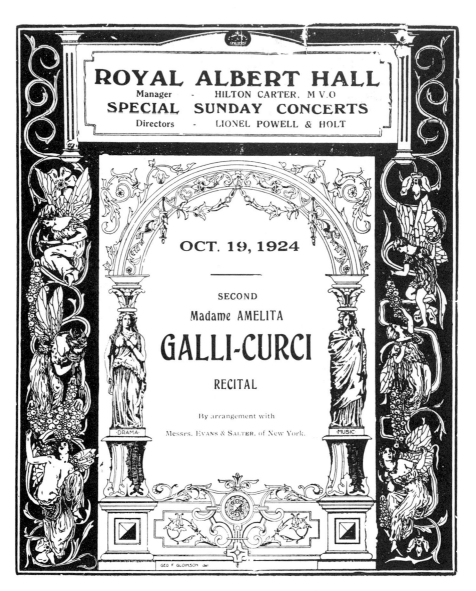

ROYAL ALBERT HALL
Manager - HILTON CARTER, M.V.O
SPECIAL SUNDAY CONCERTS
Directors - LIONEL POWELL & HOLT

OCT. 19, 1924

SECOND

Madame AMELITA

GALLI-CURCI

RECITAL

By arrangement with

Messrs. EVANS & SALTER, of New York.

·DRAMA·   ·MUSIC·

GEO F GLOINSON del

4. Programme cover for a recital by Amelita Galli-Curci

of the gallery. In 'Ah, non giunge', the finale of *La sonnambula*, the exuberance radiates energy as well as light. The middle and lower range by contrast can sound pallid, sometimes infantile. Yet Percy Pitt, who conducted many of Tetrazzini's performances at Covent Garden, used to say he always felt there was a potential dramatic soprano in her voice.

At present, among coloratura sopranos prominent on the international

5. Amelita Galli-Curci

scene are two whose voices have unusual power throughout their compass, together with easy, full-bodied top notes and a high degree of technical skill. June Anderson made her Covent Garden debut in a concert performance of Rossini's *Semiramide*, which London had previously heard, also in a concert version, with the title role sung by Sutherland. Anderson has stepped into the Sutherland repertoire, and

15

her quality is well represented by two recent recital records: one of arias by Bellini, the other of an evening at the Paris Opéra in concert with Alfredo Kraus. The second soprano is Edita Gruberova, who also sings the Italian repertoire but is perhaps best known as the Queen of the Night in *Die Zauberflöte* and Zerbinetta in *Ariadne auf Naxos*. Here records do less than justice. If they suggest an overbright, slightly edgy timbre, that is misleading: in the theatre it has been a pure, exhilarating sound, capable of softness and warmth. She if anyone has the Tetrazzini exuberance. One can hardly conceive of a performance more brilliant than her Zerbinetta, and yet the most acrobatic feats are accomplished with a smiling security in the spirit of comedy (which Zerbinetta embodies), almost as though they were something slightly comical in themselves.

In her concerts Tetrazzini would take the trills, scales and high notes of her coloratura solos quite nonchalantly while swinging the absurd mass of beads she wore – perhaps the original of Beatrice Lillie's famous review sketch where the beads would end up round her ankles. There *is* something comical about the art of the coloratura soprano: not half as comical, however, as the musical puritan who has never enjoyed a Mad Scene in his life, whose heart has never leapt at a high note, and to whom the gentle lark sings in vain.

✧ Lyric ✧

The lyric soprano is the world's girlfriend. She is Mimì in Paris, Eva in Nuremberg, Tatiana in Moscow, Liù in Peking. By comparison, the light soprano, the soubrette, is a life-and-soul-of-the-party girl, but perhaps not one for the deep and lasting relationship. Her dramatic-heroic sister is more formidable, almost alarming. Who would marry Norma? Even the assorted Leonoras, one imagines, would take a certain amount of living up to. And how often have we smiled pityingly at poor little black-coated Don Ottavio offering to draw his sword in the service of a Donna Anna who could pick him up with one hand. No: it's the lyric soprano for us. She is gentle, affectionate, and loyal, and so will remain till death us do part, as it normally does in the final act.

Vocally, we require nothing too much of her. In range, two octaves, C to C, will do very nicely, though, as Maggie Teyte used to insist, an extension of two notes will help with Mozart. No exceptionally penetrative powers are needed, though tastes differ nationally on the matter of timbre. Sheer volume is certainly not a prerequisite, and yet the large heart does not go well with the small voice. The trills, staccatos, scales and arpeggios of the coloratura specialist are to be cultivated, for nobody wants a Marguerite with a lazy trill and a smudged scale in the Jewel Song, and Mozart's Donna Elvira, Fiordiligi, Pamina and even the Countess in *Figaro* need to move with grace and agility. Even so, the lyric soprano may pass whole seasons wondering whether she has not acquired these accomplishments in vain. Purity and clarity come uppermost.

The role of Marguerite in Gounod's *Faust* is a good example here. At the same time, it is well to remember that the voice-types are more approximate than one might think. Marguerite sometimes attracts a coloratura soprano because of the Jewel Song; there is also a heavier type of voice that will not be out of place in the Church Scene and the final trio.

Purity, clarity and grace are the essentials in Marguerite's first solo. She is not heard till the opera is a quarter of the way through; then she sings, modestly, for just nine bars in response to Faust's greeting, and leaves the stage. The solo has lasted for thirty seconds, no more, yet it can have a bewitching effect. Up to this point, male voices have predominated, and so the gentle sound of the soprano falls like a benediction. The melody is beautifully shaped, the orchestra marked pianissimo, a moment of stillness in the midst of a fast-moving crowd scene: everything contrives to create a brief enchantment. But all depends on the quality of the soprano voice. At that moment the charm of a beautiful girl must come to us through the exquisite purity of a lovely voice, and in its way it is as testing for the singer as those fearsome twelve bars that Verdi wrote for the entrance of Otello.

Then, in the third act, the Garden Scene, Marguerite comes into her own. Again, the first half of her solo wants vocally nothing more than the purest lyric beauty, all in the easy middle of the lyric soprano's voice. Then follows the discovery of the jewels; the tessitura or 'lie' of the music rises and the style has a new brilliance. Now comes the demand for a real, well-sustained trill, a clear, rapid scale, and well-placed high notes. Finally, with the coda, 'Marguerite, ce n'est plus toi', Gounod asks for more still. Now he wants power and fullness: not for long but for these twenty bars, which are to culminate in a brilliant trill and a sustained, ringing high B natural to bring the house down while the orchestra plays on.

So the scope of the lyric soprano may extend beyond what might be thought of as her own special territory. Yet this role of Marguerite is certainly hers, and it returns now to a less adventurous existence well within its recognised boundaries. The Quartet is followed by the Love Duet, with its solo 'O silence, ô bonheur', which is a perfection of melody and of writing for the lyric voice. The final pages of the act are also Marguerite's, and once again she must have that something extra to draw upon as the music swells, and, whatever the composer had to say about it (he wrote the note as an alternative), the audience wants a good climactic high C. From this point on, a certain anxiety arises about the singer's stamina. These days she may be asked to include a solo scene at the spinning-wheel, traditionally omitted. That is not too demanding in itself – but immediately following is the Church Scene, and now the part goes well within the realm of the dramatic soprano. Gounod is considerate to his singers, and when the dramatic music lies low in the voice he is generally careful to keep the orchestra down; but there is no disguising its dramatic quality, and for the broad, expansive melody ('Seigneur, accueillez la prière') our soprano must find power to rise over orchestra and chorus, and having reached her high B natural again must find enough heroic reserve in her voice to bring some strong chest tones into play for the final notes which lie an octave below. When this is over, the death of Valentine brings her back on stage, and there still lies ahead the Prison Scene, when after much that is tailor-made for the lyric soprano comes the almost cruelly demanding trio. In this, at the end of the whole evening's performance, the voice must rise a tone higher in each repetition of the melody. The final verse is at fortissimo, competing with tenor, bass and full orchestra; if the singer is tired it will come out as an unresonant scream and Mephistopheles will not be the only one to curse her.

So, two-thirds pure lyric soprano, the role veers from time to time towards the dramatic-heroic type, and less frequently towards the coloratura. Going through the sopranos who have sung the role at New York's Metropolitan – once dubbed the *Faustspielhaus* – we find among the earlier Marguerites two fully-fledged heroic Wagnerians, Lilli Lehmann and Lilian Nordica. Also in early days there were Nellie Melba and Marcella Sembrich, who on other nights might be singing what would generally be regarded as coloratura roles such as Lucia. But generally the light coloraturas (Galli-Curci, Pons, Barrientos, Peters, Sills) do not appear, nor do the lighter lyrics such as Lucrezia Bori or Bidu Sayão. Otherwise the list includes (alphabetically): Albanese, Alda, Amara, Caballé, de los Angeles, Eames, Easton, Farrar, Freni, Gluck, Kirsten, Lorengar, Maliponte, Moffo, Rethberg, Scotto, Steber, Stratas, Zylis-Gara. And that amounts to a fairly representative list of the leading lyric sopranos in the house's history.

When Covent Garden mounted a new production of *Faust* in 1974, the Marguerite of the première was Kiri Te Kanawa, with Mirella Freni in a revival. These two make an interesting comparison for our present purposes. Freni was introduced to us in 1961 when, with Zerlina in *Don Giovanni*, she appeared as the most lovely Nannetta in *Falstaff*: it was (as I remember it) quite perfect, and especially so in the bell-like purity of the sound. She was careful and kept to the roles expected: Micaëla in *Carmen*, Mimì, Susanna in *Le nozze di Figaro*, Liù in *Turandot*. Violetta in *La traviata* and Elvira in *I puritani* extended her but not rashly. As her voice became more ample there came more Toscas, more Butterflys, and Aida. Recordings soon showed that a price had been paid: the perfect steadiness was compromised and for a while there was more than one anxious listener who feared the worst. Remarkably, the purity of tone remained almost unimpaired, and what we heard when she sang at Covent Garden, as Tatiana in *Eugene Onegin* (1988) was a voice in which the vibrations had loosened so that it no longer sounded fresh and right for the role (till the last act perhaps), but which retained a quality of distinctive beauty. It provided a warning nevertheless of the dangers which the lyric soprano courts when she ventures into the lyric-dramatic repertoire. In the interwar years the career of Elisabeth Rethberg also brought it home. She became widely thought of as the successor to Emmy Destinn in the role of Aida, yet as far as we can judge from records and contemporary accounts it was the quality of her singing rather than the dramatic power of the voice that earned her this reputation. As early as 1931 W.J. Henderson, a wise old man in such matters, warned of the dangers posed by the role of Rachel in *La Juive* to this voice which on her

6. Kiri Te Kanawa

19

arrival at the Met had been of the utmost loveliness.

Now, as scrupulously as any singer of her kind, Te Kanawa has kept within the lyric soprano's proper limits. She sang Tosca in Paris and in a recording, but it wasn't right for her and she gave it up. Many lyric sopranos go from Mimì to Tosca without apparent trouble, and as far as the first and third acts are concerned there is perhaps no great distance travelled; but in Act II, with its cries and protests, this is a different matter. Do this a few times too often and the purity will have gone – and in most cases, once gone it is gone for ever. Te Kanawa also sings the Marschallin in *Der Rosenkavalier*, and here it is not the voice but the role that suffers: the glory of the lyric soprano's voice is its upper half, and much of the Marschallin's music lies in the lower area where the more substantial body of a lyric-dramatic voice is wanted. Generally Te Kanawa's roles have been central to the voice-type: the Countess, Fiordiligi, Donna Elvira, Violetta, Amelia (in *Simon Boccanegra*), Desdemona, Micaëla, Marguerite, Mimì, Arabella. The list is not complete but it is representative. Listening again to the recently reissued song recital made in 1979, one hears the most beautiful sounds in creation. There are temperamental and interpretative limitations no doubt, but note by note, phrase by phrase, here is the most lovely singing – that of a pure lyric soprano whose own proper territory is rich enough in resources for her to have little temptation to go beyond it.

Te Kanawa's tone has probably as wide an international appeal as any at present; but at present national differences of taste are much diminished. In earlier times, as recently as the interwar years, the preferences were much sharper. The Russians specialised in an excitingly bright tone such as that of Nina Koshetz. The German taste was quite different: a maidenly warmth and roundness was their ideal, and it was well represented by Tiana Lemnitz. In Italy and Spain a more vibrant tone was preferred, as for instance in the two Liùs of the Covent Garden *Turandot* of 1937, Mafalda Favero and Licia Albanese. For the French, the clear definition of a Ninon Vallin had the *savoir-vivre*, the *esprit* of a heroine who would never be insipid. In England Melba's influence helped to nurture a generation of pure, sweet and, to the rest of the world, somewhat sexless voices. At best we had the technical perfection and strong personality of Joan Cross, the modestly ladylike tones of Miriam Licette in opera, the clear treble tone of Isobel Baillie in song and oratorio.

A little earlier, America had Geraldine Farrar, and she indeed was the image of the world's girlfriend. Lovely as a picture-postcard keepsake, high-spirited enough to face her Don José with a genuine *mauvais quart d'heure* at Lillas Pastia's, never looking prettier than when tending her flock of geese on stage in *Königskinder*, she was nevertheless highly gifted

7. Geraldine Farrar as Tosca

and well schooled. Prominent in her repertoire were Tosca, Butterfly and Carmen, all high-risk roles for the type of voice. Farrar could afford to take risks, however, for she made a resolution and stuck to it: at forty she would retire from opera. 'The distressing vision of prima donnas overstaying their artistic prime and inviting apology gave me the horrors', she wrote. 'Perhaps it was the soul's voice trying to be heard through the glamorous weave of the artist's controlled medium.' Well, perhaps it was; but perhaps it was the simple intuition that at forty one is no longer young, and that the lyric soprano is the voice of youth.

☙ Lyric-dramatic ❧

If the lyric soprano is the voice of youth, the lyric-dramatic is her elder sister: a woman, mature in feelings, physically and perhaps morally a more formidable proposition, very probably a fighter, almost certainly carrying within her the seeds of tragedy. So it is with Tosca, Aida, Sieglinde, Elisabeth de Valois, the Leonoras of *La forza del destino* and *Il trovatore*. For these, the voice needs more depth and volume, the style more intensity and declamatory force. A lyric soprano will often graduate to them by an insidious process so that it hardly seems as if a particularly momentous decision has been taken, but innocence once lost cannot be regained, and, though the transition from (say) Mimì to Tosca, Pamina to Donna Anna, may not be utterly and immediately irreversible, it is best approached in the spirit of an impending wedlock which, as the Prayer Book has it, is not to be enterprised, or taken in hand, unadvisedly, lightly or wantonly.

Tosca is probably the most common transition-opera. It seems natural enough that it should be so, for 'Vissi d'arte' will often follow 'Mi chiamano Mimì' in recital, and there might appear no obvious reason why the complete role should not follow just as naturally. A few rehearsals of Act II will make the position clearer, though in fact Puccini has signalled the difference between his two heroines in their very first phrases, both of them sung from off-stage. While Mimì quietly sings 'Scusi', Tosca is heard loud and clear 'chiamando stizzita', 'calling angrily'. The first voice is gentle, even timid; the second imperative, impetuous, impatient and imperious. Mimì never scolds or raises her voice in declamation, but when Tosca discerns in Cavaradossi's portrait a likeness to her potential rival she cries out on a high A and then launches her jealous accusations from the vantage-point of a low note which brings the chest-voice into play. With it comes a vocal character quite alien to Mimì's and much rougher on the voice.

In Italy, where an audience will sometimes applaud individual phrases, I once heard two of Tosca's singled out (quite undeservedly) in

22

1. Soprano

Act I. The first, rather to my astonishment, was the simple question 'Lo neghi?' ('Do you deny it?'), and the second, more predictable, was her last words in the act: 'Dio mi perdona. Egli vede ch'io piango.' Both were played for all they were worth, or rather more so, tutta forza and with grand histrionic gestures to match. Puccini can hardly be held responsible for the excesses of his audiences and interpreters but this is none the less the kind of performance, vocal and dramatic, that the role has appeared to promote in the country of its origin.

Act II brings not just the 'Vissi d'arte', which is a lyrical interpolation of the private, inner life into a violent world of public affairs, but also the fortissimo cries ringing out over a full orchestra, mounting higher till the limits of vocal and emotional endurance are reached on the high C. Then in the third act, in among passages of rare tenderness and quiet beauty, the soprano has to wish herself a Brünnhilde voice for the space of two bars ('Io quella lama gli piantai nel cor') in which she relives her assassination of Scarpia; and the final impression she leaves with the audience is of that heroic challenge with the high B flat hurled towards the Judgement Seat in 'O Scarpia, avanti a Dio'.

So there is no doubt that here is a full-bodied dramatic soprano. Yet in another sense the role is not representative of the lyric-dramatic repertoire, for though many of its demands are fearsome enough there are others that it makes not at all. Tosca does indeed have one single phrase that extends her technically in this other direction.

Early in the Love Duet she has a solo ('Non la sospiri la nostra casetta') in which she sings of the country retreat where she hopes to meet Cavaradossi that night. The first section ends with a dainty unaccompanied phrase ('le voci delle cose') which flutes up high, lightly touches the B flat, and descends as nimbly as it rose. That, at least, is how it *should* sound: an unusually charming little exhibition of vocal dexterity briefly lightening the texture and introducing a touch of eighteenth-century grace. This is a phrase that sorts out the real singers (it is, incidentally, the single memory I retain of Renata Tebaldi's Tosca at Covent Garden in 1955). Often it will be smudged or shrieked, and if this is so it does not augur well for success in the older operas, which are still at the centre of the lyric-dramatic repertoire.

Tebaldi comes to mind again, though now as illustrating limitations that have been common among lyric-dramatic sopranos this century when they turn to a role such as that of Leonora in *Il trovatore*. All may be well in the first aria, 'Tacea la notte', though even here there are some triplets that need a smooth articulation they do not always get. The aria has one of those fine, rising phrases, typical of Verdi, lying in the well-nourished upper-middle part of the voice, and then a climax, demanding indeed, but not too much of a problem provided the notes

23

8. Maria Callas as Norma

are there and supported by a considerable reserve of energy. But a different kind of trial lies ahead. Following Leonora's aria is her cabaletta, 'Di tale amor'. This abounds in trills, staccatos, scales and high notes. At a glance you would say that it was written for a different voice entirely, but in Verdi's time the dramatic soprano was evidently expected to have these accomplishments too.

Tebaldi, who sings the aria well enough, was not equipped for the cabaletta and in her recording of the opera this joyous allegro is deprived of its sparkle. At the corresponding point in Act IV sopranos have often solved the problem of the cabaletta by omitting it, but since Callas made people realise what they had been missing this practice has become less acceptable. The aria 'D'amor sul' ali rosee', which precedes it, presents the soprano with her most rewarding opportunity, and it often happens that a singer who has not made her mark earlier in the evening will do so with this; but a fully adequate performance has to include some real and well-sustained trills, a graceful scale, a fluent cadenza and a high D flat which does not sound like the screaming end of the world. This all involves a considerable extension of the skills required of a successful Tosca.

24

1. Soprano

But then perhaps the question arises, 'Why *should* the *Trovatore* Leonora be a dramatic, or lyric-dramatic, soprano? What is it that puts the role into a category of voice heavier than, say, Violetta in *La traviata*? Don't some singers appear in both roles? Isn't the difference in these instances more a matter of character and psychology, and our subjective approach to them – a feeling that Violetta, like Mimì, being consumptive and kindly, has a lighter, gentler voice whereas Leonora in a turbulent, dark opera calls for a more dramatic, dark and hard-hitting voice? Does it not have more to do, in other words, with the drama than with purely musical requirements?'

It is of course part of the nature of opera that musical and dramatic conditions interrelate in the way such questions suggest. A glance at the scores would confirm that musically the two roles have much in common – range, tessitura, grace, agility, power to come through clearly in ensemble and so forth; but a further consideration has to involve the rest of the cast. Whereas *Traviata* can take, and will probably benefit from, a fairly light lyrical tenor and baritone, the other voices in *Il trovatore* very clearly have to be of the dramatic type, and the soprano has to match. Act I of *Trovatore* ends with a loud, fast and passionate trio, in which a lyric soprano simply could not cope. In Act IV Leonora has a long duet with the baritone, the second half of which again demands a stronger, more brilliant type of voice than the duet with Germont in *Traviata*. In the 'Miserere' the soprano will have no difficulty in making herself heard as she is the only character on stage, while tenor and chorus are off; but here the tessitura comes into play, for no written note goes above A flat (sopranos sometimes inject a C) and in the low-lying phrases the tension, both musical and dramatic, calls for a robust chest-voice of the kind with which Italian dramatic sopranos usually arm themselves impregnably.

As with other voice-types, and probably more so than with most, national differences have been strong, with the most marked contrast between the German school and the Italian. A toughness, a hard-edged challenge in the Italian voice contrasts with a gentler, rounder tone among the Germans. For Italians, a bold, almost masculine chest-voice in the low notes is part of the excitement; Germans have rarely produced it, basing their objections on no doubt sound reasons of taste and musicality, but also much influenced by the concept of womanhood that seems to underlie it.

An example of the German school of earlier times is the lovely and tragically short-lived (she died aged thirty-four) Meta Seinemeyer, for some years in the 1920s a much-loved soprano at Dresden. She recorded, though only in excerpts, a fair cross-section of the lyric-dramatic repertoire, and it is good to see some of her records now

9. Cheryl Studer

available on compact disc. Her tone, pure and finely concentrated, is always that of a woman who in the very whirlwind of passion retains dignity, never opening herself to a charge of artistic vulgarity in her usage of the upper and lower ends of the range. Though her voice was not remarkable for its power, she undertook roles as heavy as Aida and Sieglinde; she was also a Butterfly and Tosca, and played a prominent part in the Verdi revival of her time, singing in *La forza del destino, Don Carlos* and *Un ballo in maschera*. Listening to her records, one feels that it was not a voice that should be subjected to too much operatic rough-and-tumble. Hers is really a lyric soprano, dramatic by virtue of timbre rather than weight, urged that little bit further into the dramatic repertoire: a good example of what in Germany they see as the in-between soprano, the Zwischenfachsängerin.

For an Italian counterpart (modified a little, perhaps, by her upbringing abroad, including primary school at Tottenham), Claudia Muzio points both likenesses and contrasts. One of the great artists of her century, she also died all too young (at forty-six), and pushed a lyrical voice (lirico spinto means just that, a 'pushed' or extended voice) into the dramatic repertoire. The uppermost notes, the Bs and Cs, are not the glory of the voice any more than with Seinemeyer, but where the German singer will rein them in, fearful of harshness, the Italian is

26

10. Aprile Millo

prepared to risk more; and whereas Seinemeyer will take no special interest in the chest register, Muzio will have this as a great emotional reserve, an area of the voice to be drawn on, thrillingly, when the tragic depths are to be plumbed by the verismo heroines, precursors of those films in which Anna Magnani or another would cry out from the very soul of afflicted Italian womanhood.

After Muzio there was Callas, a phenomenal extender of all these soprano categories, almost their extinguisher. For a while she seemed to do everything: it was prodigious, beyond nature, and soon to be paid for. As a public artist Callas died at the age of forty-one in 1964, though she lived another thirteen years. Seinemeyer, Muzio and Callas should have a place reserved for their photographs in any lyric-dramatic soprano's dressing-room: the glory of their kind, and a *memento mori* too.

At the present time a remarkable generation of sopranos has taken the field. In America alone, Susan Dunn, Alessandra Marc, Aprile Millo, Cheryl Studer and Carol Vaness come to mind; in Britain we have Rosalind Plowright, and in Margaret Price have had for many years one of the supreme lyric-dramatic sopranos of the age; Julia Varady, a patrician artist not unlike Seinemeyer in several respects; Katia Ricciarelli and Maria Chiara in Italy; Sylvia Sass, a wildly variable singer who nevertheless has a touch of greatness within her: these are among the prominent lyric-dramatics of recent years. In between them and Callas have come Leontyne Price, Renata Scotto and Montserrat Caballé. The names are sufficient to call up a wide range of sound, all falling within this one general category.

It is in many ways the most rewarding. Its appeal to the lyric soprano is very understandable: the repertoire is bolder, the dramatic context often richer, more tense and exciting. Achievement and mastery here take a singer to the very heart of international opera, for there is nothing like a well-cast *Trovatore* or *Aida* for arousing expectation and filling the house. The warmth and at the same time the awareness of responsibility must be familiar to all the sopranos mentioned above, and perhaps by none more than Rosalind Plowright whose career has taken her to the heights and yet has not always run smoothly.

She followed a sensible path, gaining experience in chorus and on tour, then in small parts, and then in a steady 'central' lyric repertoire in Mozart. Yet her first big success came in what is often played as a mezzo-soprano role, Miss Jessel in *The Turn of the Screw*. This was in 1979 and I recall the effectiveness of this strong, penetrative voice, not exactly rich or entirely beautiful in tone (to my ear) but certainly impressive, and outstanding among that cast. I also remember being surprised, not at hearing of her acclaim abroad but at the roles in which she had gained it. They included the big dramatic roles in Verdi – Abigail, Leonora, Amelia and Aida. Hearing her back at home in *I vespri siciliani* was to understand why and how, and yet to retain some doubt as well.

The sheer volume was more than merely ample, the technical accomplishment more than adequate; yet steady as the voice remained it did seem that a great deal was being asked of its upper range and that the quality had not gained in richness, purity or ease. Then there was an unhappy spell at Covent Garden, where her Senta was completed only by what seemed to be an immense effort in the midst of the most dispiriting performance of any opera I had ever seen in the house.

The more recent *Trovatore* with Domingo found her in better form, and yet the occasion which most happily and fulfillingly presented her in my experience was not in opera but a song recital, when the voice bloomed with a sense of freedom and a beauty of tone I had not encountered before. It sent the mind back to those horrendous scores, with their B flats and tutta forzas, which the lyric soprano takes as her partner, for better, for worse, in sickness and in health, when she enters the dramatic repertoire: and the warning words of the marriage service ring out their ancient wisdom.

1. Soprano

∽ Heroic ∾

Long years ago at a competition for singers in Ballarat, Australia, an ancient adjudicator fixed a young girl with his glittering eye and said, 'You are a Brünnhilde'. As far as she was concerned he might have said she was an anapaest or an isosceles triangle for all the sense it made. She did, however, conclude that it must be a good thing to be rather than the reverse, as she had just been awarded first prize.

The girl's name at that time was Florence Fawaz, but before making her Covent Garden debut in 1922 she acted on the sensible advice of the Director Harry Higgins and took the surname Austral. The opera of her debut was *Die Walküre*, the role Brünnhilde. The distinguished career which followed is a matter of history, which means of course that it is now almost universally forgotten. But she was a magnificent singer: an Isolde as well as a Brünnhilde, an Aida too, a Marschallin, Tosca and Leonore, and one who included in her extensive concert repertoire Violetta's 'Sempre libera' and the Mad Scene from *Lucia di Lammermoor*.

What, then, were the qualities which placed this in the adjudicator's mind as 'a Brünnhilde-voice'? No doubt the first consideration was its power, or its power-potential; that after all is the *sine qua non*. Austral's power could easily be underestimated for there was nothing brutish about it: she sang well within herself, apparently with ease, maintaining a capability for lightness and fluency. Arthur Hammond, principal conductor of the Carl Rosa Company for so many years, once described to me how as a young man he had attended a rehearsal for Act II of *Die Walküre*, before the start of which he found himself chatting to the nice unassuming woman sitting next to him. The rehearsal began and the time arrived for Brünnhilde's Battle Cry, but as far as he could see there was no Brünnhilde present. Then, he said, he had never been so surprised, alarmed, awe-struck and thrilled as when his neighbour started to sing. There was no more fuss, preparation or warning than the drawing of a breath. She remained seated. And this 'Ho jo to ho' came forth, glorious, full-bodied and easy, trills, top Bs, *glissandi* and all. He had worked with singers and thought he knew what to expect; but this, as they say, was something else. It was indeed the Brünnhilde voice, and a super-rarity.

Perhaps another of its qualities which might have suggested this to the adjudicator back in 1914 was that the twenty-year-old girl to whom he had just given the soprano prize had won the mezzo-soprano as well. Often the full heroic soprano voice has a mezzo or even a contralto underlay. Among Florence Austral's recordings are two duets from *Il trovatore*, one the famous 'Miserere', the other 'Ai nostri monti' which

29

was to have been sung by the tenor and another artist, a contralto who for some reason did not turn up. Austral, having sung Leonora's music for one side of the old record, instantly obliged with Azucena's for the other. The deeper tones held there in reserve provided a solid foundation, and while the range extended upwards with true soprano ease and clarity there was always this sense of a broad-based tone that added warmth and nobility.

This admixture of mezzo or contralto is common to many heroic sopranos (the relatively uncommon feature being the skill in lightening and in preserving the graces of the lyric soprano). The supremely great Brünnhilde voice of the century is surely that of Kirsten Flagstad, who retained a strong element of the mezzo or contralto in her tone. It was certainly an inspired notion of John Culshaw's to invite her, in retirement, to contribute as a mezzo to the recording of *Das Rheingold* in 1958. She sings as Fricka and there is an amusing passage in Culshaw's book, *Ring Resounding*, where he recalls a group of young singers at the first session who appeared to be wondering why the old lady was there, and whose expressions changed to wonder of a different sort when she began to sing. But well before this she had had trouble with the highest notes, the Bs and Cs, and going back to the records she made in America in the late

11. Kirsten Flagstad

1930s, just after her first triumphs there, one hears a voice that is so gloriously comfortable in the middle and lower registers that one almost begrudges the necessary excursions upwards. Even before that, in a group of little-known and not particularly attractive song-recordings made at the very start of her career (some in 1915, others 1923), it is the lower part of the voice which is recognisable as characteristic Flagstad; and I rather think that if one heard the best of them played 'blind' (not knowing who was the singer) it would be very natural to assume that she was a mezzo.

In Flagstad, with that warmth of tone which the mezzo quality strengthens, we have one archetype among the Wagnerian heroic sopranos. Birgit Nilsson, most commonly regarded as her successor, is another, and of quite a different sort. With her, there was never any question but that here was a soprano through and through: the tone was not characterised by breadth or warmth but by purity and penetration, and the high notes were its glory. The oft-told tale of her singing the Queen of Night's vengeance aria, top Fs and all, after a performance of *Tristan* or *Götterdämmerung* is – one cannot say 'no surprise', but at least it is credible to anybody who heard her take Brünnhilde's high Cs or rejoice in the fearsome tessitura of Turandot. Her top had the brilliancy, accuracy and ease of a Tetrazzini. Normally such accomplishments are paid for by a weakness in a lower part of the voice, but this was not so with Nilsson, who had plenty of power throughout though it was not of the nobly rounded Flagstad quality.

In discussing these differences there is probably no need to go beyond the voices and their owners, but with Nilsson particularly it may be interesting to speculate how much her training may have had to do with it. For three years Nilsson studied with Joseph Hislop, the celebrated Scottish tenor highly regarded in Stockholm and at that time resident there as principal teacher for the Opera. She found his manner hurtful and she distrusted his method: he seemed intent upon reducing her to tears and her voice to a reedy little pipe. She had come to Stockholm from the farm and she knew that her voice was a big one. Apart from what she thought belittling remarks about her background, Hislop would also needle her with enquiries after her 'foghorn' and with satirical observations about 'the steamboat coming into port'. She was not allowed to use her full voice and he almost appeared to be trying to make a soubrette out of her. Although in later years she still recalled those lessons with a certain amount of loathing, she did concede that there was some sense in what Hislop was trying to do with the voice: which was, as it were, to slim it, sharpen the focus and exercise it as a more wieldy, disciplined instrument. This is certainly what it became. In Covent Garden the sound was, I think, no louder than half a dozen whom I had previously heard in the roles she sang, but it was exceptionally pure, bright and compact. These are some of the qualities least common among Brünnhildes and Elektras, then and now – and rarely has there been a big voice with less suggestion of the foghorn or steamboat about it.

If these Nilssonian virtues are rare among the Wagnerians, still more so is the absolute steadiness of production that I would associate primarily with Flagstad, and indeed with Austral. There are times when listening to so many of the 'heavy' sopranos on record or in the opera house that you feel not one truly firm note has been emitted throughout the evening. The big voice is of its nature most difficult to control, and of all maladies that afflict the imperfectly controlled voice the most dreaded of all is the 'spread' tone, beat or wobble. Sometimes it has become so habitually associated with certain roles that it passes without critical comment, and of course ears can grow so accustomed to what would normally be thought of as an undesirable feature that its presence is part of the contract. Tolerance-levels vary: just exactly how many (or how few) vibrations a second are acceptable and how many degrees of deviation from pitch can be borne will vary among individuals and (to some extent) nations. There is also a curious unpredictability about it. Sometimes a wobbly voice will deliver a perfectly firm note, loud, long and high, at the very point where the ears had prepared themselves for calamity. It is not uncommon for a dramatic or heroic soprano to sing a sustained lyrical phrase with admirable firmness and follow it with a rapid declamatory passage in which she can hardly be said to be singing specific notes at all. But this is the direst peril of the voice-type and, though one sometimes reads of a singer whose wobble is said to have disappeared, the evidence of my own ears suggests that as a general rule the process is irreversible.

Loss of steadiness and acquisition of 'wear' on the voice are two of the consequences a singer risks when undertaking too strenuous a role. Sometimes a brief contact may do little harm, or none at all; Margaret Price, for instance, drew the line at singing Isolde in the opera house but was prepared to record it. Examples of singers who succumb to such temptations, whether urged on from within themselves or by a conductor, are not far to seek. Most famous of all is still the single attempt at the *Siegfried* Brünnhilde by Dame Nellie Melba. 'I've been a fool' was her unsparing comment afterwards, and she swore never to do it again; as it was, she had to rest her voice for three months.

So, exactly, one may ask, what is it that makes these roles so formidable? Why, for instance, should this brief stretch of singing in *Siegfried* (not much more than half-an-hour) threaten, as one critic put it, to smash a delicate voice as one might a piece of Dresden china?

1. Soprano

One consideration, likely to seem strange to us now but potent in the 1890s when Melba sang the role, has to do with staging. A prima donna's place was by the footlights, and here was she, lying on a rock and unable for a time to get anywhere near them. Jean de Reszke, the Siegfried, describing the sense of panic, said it was all he could do to prevent her from rushing downstage. The modern soprano has learned to live with such restrictions, and worse. A greater worry (and no doubt the principal cause of Melba's defeat) is the orchestration. Gentle enough at first, it swells at the third greeting ('Heil dir, leuchtendes Tag'), sealing the soprano in its embrace as it is to do again many times before the final high C is reached. When that point arrives the note must ring out triumphantly, with a freshness and energy that proclaim the start of a new life: no use if it comes as a last desperate cry from a voice worn out by its losing battle with the orchestra.

In Wagner the singer always has to bear in mind what lies ahead, and for the *Siegfried* Brünnhilde (still more of course for the Siegfried himself, who has the whole opera behind him) there must be the reserves for those final pages of the score when the voices hurl themselves at each other or combine in their death-defying ecstasy without restraint or thought for the morrow. It is true that there are also pages of pure lyricism: Brünnhilde's 'Ewig war ich' comes very near to being a good old-fashioned aria with beginning, middle and end. It requires some vocal grace, not only a genuine legato but a long trill and an easy, cleanly taken high C. Even so, and even though the Brünnhilde of this opera seems higher in voice than in *Walküre* and *Götterdämmerung*, there is still a need for power and fullness in the lower and middle parts of the voice. It is not merely a matter of volume and stamina but of tone-quality. The voice-type is not called 'heroic' for nothing, and its character has to be in some way the vocal counterpart of the spear and shield, breast-plate and helmet.

For the singer provided with all this armoury of power, fullness and resilience, there should be, one would think, correspondingly rich spoil from the repertoire. Wagner is her centre of operations, but she will hope also to annexe Beethoven and a large part of Strauss by right. In Mozart, traditionally Donna Anna falls to her; in Gluck, Armide; in Weber, Rezia and (scaling down a bit) Agathe. She will also look wonderingly at the Italian field: Aida will seem right, though often it is not, and maybe parts as near to the central lyric-dramatic repertoire will beckon, Tosca and the Verdi Leonoras for instance. But strangely it is from what lies just beyond this that trouble may come.

Norma is a role with which the Brünnhilde-voice has associations dating back to the days of Lilli Lehmann, who (famously) declared it to be a more daunting proposition than all the Brünnhildes put together.

33

Frida Leider, supreme Isolde in the opinion of many, sang Norma, and at one time there was a distinct possibility that Flagstad would be the first Norma at the Metropolitan since Ponselle. Another fearsomely demanding role is that of Abigail in Verdi's *Nabucco*: this also needs a soprano of heroic power and sheer toughness, a killer of a part otherwise. And then there is Turandot.

Turandot, whose aim on stage is to have the tenor's head on a pole, has generally been more successful as a slayer of sopranos. In the opera's early days all sorts of unsuitable ladies donned the silken robe, attached the thirty-foot train, ascended the steps to the throne and (metaphorically speaking) tripped. Raisa, Jeritza, Lehmann, Muzio: none had the steel and the stamina, the supply of high notes, the penetrative thrust. Eva Turner had all that, as had Birgit Nilsson (though where they were unrivalled in my recollection was in the purity and steadiness of their voices). For ordinary mortals the role must stand high on the danger-list. Wagner's writing for the voice, formidable enough, is in some ways (as Shaw was the first to argue) considerate. Once thought of as anti-vocal and declamatory, it responds beneficently to a style which gives full value to the notes and assumes lyricism till declamation is proved (in fact, listening to a recent, scrupulously sung recording by Anne Evans of Brünnhilde's Immolation, one could well conclude that there is no declamation at all). Abigail and Turandot are every bit as dangerous as Isolde and Brünnhilde, and it is perfectly possible for the unwary soprano to walk through the valley of the Wagnerian music-dramas and be brought down in the green pastures of Verdi and Puccini.

2.   Mezzo-soprano

ᥱᥲ Lyric ᥱᥲ

We know all about the happy medium, the golden mean: how sensible it is, how possessed of every virtue except possibly entertainment value. It is closely allied to 'the sound common sense of the majority'. The sense called common is one that we have known since childhood, when it is used to be attributed to us for the sole purpose of having its whereabouts rhetorically questioned. Now, if there is one sense that opera does not appeal to, it is this common variety. Such cautious, well-balanced virtues are the property of middle-age, and contrary to appearance most opera-goers are not mentally middle-aged. When Dr Johnson produced his famous phrase about an exotic and irrational form of entertainment he was not entirely wide of the mark. Opera makes scant appeal to that part of the mind that applauds moderation; much more it is one of Donne's 'things extreme and scatt'ring bright', and this applies to voices as to the rest.

The mezzo-soprano, like the baritone, is the voice of common sense, the happy medium between high and low. It does not change lady into bird at one end of the scale or into man at the other. Sensibly, it approximates the singing to the speaking voice. It minimises the risk of parody, to which other operatic voices are subject. It suggests primarily a woman of rational disposition, a mature character, not a flighty soprano nor a gorgon contralto and not a star either.

That, all too often, has been the trouble. Public taste has favoured the extremes, and particularly on high. To be the prima donna, you needed to be Aida, not Amneris, La Gioconda, not Laura, Isolde not Brangäne. As a mezzo you had to be content very often with a secondary ingénue part like Siebel in *Faust,* or with the sort of role that everybody forgets about when discussing the opera afterwards, such as Magdalene in *Die Meistersinger.* Sometimes there will be no part for you at all: no part in *Tosca* or *Bohème* for instance, *Die Zauberflöte* or *Fidelio.* Meanwhile, out there will be the soprano, the Lucia di Lammermoor, the Turandot, the star. No wonder, then, that many a voice has been given a little push upwards in training, and that many mezzos, dissatisfied with their lot and having high C well within their range, have been tempted to drop the rather belittling 'half' in their trade-description and become a whole soprano if only for a few years.

As against this, the mezzo can claim a repertoire which includes Verdi's Eboli and Amneris, Wagner's Ortrud and Brangäne, Strauss's Octavian and Klytemnestra. There are charming roles such as Mignon and Charlotte in *Werther*. There are Mozart's Cherubino, Gluck's Orfeo, Saint-Saëns' Dalila; and of course there is Carmen. In recent times the Handel and Rossini revivals have enriched the possibilities, and several singers have established themselves as public favourites, becoming whole and complete 'first ladies' in their own right in spite of the 'mezzo' and the limiting circumstances which that formerly seemed to entail.

The Rossini renaissance in particular has opened up a very different view from the mezzo's window. Technically, it has meant that the skills of coloratura have had to be much more assiduously cultivated. Any well-schooled singer of any period will have been put through exercises in scales and rapid passagework, but for a period from late in the last century to somewhere past the middle years of this, it was quite possible for a professional career to make no regular call upon that part of the training. One of the most celebrated mezzo-sopranos of the 1920s and 1930s was the Lieder singer Elena Gerhardt, who probably never needed to execute a run or cope with florid writing in all her time. She did have a brief association with opera, when her roles were Charlotte and Mignon. In today's musical climate (and incidentally no singer today specialises quite as exclusively as she did) she might well have been given a Handel or Rossini opera, the Mozart of *La clemenza di Tito* or Orsino in a revival of Donizetti's *Lucrezia Borgia*. All of these would have demanded what we loosely call coloratura, and they are far more likely to be on the lists nowadays than they were in the early years of the century. To take another example, not long ago the HMV Treasury series brought out a record drawing on the work of eleven admirable singers recorded between 1909 and 1948 and entitled *Great British Mezzo-sopranos and Contraltos*. In this, once Dame Clara Butt's trill in 'Ombra mai fu' is over on the first band, nothing either in the recordings or the biographical notes supplies evidence of any skill whatsoever in florid singing (which is not to say that it was not available). A similar anthology from 1950 onwards would have a wealth of material at its disposal, including brilliant performances of Handel's operatic arias by singers such as Monica Sinclair and Dame Janet Baker who only a generation earlier would not have had the opportunities. The extension of the Handel repertoire was a particularly strong influence in Britain; internationally, and as far as the mezzo was concerned, the composer whose newly revived fortunes have made most difference has been Rossini.

In Rossini you cannot go far without a run. An aria may start plainly and innocently, as does the famous 'Una voce poco fa' from *Il barbiere di Siviglia*, but soon, just as the little minx herself shows that she is not so simple, so does the vocal line. Scales and groups arise asking for that kind of rapid execution which will make them sound like the easiest thing in the world. In return Rossini offers star parts: for the heavier mezzos there are the trousers roles such as Malcolm in *La donna del lago* and the title-part in *Tancredi*. For the lyric mezzo there are the comedies, including the delicious prospect of reclaiming Rosina in *Il barbiere* from the high sopranos who had monopolised her for so long. The tessitura is of course right for the mezzo, who can sing it as written rather than having to adapt or transpose (which makes life hell for colleagues in concerted numbers). What is less obviously right is the timbre; for the mezzo, as we said, is the voice of common sense and maturity, and here she must sparkle.

Many have done this in our time, some with a gentler kind of radiance than others. A mezzo who has enjoyed stardom for a spell is Frederica von Stade. She came to us as Glyndebourne's Cherubino in 1973: 'irresistible ... infinitely touching' in Spike Hughes's account, and possibly 'the best of them all'. In many ways she represented the ideal concept of the lyric mezzo, with a stage appearance that had nothing of the middle-aged female relative about it, and a personality that drew attention through sympathy rather than anything more ostentatious: she might indeed have won hearts through the eyes alone. But we are concerned here with what the ears tell, more particularly with what is characteristic of the voice rather than the style or expressiveness of its usage. Apply to recordings: to the song recitals, the Mozart and Rossini arias, and perhaps most especially the *Cendrillon* of Massenet (but not the *Cenerentola* of Rossini). As with so many of the best artists among singers, it is difficult to abstract pure voice, for each note seems to be *expressing* something so that one's first reaction is not a comment on tone ('rich', 'thin', etc.) but on emotion ('sad', 'radiant'). In this, Cinderella's first words, 'Ah! que mes soeurs sont heureuses', the first note itself has a sound that is utterly characteristic, much of the character lying in the sadness. Disentangling the strands, one finds a distinctive, natural beauty of tone in the middle register, a surprising depth on lower notes (hear her *Béatrice et Bénédict* solo or Marguerite's 'D'amour l'ardente flamme' from *La Damnation de Faust*) and a reliably available upper register with the high Bs for Rossini all securely in place. There is a change in quality, however, as the voice rises high on the stave and above it, especially when anything more than a mezzo forte is involved. Back to the *Cendrillon*, and all is of the utmost beauty till, loud and high, something in the hardening, the edging of the tone reminds us that the part was first sung by Julia Guiraudon, an exquisite singer, Paris's first

Mimì – and a soprano. Memory confirms what the records tell. In recital all was well till at a certain height the mezzo's gentleness was replaced by a soprano's brightness in which there was also a slightly harder, less pure quality. In true mezzo roles, such as Cherubino, Penelope and Charlotte, the quality could remain consistent, and then, without ever being a plump, lush sound, it had a special and unforgettable loveliness.

That, essentially, is the hard lesson that mezzos have to learn. So often they can sing the notes written for soprano; for the space of a single opera they may even deal successfully with a soprano role, and provided it is not undertaken too often it may have no harmful effect on the voice. But caution is essential for long preservation, and care is needed even in the roles broadly designed for the lyric mezzo. To a large extent it depends on the quality of the individual voice. Von Stade's lovely tone tended to lose quality in loud upper notes, so it was with some regret that one found her going in for those high-flying Rossini solos which nowadays are regarded as being so important in the repertoire. Yet there are singers with a similar compactness of tone, adequate in volume rather than imposing, who appear to suffer no loss of quality. Della Jones is one. With a technical assurance that will stand comparison with any of the international virtuosi, she has a voice which may be all the more likeable for being neither thick-toned enough to suggest weight nor so sharp-edged as to be formidably penetrative. In the excellent Opera Rara recording of Donizetti's *L'assedio di Calais* she sings the travesto part of the young hero and, demanding as the role is upon a mezzo in terms of range, agility and attack, her performance never arouses the slightest doubt as to whether the voice is being overstretched: its quality remains unspoilt throughout.

The brio and rapidity which such operas as this of Donizetti's and the whole corpus of Rossini's require are no doubt commanded more easily by the relatively light, compact type of voice represented by von Stade, Jones or Teresa Berganza. Even so, heavier, richer, broader voices have also managed with great success, most notable among them being that of Marilyn Horne. Here is the outstanding example in our time of that other kind of mezzo tone, rounder and more opulent, more than half contralto in quality yet capable of reaching well above the stave and retaining richness and ease of production while doing so. Hers is a voice-type that gives a more exciting lustre to the name of mezzo-soprano, a royalty that commands more than the middle ground of common sense, moderation and rational compromise. It also extends into the realm of the dramatic mezzo, who will be considered later.

Meanwhile there is another variety of lyric mezzo in the voice of the singer who was most closely associated with the Rossini revival in its early years. Lustre, glamour and excitement were certainly among the vocal attributes of Conchita Supervia, but, tonally, a continent, an ocean, even a civilisation, separate her from the others. In a singers' identification-parade she is instantly recognised by the fast vibrato, though her singing had other personal characteristics quite as marked and individual as that. The subject is a fascinating one: how far (for instance) the vibrato can be called an integral part of the voice and how far it is caused by a method of breath-control; how prominent it was in the impression Supervia gave 'live' as opposed to what we hear on records; and, indeed, whether it is considered attractive or repellent. In general it seems to have been more acceptable in the early part of the century than it is now, and to have been liked by the Latin races more than by Northerners. Perhaps a last, and moderated, flicker was to be found in the singing of the American mezzo Nan Merriman, who, like Supervia, had a special interest in Spanish song and whose warmly coloured tones (as I remember them) gained in character from the admixture of a rapid vibrato which never seemed to be an obtrusive element 'in the flesh'. Supervia, who died at a tragically early age in 1936, was before my time, but I have spoken to people who heard her – and it has been interesting to observe that none has mentioned the vibrato till prompted. All recall the personality, some the immediacy of her voice (a feeling that it was 'in front of you', even in a place as large as the Albert Hall, and not attached to the singer on the distant platform). One told me how, after hearing her in a concert, he went out to buy a record, and when he played it over in the shop felt so strongly that it was not the voice he had just heard that he came out empty-handed. Yet the recordings themselves differ in the degree of vibrato present, and modern reproduction will often see it settle into place much as it did in the live experience. The same acquaintance who rejected the recording in the 1930s eagerly recognised the voice heard in some examples that I played him many years later. Significant too is the absence of comment on vibrato in the press accounts of the time: critics noted the changes of register, the use of aspirates in runs, the limitation of power (no trouble in Rossini, less satisfactory in *Carmen*), but the rattling vibrancy which so captures attention on records drew no special remark in the contemporary prints. Perhaps they felt that it seemed to be one with the zest of singing which in turn was inseparable, in this singer, from the adventure of living.

She was – and still is, on records – an adorable artist; but it also has to be admitted that (leaving the vibrato aside) some of her distinctive qualities can be classified as defects. One of her London critics described her as the fortunate possessor of not one voice but three, and her Rossini recordings show just what he meant. When a strong chest-voice flavours the whole production, as with Supervia and also

Horne and Agnes Baltsa, there is always a high risk that the break between registers, even if sealed during training, will come apart after some years of singing.

These, however, are the singers who live dangerously, and the operatic will-to-excitement owes many of its thrills to those who challenge the rules and risk the avenging arm of technical orthodoxy.

ഗ് Dramatic ഗ്

The mezzo-soprano, being the most natural, 'average' singing-voice among women, no doubt goes back in time as far as song itself: Eve, I expect, was a mezzo-soprano. The term, on the other hand, is relatively modern. Early sightings occur towards the middle of the eighteenth century. Before that time there could have been no great need for a word which would denote an intermediate voice between soprano (or treble) and contralto (or alto), because in song and opera the soprano range was generally not required to extend far beyond the high G, and this is well within what we now regard as the normal compass of the mezzo. The distinction became important when composers found that they wanted to exploit the upper register of the operatic soprano voice and to be able to take its general availability for granted. Naturally, many singers were not averse to such exploitation, but the development was not simply a matter of the topnote cult; rather that with the rise of Romantic opera came an ever more uninhibited and passionate mode of expression in which the upper extreme of the voice, both male and female, provided intensity and emphasis. So the soprano ascended, as did the tenor. Basses and contraltos more or less stayed put, which left an opening for the mezzo-soprano and baritone.

Among the women, singers who would previously have considered themselves sopranos found that life was becoming difficult. This was not so much because composers introduced some formidable high notes, but because they did so repeatedly and with increasing orchestral competition. The voice that could take the soprano part in Handel's operas, for instance, needed significant extension to cope with Mozart's Donna Anna or Elvira. In turn Bellini's Norma, Donizetti's Lucia (which to judge from the score was not written with the leggiero-coloratura type in mind but rather the lyric-dramatic), and then roles such as Verdi's Abigail and the *Trovatore* Leonora drove the wedge in still more firmly. These, of course, were the parts for the prima donna. The mezzo had to accept this as a fact of life, and be grateful when a role like Adalgisa in *Norma* gave her something approaching parity. Adalgisa's duets with Norma assign the lower voice to her when the two sing together, but there are imitative phrases in which both voices in turn are to sing above the stave and even up to the C. The assumption is that the 'half'-soprano will be able to do this occasionally during the course of a performance, but not too often. It is very arguable, in fact, that this is a true mezzo-soprano role, in the sense that what is wanted is a singer whose voice is that of a soprano in timbre (because a deeper voice creates the wrong age-relationship between the two characters) but not in ability to sustain a soprano tessitura throughout a long role. The parts have sometimes been interchanged by singers: at least, it is not uncommon for an Adalgisa to become a Norma (starting with Grisi who sang Adalgisa at the première to Pasta's Norma), though the reverse procedure (as when Caballé, herself a renowned Norma, became an apt and honoured Adalgisa in the second Sutherland recording of the opera) is something of a rarity. Norma's prima-donna status is reaffirmed in the final scenes when Adalgisa is heard no more. And that was the general rule: for 'prima donna' you could read 'soprano', and 'mezzo' implied something like 'seconda'.

This had some unfortunate effects. Most particularly it meant that there was a powerful incentive for women to push their voices higher than was good for them. Some trained as sopranos when by natural endowment they were closer to the mezzo. Many who started as mezzos moved upwards, temporarily or permanently, and more often than not with a loss of quality. Of these, personal experience over the years can review a whole rank of eminent singers, whose originally bright image has been tarnished in memory subsequent to their elevation. The last

12. Fiorenza Cossotto

13. Margarete Matzenauer as Waltraute in *Götterdämmerung*

time I heard Fiorenza Cossotto was as Santuzza in *Cavalleria rusticana*, a part often taken by mezzos but better left to the sopranos: a powerful but coarsened sound on that occasion, as I recall it, and a saddening deterioration of the indomitable voice heard so often before. Grace Bumbry, who was the most golden, opulent Amneris of her time, has now turned to Aida, and I have not heard her in the role; I do, however, remember her Tosca as long ago as 1973, when the gorgeous rounded quality of earlier seasons had been replaced by a more thready tone in the main body of the voice, though well able to cope with the high Cs.

Of Shirley Verrett, never golden in quite the same way, but in other respects more appealing, I took a regretful farewell at the time of her Covent Garden *Norma*: she sailed through the part with apparently easy technical control but did not touch the heart of the role (or my heart, as a listener); it was clear that her voice had hardened with the loss of the mellower mezzo quality which had been such a feature of its attractiveness. I never heard Christa Ludwig in the earlier stages of her career, though I knew and greatly admired her records. Later, in the flesh, I found the power and richness possibly surpassed expectations, but the steadiness of production did not seem to have the absolute firmness I had thought to find. Then it occurred to me that the first time I had had this feeling was in 1962 with the famous Klemperer recording of *Fidelio*, in which she, a mezzo, sang the soprano Leonore. I also recalled the story about the origins of this surprise casting. Elisabeth Schwarzkopf had heard her colleague vocalising in the next dressing-room and had marvelled at the fullness and freedom of some very high notes. The quest being on for a suitable Leonore, word passed to the Power-that-was, and Ludwig was offered the part. The idea seemed to be a good one and a single excursion such as this would be unlikely to do harm; but even in that recording there are some warning signs. It was not the first time a mezzo had sung this dramatic soprano role. In the nineteenth century Malibran and Viardot sang it; earlier in the twentieth century there was Margarete Matzenauer. We do not know how they sounded in the part, though we do have Matzenauer's recording of Brünnhilde's Battle Cry where she tortures her magnificent voice beyond endurance: and we do have Viardot's touching admission that, wanting to sing everything, she had spoilt her voice.

To revert to Matzenauer: she is a singer who will be remembered by older American readers, and almost certainly with veneration. Henry Krehbiel, the New York critic, described hers as a 'royal purple voice'; Max de Schauensee is said to have considered it to have been the only voice comparable in texture to Rosa Ponselle's. That is an association I have sometimes made in my own mind and it is in this connection that she has a special relevance now.

From 'royal purple' you would have to move upward somewhat in the colour-circle to reach Ponselle: but not all that far, stopping perhaps at deep crimson. Ponselle's voice has been probably the most stimulating of all to the metaphor-hunters: port wine, the damask rose, the heart of the pansy: a fine garland of poetic images could be made out of compliments paid to this soprano. It is also a familiar motion for debate as to whether she was a soprano at all. On the face of it, such an inquisition might seem absurd. After all, her debut role (and the part she sang most frequently) was Leonora in *La forza del destino*, and her most famous roles included Aida, Norma and Violetta. Ah yes, comes the answer; but Aida she sang quite rarely (see p.140), and the other two roles involved transposition. Those for Norma are outlined in an article by John Ardoin (*Opera*, May 1976), who was able to study the score owned by Marion Telva, Ponselle's Adalgisa at the Met, where cuts and transpositions are noted (also relevant is the mutilated version of the score which Kirsten Flagstad was shown – presumably inherited from the Ponselle days – when it was suggested that she might sing the part at the Met). Transposition of the great solo in Act I of *La traviata* is an evident feature of the 'live' recording of Ponselle in the opera made in 1935. She dreaded the top Cs, and though the critic Charles Jahant, whose memory was phenomenal, said that he never heard her sing a bad C, recordings show it as a somewhat uneasy and unresonant note, on which she would dwell no longer than necessary. Her old colleague and fervent admirer George Cehanovsky said, 'It's a known fact that Rosa is a mezzo-soprano' (he spoke of her in the present tense after her death): she was born a mezzo, he said, and only diligent study enabled her to sing the soprano repertoire. Personally I think that I have only once said to myself during a performance, 'That might almost have been Ponselle', and that was when I first heard Marilyn Horne in the early 1960s. Ponselle's records, for what they are worth, tell of a soprano with mezzo qualities and a contralto's depth. That description might also apply to two of the most admired sopranos of more recent times, and I think it calls for an addition to the familiar categories.

When Victoria de los Angeles in her prime sang Manon or Mimì or Butterfly the voice always rose to meet the demands upon it, but one just slightly wished it didn't have to. In recital it was another matter. There the programme rarely required anything much higher than a G. She, too, could sound 'like a soprano' but the range in which she was comfortably her best self was that of the mezzo, and there was an especially deep glory in the lower part of her middle register. Concert-goers who heard her only after about 1970 (or even before that) cannot know at first hand how beautiful that voice had been, but the recordings tell pretty faithfully, and what they show is a voice which, for want of a better term, I will call a soprano-mezzo.

Jessye Norman also belongs in that category. She too answers all the vocal requirements of the soprano roles she undertakes. As Strauss's Ariadne, for instance, on stage as on record, she gives a glowing account of the music, arousing no anxieties about range or tessitura. Early in her career she established herself in the affections of record collectors by her performance as Weber's Euryanthe, the voice unequivocally that of a soprano, with a quality which in the search for similes brought forth cream, and in the quest for vocal comparisons suggested Tiana Lemnitz. Her recordings also include an account of Brünnhilde's Immolation

44

where there is no skimping of the high notes so clearly exposed. But there is also no doubt about the mezzo-admixture. It is an essential feature of the Norman tone, a source of richness, roundness and depth. Going with it is a liking for roles and music which make use of this, and a willingness to sing (for instance) as alto soloist in the *St Matthew Passion*.

Carmen has lured all three of these singers: Ponselle to what many regarded as her doom on stage, de los Angeles and Norman to recordings of a role for which neither of them seems to have been temperamentally well suited. Nor were they her first victims. She, after all, is a star, and to many a prima donna (always a soprano) it must have come as an affront to the Divine Scheme that Carmen should have been conceived as a mezzo. Patti was tempted, and fell. Within weeks of singing Violetta, Semiramide and Rosina, and within days of adding Martha and Linda of Chamounix, she gave her first Carmen at Covent Garden in 1885. The performance 'fell painfully flat', according to Herman Klein, and she never tried it again. Among sopranos who enjoyed a popular success in the part was Geraldine Farrar, who had an enchanting way with the music as her records show; but what they bring home is the need for a colourful chest voice and at least an admixture of mezzo tone throughout. An LP collection of Farrar's Carmen records included her slightly earlier and admirable recording of Micaëla's song, which shows her as the lyric soprano she naturally was; it is remarkable that she turned as successfully as she did within a short period from Micaëla to Carmen, but it can't be done with justice to both roles. Carmen must be a mezzo-soprano or at least a soprano-mezzo.

In outlining a repertoire for such voices we are essentially thinking of what is a fairly well-known area, usually traversed by mezzos on the way up, though I think the traffic should be far more of a two-way system. A first step into the borderlands is Santuzza in *Cavalleria rusticana*; Kundry in *Parsifal* and Venus in *Tannhäuser* also seem to be agreed common property. A little further along those lines and we are with Sieglinde and Elisabeth in Wagner, Lady Macbeth in Verdi, Adriana Lecouvreur and possibly La Gioconda in the later Italian repertoire. If there should be a Meyerbeer revival then Valentine in *Les Huguenots* and Selika in *L'Africaine* come into view. Travellers from mezzoland also tend to favour Tosca, though I would have thought that was asking for trouble. Salome, adopted by a whole line of intermediaries from Olive Fremstad to Maria Ewing, seems to me to be a mistake, if not from the singer's point of view then from Salome's: the infusion of a mezzo's richness is inimical to the fresh, silvery, girlish tone that should characterise Strauss's enfant terrible. Similarly, in English opera I always think it was a mistake for Walton to have adapted his Cressida for a mezzo: the capable, adult voice spoils the image of fragility and youth which the lyric soprano of the original version could supply. Where the type of voice we are considering should find its star-part in English is in Britten's *Gloriana*. Opportunities to sing the role are regrettably few, but the tessitura is right and the voice-character needs just such reserves of majesty and opulence.

Years after her retirement Rosa Ponselle confessed that she would often stand in the wings and desperately envy the mezzo-soprano on stage: 'How I wanted to sing those parts ... without worrying about the next high C coming up.' What a pity she could not have taken the further step: she might have been *the* Amneris of her time, perhaps of the century. What a pity too that Victoria de los Angeles could not have sung Eboli in *Don Carlos*: she might not have had the power for the climax of 'O don fatale' but her Veil Song and general characterisation would have been something to remember. There is, of course, still time for Jessye Norman to do something of the kind. I don't know that I pine to hear her as Aida or Elisabeth de Valois, Isolde or even Elsa of Brabant; but Amneris or Eboli, Brangäne or Ortrud, those would go down in the annals.

These are, of course, the great roles for the dramatic mezzo. In them she stands at the centre of the drama, and in the two Verdi operas she has moments of glory in which the voice may ring heroically through the house and the house will rise to greet it. As Amneris in *Aida* curses the 'empia razza' of the priesthood she can give all her power, just as Eboli in *Don Carlos*, aglow with energy, resolution and the anticipation of triumph, brings the act to a close with her curses upon the fatal gift of beauty. For such moments we have been fortunate in our time to have the great cleaving tones of Fiorenza Cossotto, and in recent years the vibrant glow in the tones of Agnes Baltsa, whose appearance at Covent Garden in the last lamented days of the Visconti production remains as one of the most urgent and vivid in the memory.

3.   Contralto

Under the heading 'Some Lighter Reading on the Subject', Percy Scholes' *The Mirror of Music* (Novello and OUP 1947) has a quotation from Ernestine Schumann-Heink, dated 1928: 'I am looking for the contralto singer who will be my successor. She must be *the* contralto.' To catch the full majesty of the utterance, the last sentence must be spoken allargando and in the accents of Lady Bracknell and Chancellor Bismarck. It helps also to have in mind a photograph of the great lady in Wagnerian costume: a fine figure of a woman, no doubt, but perhaps not what one would choose to find sitting in the other armchair after a hard day at the office.

By all accounts, Schumann-Heink was a delightful, lovable and particularly homely woman as well as a great artist, but it appears that there is something about the contralto, or the 'image' of the contralto, that encourages ribaldry. Gilbert and Sullivan found it irresistible. When Ko-Ko has to take under his wing (tra la) 'a most unattractive old thing (tra la) with a caricature of a face', the 'old thing' is inevitably the company's contralto. A whole tribe of basilisk female predators haunts the Savoy operas. Quiller-Couch may well have been justified in thinking this an ungentlemanly streak in Gilbert's character, but contraltos themselves will probably place more of the blame upon Sullivan's share in the ungentlemanly conduct, for he never seems to think of casting the gorgon in question as a soprano or mezzo.

It may be the 'image' that has done most to cause the flight from contralto to mezzo, for there are precious few avowed contraltos around today. One searches for the really deep voices and they seem to be almost an extinct species. *The Mirror of Music*, in its catalogue of 'Vocalists Popular in Britain, 1844-1944', lists twelve foreign mezzo-sopranos to ten foreign contraltos, and ten British mezzos to twenty-five British contraltos. What is more, the names of the British contraltos from the 1890s onwards are still remembered, while, with the exception of Louise Kirkby-Lunn, the mezzos are not. But then, at the head of the list of contraltos stands another majestic and formidable figure, that of Dame Clara Butt. She, I fancy, had much to do with the high status of the contralto voice in that period, and equally, much to do with its subsequent demotion.

14. Clara Butt

She was, of course, a national insitution. In a schoolboy quiz of 1914, the question 'Who was "the God-gifted organ-voice of England"?' would have been more likely to elicit the answer 'Clara Butt' than 'Milton'. When she *sang* 'Land of Hope and Glory' it was generally felt that she *embodied* it; when she sang 'Abide with Me', so warm was the invitation, so capacious the envisaged accommodation, that it was hard not to confuse the Diva with the Deity. Not that such operatic terminology was entirely appropriate, for with all the massive tones (and the six-foot physique to match) she remained in some way a homely personality, and very English. She had accordingly a tremendous

48

influence. We know little about the kind of sound made by contraltos before her, so it would be too much to say that she *created* the British contralto voice, but she was certainly its apotheosis. With her, the voice gained status, and, since hers was such a characterful sound, she often seemed to provide not so much an example as a definition. Her voice was rich and it could boom and it was very, very deep: that, it seemed, effectively defined the contralto.

Such was the popular and, I should say, the posthumous 'image' of Dame Clara Butt. It is only part of the truth, however. We are concerned here with voice-types, not with the complete art of the singer, and individuals occupy our attention only in as far as they exemplify a particular voice-type. But sometimes the 'image' obscures the true picture; and the nature of a voice can be falsified. Its relevance in this instance is that Clara Butt's influence might hardly have carried as far as it did had her art not so readily provoked caricature. To catch the reality, it is worth making an effort to hear more of her records. First there are the obvious surprises: the excellence of her trill, the fluency of her runs and arpeggios, the extensiveness of her upper range, the delicacy of her pianissimo. Then there are the contents of her repertoire; gramophone records have her in excerpts from *The Dream of Gerontius*, the brindisi from *Lucrezia Borgia*, songs by Dvořák and Fauré. Her single operatic role on stage was Gluck's Orfeo, with four performances at Covent Garden in 1920. The critics gave heavily qualified praise, but to one young singer in the audience Butt's singing on the occasion was greatness itself. This was Astra Desmond, duly listed in *The Mirror of Music* among the leading British contraltos of the next generation. She had heard Clara Butt first at the age of two: the famous singer visited her father's home in Torquay when the sound of the great voice brought her out of her cot, and she was found with her head through the banisters listening to this huge sound. That was how Astra Desmond herself put it in a broadcast (15 July 1965). The caricature-voice of Clara Butt, the 'image', would have been enough to put the child off singing for life, but the reality was different. 'Oh, it was a marvellous, marvellous voice' she said. And this, mind, is from an artist who developed for herself a particularly specialised, refined repertoire, and who would certainly in the present age have been known not as a contralto but a mezzo.

So, one might ask, what repertoire was open to these British contraltos: they can't have spent the whole of their time singing *Messiah*, *Elijah* and 'Abide with Me'. In fact, though it comes as something of a surprise, most of them had experience in opera and in some instances their parts included the great roles in Verdi which we see as essentially written for a mezzo rather than a contralto. Astra Desmond, for instance, says that she was pushed out (by her celebrated teacher

15. Muriel Brunskill as Amneris in *Aida*

Blanche Marchesi, and before she was ready) into the Carl Rosa, and in
at the deep end. Without any more training, she sang Carmen and
Azucena, and Amneris in *Aida* without a rehearsal. Amneris was almost
always sung by a contralto in those days: Edna Thornton can be heard,

magnificently regal, on an early record of the Act II duet with Florence Austral, and at Covent Garden in 1933 Muriel Brunskill sang the part with such spirit that the critics sensed she was rejoicing in the newfound freedom to expand a naturally sumptuous voice. Mary Jarred, another of the contraltos who came along in the wake of Dame Clara, also enjoyed a conspicuous success the same year, but in one of the few genuine contralto roles, Erda in *Rheingold* and *Siegfried*. On records we hear nothing of this: Brunskill recorded the usual *Messiah* and *Elijah*, and Jarred was best known for a wartime recording of The Lord's Prayer. We were not, in those days, very clever at making the most of our native talent.

The advent of Kathleen Ferrier brought about a change. But Ferrier, as well as being the first of the postwar line of internationally active British singers, was also the last in the old line of British contraltos. Her successor in general esteem was Dame Janet Baker, who has always classed herself, and been classed, as a mezzo. Ferrier was always 'contralto', and indeed there was extra depth to her voice. But one wonders: swop generations, and would not Baker have been 'contralto' and might not Ferrier have been 'mezzo'? Would the voices themselves have been different, and, in any case, what accounts for the shift that has undoubtedly come about in the recognition and use of the two voice-types?

It is tempting to conclude that more is in the mind than in the throat: a

16. Kathleen Ferrier

voice can often 'think' itself higher or lower if the mind sees good reason to do so. In the contralto age (the Clara Butt period, let's say) they 'thought' downwards. The depth, the boom even, were desired qualities. It was so in the bass voice too, and, not unconnected, it was also an age when they liked bass-heavy performances of Bach and Handel. Modern taste has reacted against that, and has wanted to liberate the old composers from what it finds a ponderous style of performance. As in instruments, so in voices: the old type of bass and the old type of contralto have all but disappeared from the choirs; and choirs, after all, are full of aspiring soloists.

But the voices change in accord with the repertoire. The development of the choral repertoire is another subject; for the contralto and/or mezzo soloist, things have certainly changed. Take, for instance, the English specialisation in Handel, and look at the style and repertoire in use even as recently as Ferrier's time. In all of Ferrier's Handel recordings there are scarcely any allegro movements, and we hear no decoration of the vocal line. All is plain and most is slow. A very few years later, she would have been confronted with the Handel opera renaissance, which brought with it the restoration of embellishment as a legitimate and indeed required practice. How all of that would have affected the centre of her vocal *thinking* is an open question.

The chapter called 'Top A' in Winifred Ferrier's biography of her sister (Hamish Hamilton 1955) inevitably comes to mind. Ferrier's first opera was *The Rape of Lucretia*, which had its première at Glyndebourne in 1946. She had many problems to face, most of them to do with stagecraft but, as Britten himself saw very clearly, some were concerned with the high tessitura of her role. A single high A appeared to be 'quite out of her reach', so Britten substituted an F sharp. He then found himself startled at one of the last performances when she sang the original A with no apparent trouble and with ringing tone. She had become absorbed in the part, had forgotten her inhibitions and was as surprised as he was to find the note coming from her. After that time she always sang it and the difficulty was over. There are many stories of singers similarly surprised, or sometimes tricked, into extensions of their range. It is also true that most, perhaps all, singers worth their salt will have the ability to sing notes at either extreme of the voice which the public never hear. The contralto Mary Jarred had a high C, but its practical usefulness lay not in public exhibition but in promoting confidence in the top notes that she had to sing: she knew, and the public guessed, that they had not stretched her uncomfortably to the furthest boundaries of the voice. It may well be that Ferrier's inhibition about the top A was not really a 'hang-up', but as healthy in its origins as the highly useful instinct of fear in humans and animals. We tend to think of this movement from contralto to mezzo as a liberation (just as mezzos count it liberating when they can move into the soprano repertoire); but there is very often an account to be settled later, not the least important item in which is a loss of richness in quality. The contralto, in other words, does well to stand her ground and not be pushed up.

The movement downwards (from soprano to mezzo or contralto) as remarked in discussion of the mezzo voice, is comparatively rare. I do recall, however, a performance of *Un ballo in maschera* where, not having looked ahead in the programme to see who was singing the secondary roles, I was excited to hear for once a real contralto Ulrica. The part is magnificently written to bring out the full richness of a contralto timbre in the opening solo, and this voice was of the full-bodied, opulent kind that one may have dreamed of but hardly expected to hear. The singer proved to be Regina Resnik, who for several years had sung soprano (the Met's first Ellen Orford, for instance). I'm sure that this remarkable lady has done many wise things in her life but moving down was certainly one of them.

In many of the reference books Resnik is designated mezzo-soprano. Where then does the division come, or are they two names for the same thing? In practice that is how it often seems to work out, the terms telling more about attitude and intention than about the voice itself. But it should not be so, for the distinction is real enough. It is not to be settled, however, by repertoire and range.

In America, Resnik herself would have entered a scene not entirely unlike the British, for there too 'contralto' was a word with old-fashioned connotations that applied beyond voices to their owners as women. The nearest American equivalent to Clara Butt was Louise Homer. She was Samuel Barber's aunt, very grand in the musical world of her time and too busy, one gathers, to bestow more than a benevolent glance upon little Sam's first compositions. She had a sumptuous, powerful but somewhat pokerbacked voice; pokerfaced too, for in duets with Caruso it would be hard to guess what is her exact, or even general, emotional disposition at any given time. I fancy – and indeed have seen the opinion expressed in an American review – that hers is the vocal 'image' of a past left behind without regrets. But she was, definitely, a contralto; so that view, of a matriarchal figure, a Queen Mary among singers, becomes part of the contralto's image. Ernestine Schumann-Heink, despite her German nationality, was the other and greater contralto in American national life – for she became a national figure, associated with 'Stille Nacht' at Christmas and, in wartime, with songs for the troops, who allegedly knew her as 'mother'. The 'image' here was of a less unbending female grandeur, homely in a Germanic way, but decidedly maternal (rather than young) and soon grandmotherly.

The repertoire of these ladies, as with that of their British counterparts, included the role of Amneris in *Aida*: it was Schumann-Heink's début role at Hamburg in 1895, and Homer's at the Metropolitan in 1900. This has been taken as an index, a crucial role, in the repertoire of the dramatic mezzo-soprano in our time, and I think it would be true to say that it would never nowadays be attempted by a singer who called herself a contralto. But in those days, in Germany, Britain and America at least, Amneris would be a professed contralto. Now, did these people not know their own voices? Did they sing parts of the role transposed or adapted (like Ferrier's F sharp)? Did they sing most of the role *as* contraltos and risk their luck, or make skilful adjustments, over the high notes? Records suggest that they sang with their contralto timbre.

To add to the discussion some contraltos of the interwar generation: Sigrid Onegin and Maria Olczewska sang with a contralto's tone, deep and rich; but when the high notes came, to some extent they ducked. There is a marvellous record of Onegin singing an arrangement of a Chopin Impromptu, where she shows all the flexibility of the most highly trained coloratura soprano but where the notes above the stave – all beautifully toned and obedient to call – are only lightly touched. We find something similar in her operatic records, such as Eboli's 'O don fatale' or Fidès's solos in *Le prophète*. She also sang a bolero by Arditi called 'La gitana', previously a favourite display-piece of Schumann-Heink's. Onegin takes cautiously the high notes which her predecessor, in spite of the primitive recording, gives in something like full voice. The full-voiced high notes can sometimes turn sour – powerful but lacking in

17. Cecilia Bartoli

resonance, as in Homer's *Aida* Act IV duets with Caruso.

Obviously in such a repertoire there are advantages in 'thinking upwards' and confronting those high notes as something other than the furthest extreme of the voice. Yet in the process, many voices forfeit what they might have had of contralto depth and richness, the kind of thing which these early, fully committed contraltos retained. Perhaps Marilyn Horne found the right compromise, for her dramatic mezzo kept its contralto qualities. Perhaps, as a lyric mezzo, young Cecilia Bartoli will manage to do the same, for a distinctive and enriching characteristic of her tone is the underlying element of contralto. When a real contralto voice turns up, we know it: one such was Oralia Dominguez, another Monica Sinclair, both of them true contraltos with an extensive range and great technical skill. The vital point now is to re-establish the word itself: contraltos should stand up and be counted.

4.   Alto or Countertenor

Angels are disinclined to enter hornets' nests, and we know who rush in. Nevertheless …

I remember. I remember that before Matins and Evensong we trooped into the Mercers' Chapel to sing an introit. In something that was not quite a semicircle we stood for a relaxed moment which terminated in the precipitate arrival, up the vestry steps, of Mr Stephenson. As an outraged eagle he inspected our ranks. No visiting General could have caused a better-justified sense of trepidation. The complexion promised apoplexy; the profile cleaved the ranks of Decani and Cantoris. A black cassock with a black belt encircling it, two black shoes about to ascend the organ loft and tread out heaven knew what ceremonial upon the bourdon and the 32-foot, asserted the least questionable authority in the world. Within a year the whole cathedral would be blown to smithereens, but with the grim faith of the twelve-year-old I still believed that if choir practice had been ordained for twelve the next morning no absentee would be forgiven by Mr Stephenson.

For the introit, a note appeared in the air and we sang. 'Let thy merciful ears, o Lord', we requested; 'Lord, for thy tender mercies' sake', we urged. But my favourite introit suggested a more conditional piety. This was 'If ye love me' by Thomas Tallis, and it informed my young mind of nothing less than what music truly *was*.

It involved a most delicious interplay of voices. Previously I had thought that we, the trebles, having the tune, were the important ones. But no: it passed to the tenors, then there it was in the basses, and ah, what was that? That, I came to realise, was Alto Smith. It was a sound from outer space, it was not of God's earth. Over and above us trebles came this phrase, 'even the spirit of truth'. And Tallis, lovely man, had arranged for it to be repeated. Knowing that our part was for once subordinated to other voices, we trebles could look around for the source of this celestial impertinence, this surplice-clad voice of astonishing height, power and purity.

It was not, I noted, Mr Collier. This surprised me, for Mr Collier was an alto of immense hootage who sang immediately behind me in the stalls and who seemed to be the most likely perpetrator. He indeed was singing, but the source of this sound was elsewhere, to my right. For years it spearheaded my quest for fuller understanding of the human voice; for some time it even directed my personal ambitions.

So let me recall this voice a little further. Alto Smith had sung in the choir as a boy; then, when his speaking voice had broken and he was able to sing bass, his unbroken but lowered boy's singing voice had remained with him, and his choir-master had pronounced him 'a natural alto'. His range, I remember, included the high C but he never offered anything beyond. The most thrilling occasion of the church year was the Sunday on which he and Mr Collier led off in Mendelssohn's 'How lovely are the messengers', with its Cs and its exposure of the alto voice naked and unashamed. Mr Collier enjoyed his high notes, and would blastingly give forth on the high Ds of the anthem we had from Dvořák's *Stabat Mater*. But later Alto Smith would confide in me the word 'Falsetto!'

'Falsetto?' I asked. This was a distinctly third-rate sort of thing to be, and there was apparently a low class of alto who really sang falsetto. Was Mr Collier a falsettist? Well no: his was a powerful, though suspiciously high-reaching, alto. In the meantime, pottering around among old volumes, I had come upon some eighteenth-century verse-anthems that seemed not to have heard of the alto voice at all but to require something called a countertenor instead. I noted that these were more in Alto Smith's line than Mr Collier's, but in the distance the hornets were buzzing.

And now we'll leap across decades right into the nest. The year is 1982 and the countertenor has come into his kingdom. In *Gramophone* magazine, my colleague Lionel Salter reviews a recital record, newly reissued, by Alfred Deller who, he says, 'put the countertenor voice on today's musical map'.

This set off in the correspondence columns a long and well-informed exchange which still provides a useful summary of the current state-of-play in the alto/countertenor controversy. Briefly, it was held on the one hand that the true countertenor is something quite different from Deller and his fellow 'altos' brought up in the traditions of English church music. High tenors, whose range extended upwards with the help of a properly supported head-voice and whose ranks in past ages may have included opera singers as famous as Rubini, were suggested as candidates to fill the vacancy. On the other side it was shown that, historically, the terms 'alto' and 'countertenor' became interchangeable in early Victorian times and clearly referred to the same kind of voice. This, moreover, was the conclusion reached by Peter Giles, whose book on the subject provided the best authority. He also distinguished

57

between three different kinds of countertenor (or alto) voice, covering the various types instanced in the controversy. Personally, if nomenclature is still in question my own vote would go to 'alto' rather than 'countertenor', which denotes a function in polyphony (the part next to the cantus firmus held by the tenor) rather than describing a voice, whereas 'alto' much more aptly denotes the highest adult male singing voice. Against that, it has to be admitted that in the last forty years or so 'countertenor' has established itself; it is what the owners of the voices generally prefer to call themselves and, because of its associations with early music, it carries a certain dignity, conferring what Henry James might call the tone of time.

Whatever the term, whatever the category, something new has entered the discussion with Jochen Kowalski. Now in his thirties, he has been exceptional in his close association with the operatic stage. In addition to Oberon in Britten's *Midsummer Night's Dream*, and the Handel operas in which nowadays it is no surprise to find a countertenor (or alto), he sings Gluck's Orpheus, Feodor in *Boris Godunov* and Orlofsky in *Die Fledermaus*. His special contentions are that the voice can be a passionate instrument, that so far from being sexless it can be powerfully erotic, and that an essential element in this is vibrato. He consciously dissociates himself from the English school which he considers to be restrictive in emotion and vibrancy. Recordings show why. Most characteristic are the four arias of Farnace in Mozart's *Mitridate*, where he gives himself to the drama with an almost reckless commitment, in spirit more like an old-style Italian tenor (Aureliano Pertile, say) than an English ex-choralist trained in anthems and cantatas. His recitative tends to be emphatic; he treats words with the dramatic intensity of a Fischer-Dieskau. The emotional range also extends to tenderness and warmth, when he can sing with smooth production and well-rounded tone. Yet in turbulent music he will encourage a style and method of production that put music essentially at the service of drama. This is of present relevance because it has a bearing on the kind of voice, which he has fashioned into a thrusting instrument, used for purposes of singing 'out', and carrying this into the upper register, where there is no feeling that the tone needs covering or that the singer would be happier if he resorted to the soft, flutelike tone which Alfred Deller, for instance, generally preferred to use in notes beyond the middle register.

Deller, indeed, might seem to be at the furthest remove from Kowalski, yet in one important respect they are alike, in that Deller's voice could also be exceptionally vibrant. In his prime, when he sang at a forte in the middle of his voice he had a resonance and richness of tone that distinguished him from the others who came to share and develop his repertoire. His voice was relatively low in its centre, and though he sang quite easily a solo such as the 'Agnus Dei' from Bach's *Mass in B minor*, with its sprinkling of D naturals and touching the E flat, he liked to use a light head-voice for those notes. It was in matters of this kind that, as I remember it, such a contrast arose when the American Russell Oberlin was brought in for the *Midsummer Night's Dream* performances at Covent Garden. Oberlin's voice was higher in timbre, very 'unplummy': not rich in vibrancy, but extremely accurate in focus. Interpretations are not our concern here, but memory has a sound-picture of his Oberon as very straight, effective in its way, but without the dappled lights and shades that are preserved in Deller's recording of the part.

When Britten devised what is still the most outstanding operatic role written specifically for countertenor, he showed by self-imposed limitations that he understood very well what the voice could and could not do. He had Deller clearly in mind, and the main solo 'I know a bank where the wild thyme blows' exploits the supple scales, the sudden softenings, the honeyed languor, that characterise his singing of songs such as Purcell's 'Sweeter than roses'. Britten is also very sympathetic in limiting the range and tessitura. From the low A he lets the voice rise to C sharp a tenth above and once lightly to touch the D, but mostly he works within a small area in between. Other countertenors are happy to go higher, and in *Death in Venice* the off-stage voice of Apollo is given some strong high Ds and, at the climax, an E. Still, the limitations remain, and composers have not in any large number followed Britten's lead. Deller also sang the part of Death in Alan Ridout's one-act setting of *The Pardoner's Tale*, and Michael Chance enjoyed something of a triumph in Judith Weir's *A Night at the Chinese Opera*. More conspicuously, Aribert Reimann uses the voice to chilling effect with the maddened howling of Edgar in his *Lear* (though when Edgar is himself again and no longer in his assumed role of poor Tom, the singularity of voice makes it doubly strange that his father – blind but not deaf – does not recognise him). There is also the question of power, and we note that Britten in *Midsummer Night's Dream* has been particularly careful not to let the orchestra mask the voice: harps, harpsichord, celeste, a muted horn, pianissimo strings are magically but sparingly used. He makes a virtue out of necessity too, for this accompaniment invests Oberon with the shimmer of moonshine, just as the voice itself puts him at a remove from earthly substance and sexuality.

Subsequent memories of the role are dominated by the sturdier, thicker, formidably projected tone of James Bowman. He, if anybody, is probably most widely seen as Deller's successor, and among his services to the voice is an extension of the repertoire into twentieth-century song. Several composers have written for him, showing that, where there is an understanding of the voice, modern music can suit it as well as the Elizabethan lute-song. A recorded recital by Bowman also helps define boundaries, for it begins with Vaughan Williams's 'Linden Lea', and the voice simply does not tell of 'brown-leaved fruits a-turning red'.

However robust the style and powerful the tone, there remain very distinct limitations to the alto/countertenor voice. Even if we rechannel the term 'countertenor' to cover those high tenors who have developed the ability to pass almost undetected from their tenor-tone to a well-supported mixed-voice, there would still remain limitations of colouring and fullness. At some point their comparability with the castrati must also enter the discussion. Several countertenors have taken the castrato repertoire on board. The American Drew Minter, for instance, sings a programme of music written by Handel for Senesino, an alto castrato and the first Giulio Cesare. Minter has marvellous precision, fluency and sweetness, with a more feminine tone than the others mentioned here, his version of 'Vivi tiranno' from *Rodelinda* making an interesting comparison with Kowalski's. Another remarkable artist, the Greek Aris Christofellis, has managed to sing the music of the soprano-castrati, his voice ascending without evident difficulty to the upper notes. Disappointingly, the sound itself is not attractive, and it seems unlike the little we know of the castrati through the evidence of our own ears.

One sole castrato voice, that of Alessandro Moreschi, remains to us on a few primitive recordings made in 1902 and 1903. In most respects they are terrible, but two points are worth making. One is that, like Kowalski, this last of the castrati seems genuinely intent upon demonstrating the emotional power of the voice. The other is that just occasionally there comes a sound, a true soprano note above the stave, when for a second a door is opened into a theatre box looking down upon a stage where stands a strange figure whose unearthly voice fills the house. The ears, they say, were ravished; and the world, with its store of altos and/or countertenors untold, has since known nothing like it. The nearest thing, I daresay, was to be heard in the Mercers' Chapel before Matins when, in Thomas Tallis's introit, there arose in notes of astonishing height, power and purity the voice of Alto Smith.

5.   Tenor

☙ Tenore di grazia ❧

The Italians are almost as good at hurling abuse at one another as were our Elizabethan ancestors. The vocabulary is rich and the choices are many; but in vocal circles, certainly in operàtic ones, you can make a start with 'Tenorino!' It is what the young Caruso was told he would be, and by way of consolation he was assured that with luck he might eventually manage to sing such roles as Wilhelm Meister in *Mignon*. 'Will ye hark to the little feller', John McCormack would say, if his old record of the trio in *Faust* was brought out. There he was, sandwiched between Dame Nellie Melba, as imperious a Marguerite as ever knocked on Heaven's door with every intention of getting in, and Mario Sammarco, brought along for the occasion as he happened to be within call, no Mephistopheles really but a baritone and a formidable one at that. In the middle, the Irish tenor can be heard quite clearly, thanks to his good production, but the heart goes out to him and he does indeed sound as if in danger of submersion though he never actually goes under. The plight of 'the little feller' is the lyric tenor's nightmare; the demon taunt of 'tenorino' is his personal hell.

'Lyric tenor', however, is a term that admits of a wide definition. When Caruso first came to London and New York it was as a lyric tenor that he was welcomed. 'His voice was originally purely lyric, a smooth, mellow, sonorous but not heavy voice, but beyond all question the most beautiful tenor heard by any living opera-goer': thus W.J. Henderson in 1921. Gigli was a lyric tenor; Tauber also and, in more modern times, Wunderlich, Vanzo, Pears, the young Di Stefano, Pavarotti. There is variety enough there, but all of those are in a different category from another type at the head of whom, by general estimation, stands Tito Schipa.

To many opera-goers and record collectors of my own generation the name of Schipa and the term 'lyric tenor' are virtually synonymous. He himself was partly responsible for this because of the care he took to ensure that people understood what he claimed to be and judged him accordingly. In the record catalogues, where Caruso and the rest were simply 'Tenor', he (and he alone) was 'Lyric Tenor'. This helped to set him apart, which his own voice-character did anyway, and it also bestowed a distinction, almost a mystique, upon the voice-category.

With it went certain limitations. One was the matter of weight, which was light; another and separable question concerns power, where the answer is not so simple, for, while this may not have been a voice to take with you into battle against a noisy orchestra, it did have remarkable carrying-power in a large auditorium. Range was limited in the expected way towards the lower end, where it became husky and colourless, but also at the top where at no very great age Schipa came to be wary of anything above a B flat, transposing if he felt the need. In repertoire his limitations act as a useful guide to the core-curriculum. What he sang, lyric tenors of his type must sing too. For some of his best years, from 1920 to 1929, he was in Chicago and appeared with fair regularity in twelve operas (*Don Giovanni, Il barbiere di Siviglia, La sonnambula, L'elisir d'amore, Don Pasquale, Lucia di Lammermoor, Rigoletto, La traviata, Martha, Lakmé, Mignon, Manon*). His nine operas at the Metropolitan were all drawn from that list, and at La Scala, after 1930, essentially it was the same repertoire but with the significant addition of *Werther*. A handful of others crop up in Milan, Chicago and at various stages, but basically one can say that his was a career founded on a repertoire of a baker's dozen, all of them roles which make very moderate demands on the vocal range and, with a few exceptions, are scarcely more arduous as tests of fluency in passage-work or other aspects of singing that may be thought of as the province of the virtuoso.

So: how to describe this voice which has so lodged in the shared memory that the sound of it is heard mentally whenever the term 'lyric tenor' is mentioned? Of course the memorability of a singer does not have to be primarily a matter of voice, and with Schipa it was certainly in large part the art of its usage and the personality inherent in it. Still, the starting-point is the voice. Light in colour, with not the faintest suggestion of a baritonal tint, it seemed to bypass the dangerous corner, the so-called 'passaggio' where the middle register moves into the upper and where the 'open' production gives way to the 'covered'. It is as though, perhaps because of the physiology (and related to the high speaking-voice), the singer is 'at home' in the area (roughly) E flat to A flat in the way most tenors are 'at home' in the C to F range, or a baritone in the A flat to E flat. Even in later years when his range had become embarrassingly short, that particular area remained open and free; the notes were also quite powerfully projected. One felt that if one were to try to sing like Schipa there might be a total absence of sensation not only in the throat but in the lower half of the face too: the sound would all be aimed high and forward. No doubt this is cognate with the notion of 'poise'. It is a word that regularly came to mind in association with Schipa, and it has much to do with the elegance of style which in turn is inseparable from the nature of the voice and its production.

Now while this – not the art so much as the voice – is representative of a certain kind of lyric tenor, it is very far from covering the whole category, even of those who share the same repertoire. Over the last two or three decades the tenor who most calls Schipa to mind has been Alfredo Kraus, and I hasten to say that it is for contrast as well as comparison. Kraus does not share the whole repertoire, but he has long been pre-eminent among the Donizetti tenors of our time; Schipa's roles in Verdi are his too, and he is also considered by many to be the most worthy inheritor of Schipa's favourite role of Werther. Several features of his singing are Schipa-esque. He too has something of the poise, the forward projection and freedom from the throat; he can lighten the tone gracefully as Schipa did; and sometimes there is even a similarity of pronunciation or at least vowel-sound. In other respects Kraus is a far less restricted singer. The power of his voice, somewhat reedy as I remember it in younger days, has become more robust. His range is far more extensive. His survival as a fully active operatic artist is a good deal more impressive (Schipa sang in public at the age of seventy-three, but even in the mid-1930s, before he was fifty, the word 'passé' began to be heard). In the *Concise Oxford Dictionary of Opera* Harold Rosenthal concludes the entry under Kraus (b. 1927) with the phrase: 'Regarded by many as the best *tenore di grazia* since Schipa'. But again one has to reflect that if that term 'tenore di grazia' really suits Kraus, then a considerable extention of its coverage is implied. Who, for instance, could imagine Schipa singing the 'Ah, mes amis' solo from *La fille du régiment*, with its volley of high Cs, as Kraus did in Paris as recently as 1986?

Adding Kraus's repertoire to Schipa's, the tally for the lyric tenor begins to mount up. An opera that now looms as a likely challenge (and figuring in Kraus's repertoire) is *I puritani*, with its aria 'A te, o cara' a famous test-piece of bel canto singing (a C sharp casually thrown in as a written embellishment of the melody in the second verse), and then in the last act the infamous 'Credeasi, misera!' which eventually looks so preposterous on paper that one thinks there must be a printer's error. The question now is the vexed one of how such high notes were expected to be sung. Giovanni Rubini, for whom the role in *I puritani* was written, worked (it now seems to be accepted) on a technique which enabled him to extend beyond the tenor notes using a voice variously described as mixed, pharyngeal, reinforced or just falsetto. In later years Italian taste became very hostile to any kind of falsetto mix; but then this development coincided with that of a taste which on the whole rejected such operas as old-fashioned. Nowadays it occasions no special wonder if a tenor includes 'A te, o cara' with its C sharp in his recital on compact disc, and whether he uses pure tenor tone or some kind of falsetto-mix seems to worry most listeners neither one way nor the other.

A feature of this same revival which has brought back that opera of Bellini's is the ever-extending investigation into the forgotten works of Donizetti and, from the singer's point of view, still more challengingly into those of Rossini. It is not so long ago that these were considered unsingable: or rather, it was held that there would be no possibility of a modern production because singers were no longer trained to cope with such virtuoso writing. A few sopranos and mezzos might conceivably be found, but never the tenors. And this seemed no more than realistic. We would listen, in awe, to the recordings of Fernando De Lucia singing Almaviva's solos in *Il barbiere di Siviglia*, particularly the 'Ecco ridente in cielo' recorded in 1904 with such well-practised fluency as came from quite another age. There were versions from a later generation of gifted and elegant singers such as Dino Borgioli, Heddle Nash and Schipa himself, but De Lucia's virtuosity was of a different order, singing of a type to which the key had been lost. Emulation, study and practice, however, have produced a new generation of tenors, some of whom have certainly developed a technique that will cope, not only with Almaviva's music (which at least is moderate in its range) but also with roles such as that of Idreno in *Semiramide*, which, if sung without convenient cuts, takes the tenor soaring aloft as well as tying himself in knots with complex runs of dizzying rapidity.

The prime exponents here have come (not surprisingly) from America; what may be less predictable is that they have been so acclaimed in Italy and have become such favourites there. It is also interesting that though we might admit Chris Merritt and Rockwell Blake into the broad category of lyric tenor on account of the repertoire, neither of them answers very well to the description of the lyric tenor as so far discussed, or to the assumption that tenore di grazia might be a valid description too.

They sang together at the 1988 Pesaro Festival in Rossini's *Otello*, and it was noted that whereas Blake's Rodrigo (a major role and not the counterpart of Shakespeare's poor creature) was pure tenor, Merritt's Otello had by comparison a baritonal tinge. That of itself sets him apart from the lyric tenors in general. Blake ('the fastest tenor in the West' according to the advertisements) sings with an ardent, almost febrile style that also seems remote from the normal concept of lyric tenor. Yet, to judge from reports as well as recordings, it is a voice that is rightly placed in Rossini and Mozart rather than in the later, 'dramatic' repertoire. With Merritt, the opportunity to hear him extended well beyond the lyric repertoire has come with *Guglielmo Tell*, the Scala production in which he appeared being now on records. At the Scala (as in the recording) his voice struck me as having neither the metallic ring nor the interest of coloration which this notoriously demanding role of Arnoldo requires – and yet it seems the height of ingratitude to say so, when the man accomplishes so reliably and with apparently complete ease the various Herculean tasks that Rossini has set before his tenor, in a part which is essentially heroic in character.

Whatever assessment one makes of their performances, it surely stretches the definition of this already generously inclusive term of 'lyric tenor' to admit these singers within it. One can only note that once again repertoire does not define the voice-type. Yet just as most of Rossini's tenor roles have traditionally been sung by a lyric tenor, so most lyric tenors have had Rossini in their repertoire (even if only *Barbiere di Siviglia*), and most of the robusto, heroic types have not.

Reverting then to the modern lyric tenor cum Rossini specialist we could take the Argentinian Raul Gimenez as a working example; but let's look at a particularly interesting newcomer to most record collectors (though, like Gimenez, no youngster in point of years), Giuseppe Morino. This was the tenor who in the Valle d'Itria Festival of 1986 made such a memorable impression in *Semiramide*, especially with the restoration of the Act I solo, 'Ah, dov'è il cimento'. A recital record has recently appeared with this aria in the programme and, leaving aside the grotesque aspirating of runs, it presents something near to the once unapproachable ideal in its combination of a naturally sweet tone with the most cultivated arts of voice-management in rapid motion over a two-octave range. For the highest notes (above C sharp) he employs what appears to be a well-supported, skilfully integrated falsetto, and this seems entirely legitimate. In the other Italian arias, mostly by Bellini and Donizetti, he shows very clearly the advantages of an Italian voice – by which I don't mean to imply that its owner must *be* Italian – in that it makes a prime virtue of beauty of tone. It is also worth noting that when it comes to the French repertoire (arias from *Faust, Roméo et Juliette, Le Roi d'Ys, Pêcheurs de perles* and *Manon*) he also has something of the old French school as represented by, say, David Devriès and Charles Friant. As far as one can judge from these recordings, Morino has his share of faults, but it is nevertheless through such artists that the noble traditions of European singing survive.

☙ Lyric and spinto ❧

One of the limitations of the tenore di grazia is that people tend not to take him very seriously.

The tenor is almost always 'good': aesthetically, that is his affliction. There is an occasional ambiguity (Grimes, Eléazar, Hermann) or contradiction (Peter Quint, Busoni's Mephistopheles) or grotesque (Mime, Herod), but essentially 'hero' is tied like a label round his neck. Usually he is a romantic hero too, though the heavier types of tenor often have something else on their mind, such as patriotism (Radamès), social injustice (Chénier) or religion (Tannhäuser). The robusto or Heldentenor, morever, may be a divided, tormented soul (Parsifal, Otello, Canio), which makes life more interesting. As Siegfried he may have another outlet in physical exercise; as Florestan there is the sublimation of suffering. But for the lyric tenor, uncomplicated goodness is much more inescapably the general doom. Being male, he is not expected to be as pure and blameless as his opposite number, the lyric soprano: he may even be Faust to her Marguerite, Pinkerton to her Butterfly. On the whole, however, he has our sympathy, for he is (vocally) young and handsome, and almost invariably he is in love. When trouble comes we look to him for the virtues: his depths will be sounded. But character in opera is only in a nominal, superficial way established by the words or by developments in the plot; basically, it is realised in, or through, the music. The music in turn comes to us to a very important extent through the voice, and voices themselves have character. On the whole, the light voice expresses the light nature. As with the soubrette, some of the tenore di grazia's best roles are in comedy, and when, say, Ernesto in *Don Pasquale* has his sorrowful aria in minor key ('Cercherò lontana terra') we are not unduly perturbed: in fact we don't take him seriously. In a tragic role the tenore di grazia commands sympathy for his sad plight, but a bright and slender voice, as most of these are, is not suggestive of a deep nature.

Generally it is felt that when the voice adds to itself a little depth and weight (and it need not be more than a little) the character puts on something of those qualities. Together they are suggestive of warmth, of manliness too, so that the voice-character moves further towards the centre and gains a more complete kind of humanity. As a lyric tenor, the singer will still present a picture of romantic youth and we shall not normally expect to find him rallying the troops or wrestling with problems of state. But the full human-being in him takes a step forward and to that extent he is not simply or primarily 'the tenor'.

Yet, paradoxically, if we say 'tenor' without specifying a particular type, this – we'll call it the Rodolfo voice – is what we normally mean. Though the light kind of lyric tenor (Tito Schipa, for instance) will probably have *La Bohème* in the repertoire, he is likely to sound very much the proverbial 'little feller' in among the big boys when the noisy orchestration makes all four Bohemians give forth as robustly as they can. Moreover, the emotional fullness of the part demands a more full-bodied tone. 'Che gelida manina' is not associated in our minds as much with Schipa (though he recorded it) as with Gigli, or with Alfredo Kraus as with Domingo or Pavarotti.

That famous solo and what we'll call the 'central' lyric tenor suit each other to perfection; part of its magic is the way in which it unfolds the beauties of a voice, pleat by pleat, till all is laid out, the whole fabric admired, its colours, texture, strength and softness.

The aria begins as a monotone. The voice is at its easiest, a quiet exercise of the medium range followed by a gentle excursion into the easy upper notes in which lies the nectar of a natural lyric tenor voice. A little warming, a first suggestion of the passions in store, then a momentary return to the monotone acts now as a prelude to the first flowering of inspiration, the first high-note and the opportunity to phrase on forwards, unashamedly glorying in the sound. Because an opera singer is more than a singer and because variety encourages appreciation, the tenor now welcomes a few phrases of quasi-recitative. Then the new lyricism ('In povertà mia lieta') again starts softly but soon culminates ('l'anima ho milionaria') in a heaven-sent opportunity for an open-throated uncovering of some of the richest notes in the voice. And then, as Rodolfo himself gains inspiration, so does the composer, not least in his instinctive Italian's knowledge of what it is like to be a singer. When does a tenor sound most as though praising his Creator for making him what he is? Isn't it when he launches into 'Talor dal mio forziere', the glowing affirmation of the whole opera, and all made in that part of the voice in which the tenor enters into his kingdom. More middle-ground now, and then, when the high C comes, the thrill of its vantage-point as the summit of the world is maximised. There remain the four final phrases, the passion within them briefly swelling and diminishing, and nothing here (one would think) need give the singer any trouble when he has come through all the rest. Strangely, it often seems that the one note which Puccini did not 'sing' with the singer is his last. After the many repeated E flats, Rodolfo's 'vi piaccia dir' quite frequently causes a moment of anxiety which never attended the high C. At the end of his labours the tenor must return to that E flat and sustain it softly on the 'ee' sound of 'dir': tricky and sometimes perilous.

The role of Rodolfo expands to include some tense and tragic utterances. In Act III bitterness enters his voice for the first time, and perhaps it is then that the listener reaches out mentally for another sort of tenor. Yet the Quartet brings back a gentle lyricism resembling the love music of Act I, and so does the duet in Act IV, 'O Mimì, tu più non torni'. Here indeed, at least for the opening solo, the Schipa type of tenor might be ideal (he did not record it but John McCormack did, and

67

18. Beniamino Gigli as Cavaradossi in *Tosca*

with him we hear the fine line and clean tone that would tend to forfeit something of their poise in a voice that had more weight and breadth).

Now, placed in a structurally similar position to that of 'Che gelida manina' in *La Bohème*, and in an opera originally produced just one month later in 1896, the 'improvviso' ('Un dì all' azzurro spazio') of Andrea Chénier runs it a very close second in its expert matching with a certain kind of tenor voice. The dramatic situation is of course very different, but again there is a young woman who has newly caught the eye of a young poet. Here the scene is set not in a Parisian attic but an aristocratic salon not so far away in Coigny. Chénier, brought to the reception by a friend, is put on the spot when asked to improvise a poem, and all is well as he begins with the conventional pastoral description. When the eyes of imagination explore further and find poverty, disease and ignorance, he gives offence, as indeed he intended, to all except the young woman in whose eyes he can see sympathy and even love. The emotions range wide, but clearly they take a fiercer, more turbulent form than anything in 'Che gelida manina'. The writing for the voice becomes correspondingly more strenuous, and encourages a more declamatory manner. It does not call, necessarily, for the power of a tenore robusto;

19. Giovanni Martinelli as Cavaradossi in *Tosca*

much of it and the rest of the role are essentially lyrical in style; yet it is indisputably beyond the tenore di grazia and may not be suitable for the *Bohème* tenor either. This is where the lirico spinto enters the scene.

In fact he entered briefly a little while ago when our survey of the role in *La Bohème* paused to take in the more stressful moments of Act III. Rodolfo's manner and vocal style change with his sneering criticisms of Mimì ('Mimì è una civetta') and then with the impassioned, bitterly charged torment of 'Invan, invan nascondo la mia vera tortura'; and it is here that the lyric tenor has to do his best to increase the dramatic thrust and intensity of his singing. He has, in a manner of speaking, to push. And this is the nature, the speciality and rationale, of the spinto – who is also, incidentally, a past-participle. The verb spingere means 'to push; shove; drive; thrust', and the lirico spinto type of tenor arises out of music which has a particularly thrustful emotional emphasis. Andrea Chénier is a case in point; an earlier opera is *La forza del destino* where the role of Don Alvaro, despite some purely lyrical passages, drives his voice with bitter intensity against a malevolent fate. In vocal terms, 'push' does not necessarily mean 'strain'; essentially it is a lyric tenor voice intensified for dramatic purposes.

The two types, the 'central' lyric tenor and the spinto, are best illustrated not from our own time but by two famous tenors of the interwar years, Beniamino Gigli and Giovanni Martinelli. They contrast quite sharply, Gigli's tone being rounded, Martinelli's pointed, Gigli's delivery suggesting ease, Martinelli's danger. Part of Gigli's 'ease', especially in later years, lay in the use of a sweet-toned head-voice for his softer singing, distinct in tone and method from the voice at forte. Part of Martinelli's 'danger' was that when he wanted to sing quietly it was with the same 'unmixed' tenor tone as the loud singing but reined-in under a tighter control. This carried through into stylistic matters, which are not our concern here, so that while Gigli gave the impression of breathing 'naturally' – and, accordingly, phrasing without any special breadth – Martinelli would achieve an exceptional span of melodic continuity on a single breath but at some cost to the sense of freedom in the tone, which was thinned and concentrated by the necessary compression or retention of air in the lungs.

To these two fell the major share of the spoils at the Metropolitan after Caruso's death in 1921 (though both would have abhorred that way of expressing it). Gigli took the more lyrical roles such as the Duke in *Rigoletto*, Alfredo, Des Grieux, Lionel in *Martha*, Nemorino in *L'elisir d'amore*. Martinelli became the regular Don Alvaro, Manrico, Radamès, Canio, Eléazar in *La Juive*. They had many roles in common, Chénier for instance, Cavaradossi, Enzo in *La Gioconda*. On records and (for Gigli) outside the Metropolitan there was a bigger overlap as Gigli came to undertake heavier parts in the 1930s. Comparison of recordings does not suggest (as might be expected) a greater power or volume in Martinelli (to judge from press reports, his voice became an instrument of considerable power in the first decade of his singing and seems to have lost some of this in the 1930s). The differences are principally in timbre, method and style. Sometimes the general notion of the lyric tenor and spinto will find Martinelli closer to a pure lyricism (compare his finely-bound line in the *Lucia di Lammermoor* solos, for example) and Gigli the more emphatic and overt in emotional utterance. But when they are being their most representative selves, as singers, they each provide an admirable definition-by-example of their respective types. Perhaps it should be added that push came to shove when Martinelli took Otello into his repertoire (and, in a single performance only, Tristan), but that if he had not done so we would have lost what, on records at least, is a performance of unsurpassed intensity unequalled (I think) in its power to impress itself upon the memory and imagination.

∽ Robusto and Heldentenor ∾

The *tenore robusto* is a splendid fellow with swelling thorax, bristling mustachioes, arms akimbo, or a gleaming sword aloft in his right hand, and all five-foot-eight of him aflame with devotion to mistress or mother, native land or the week's good cause.

In repertoire he overlaps with the spinto and even with the lyric tenor. He will not necessarily wish to renounce his Dukedom of Mantua just because he has been appointed commander of the army in Egypt. Though in practice opera's favourite double bill will assign to him the motley and heartbreak of Canio in *Pagliacci*, he may still be interested in the earbiting stuff of *Cavalleria rusticana*. Drawing a deep breath and offering an urgent prayer, he will eventually agree to sign on for *Otello*, but will still want to keep his lodging in *La Bohème* and be shot at from time to time by Scarpia's firing-squad in *Tosca*. In the French repertoire he will probably forsake *Faust* but cling to *Carmen*. The slimcut roles which won him his first laurels in youth – Gérald in *Lakmé*, Wilhelm in *Mignon* – will now be outgrown, and the Singalese diver's outfit for *Pêcheurs de perles* will be exchanged for the rags of poor Samson, eyeless in Gaza at the mill with slaves. Adventurously he might consider Handel's *Samson* too, and then Britten's *Peter Grimes* and perhaps Walton's Troilus. The unloved heroes of Weber, Max in *Der Freischütz*, Huon in *Oberon*, come into view; Beethoven's Florestan certainly, and then Wagner. Aspiring beyond Lohengrin to Tannhäuser and even Tristan, our tenor's robustness may finally quail at the prospect of

Siegfried. Yet some have faced that challenge too and quite a few have survived it.

Home-ground for the robusto is Manrico in *Il trovatore*. It is not such a heroic role that it cannot be taken by the lirico-spinto, and some of its noted exponents have come within this category. Martinelli sang it 69 times at the Metropolitan, and with Radamès and Canio it shared a position at the head of his regular repertoire. All the same, though his remained a 'lusty' performance (that was the usual word), when he was in his prime and sang in the first performances under Toscanini the aria in which he shone was the lyrical 'Ah, si, ben mio', not the heroic 'Di quella pira'. This was so too with comparable later tenors such as Björling and Bergonzi. For full justice, Manrico needs Caruso.

Caruso's *Trovatore* recordings are among his finest. His 'Ah, si, ben mio' and the solo verse of 'Mal reggendo' have an ease and continence such as any lyric tenor might envy; the Miserere has all the thrust and brilliance of the finest type of spinto; and the 'Di quella pira' might well provide, by example, the best working-definition of what is meant by the tenore robusto. Among the many remarkable qualities of that last record (made in 1906), a notable feature is the fact that the top notes (they are Bs, not Cs) are thrillingly forward and even in their resonance, while the general tone-quality has a breadth and roundness about it that are closer to the tones of the heroic baritone. It is this extra roundness and 'body' of tone, together with the impression of giving greater volume of sound, that distinguish the true robusto from the spinto; and it is probably an awareness of this quality that leads him on, from Manrico and Radamès in Verdi, to Otello.

So *Otello* in Italian opera, *Siegfried* in German, appear to be the terminal points, the ultimate extension, for the robusto, and by this point he has moved into the full heroic territory which, after all, is that of the Heldentenor. So the question then is whether this development involves a difference in kind; otherwise the heroic tenor is simply a particularly powerful robusto. A supplementary question concerns the Heldentenor. Is he a different species entirely, and if so is it by virtue of his predominantly German (and Wagnerian) repertoire, or is there a special kind of style and voice-production that earns him this description and the 'image' that goes with it?

We all know a Heldentenor when we see one. He carries a spear and wears a helmet, travels by swan, plays with bears, talks to birds and laughs at dragons. He is very big and very strong and very brave and (as Anna Russell says) very stupid. If you have a sword stuck in the tree that grows in your living room he is the man to extract it. He needs to possess an exceptionally stentorian voice in order to compete with his Isolde and Brünnhilde, who (as Anna Russell also observes) are in the habit of

72

winning. For many years the Heldentenor was almost invariably
embodied by the great Dane, Lauritz Melchior. A fine figure of a man in
early years, he came (according to Rudolf Bing) to look like a walking
sofa on stage at the Metropolitan towards the end. Nowadays when we
gaze around for a comparable embodiment, it is almost as though most
of the contenders have tried on the magic Tarnhelm and become
invisible: an extinct species, we sometimes suspect.

Perhaps that is all there is to it: a tenor who sings Wagner and
therefore has exceptional power. But this is a definition of voice-type by
repertoire, which is never entirely satisfactory, for several different kinds
of voice may sing almost any particular role. Perhaps as a way in, we may
listen a little more closely to this archetype of the Heldentenor, Lauritz
Melchior. We might hear him first in Siegfried's Forging Song. Power
there is certainly; poor little Mime, when he starts to chatter his
malicious encouragement, is dwarfed vocally as well as physically. The
power, too, is not unlike the sword he is forging, shining brightly and
cutting cleanly. The range extends upwards to the repeated high A,
sometimes with a short glancing blow, sometimes with a sustained
frontal assault. Melchior seems to rejoice in it, swelling fearlessly, giving
the impression of an athlete in tiptop condition who could go round the
track another couple of times and think nothing of it. With many, the
sheer power is lacking to make this the effective climax of the Act,
sometimes the stamina to carry it through after all that has gone before;
or years of service may have loosened the vibrations and the dreaded
wobble may afflict those sustained notes. Or it may be that the tenor
sounds heroic enough on the full-bodied middle notes, but has no
natural tenor resonance for the As. Nearly always, if you know
Melchior's recordings, the night's Siegfried in current performances
seems a poor second-best at this point, even if he passes muster in the
rest.

Melchior's artistry and musicianship were sometimes impugned, but
in sampling the voice as an instrument fashioned to meet Wagner's
requirements, many other records show him using it with great art. It is
worth looking out, for instance, his 1929 recording of the *Tristan und
Isolde* love duet with Frida Leider to hear how in the quiet, lyrical section
('O sink hernieder') he moderates his tone so that it exactly matches the
soprano's, and how he meets Wagner's challenge to the Heldentenor,
virtually asking that he should lighten his voice so that he sounds almost
like the lyric tenor of Italian bel canto opera, Ernesto in *Don Pasquale*
perhaps, gentle and honeyed as in his nocturne-duet, 'Tornami a dir che
m'ami'.

Another aspect of the Heldentenor repertoire, and an important one,
presents itself if we listen then to Melchior in *Die Walküre*. Take the

opening of the third scene in Act I, with Siegmund's narrative 'Ein Schwert verhiess mir der Vater'. It contains the great cries of 'Wälse! Wälse!', the name by which Siegmund knows the father he lost in boyhood. These call for all possible fullness of voice supported by maximum lung-power and control: as a challenge, they are to the Heldentenor what the top C of 'Di quella pira' is to the Verdian robusto. Melchior impresses mightily, in his many recordings both 'live' and in the studio. But another point about this solo is its depth: that is, the extent to which this writing for the tenor voice presupposes a baritonal strength and richness in the lower notes. It ends with a phrase set deep in the voice, reflecting the dark recesses of the heart where the fire burns: 'tief in des Busens Berge glimmt nur noch lichtlose Glut'. From the voice that shone so brightly as pure tenor in Siegfried's Forging Song come notes that would be superbly ample in a baritone, or even a bass. They remind us that Melchior started his career as a baritone and they provoke further speculation on the true character and definition of the Heldentenor voice.

This role of Siegmund in *Die Walküre* is, in fact, of all standard operatic roles, the one in which a tenor part could most readily be taken by a baritone: it would be highly inadvisable to try it, but note by note, phrase by phrase, it could almost certainly be done. But something similar could be said of Otello, which is the 'terminal' role for the heroic tenor in the Italian repertoire, and perhaps we should make a brief inspection of Otello's music before going further.

It is not an exceptionally long part, and certainly not high. Otello sings something like two and a half thousand notes, of which, according to my unreliable calculations, just about eighty rise above the high G. One optional C (a brief stabbing note for dramatic emphasis), a single exposed B natural with another as a quick, if awkwardly placed, appoggiatura, five B flats, a few A naturals – and these are well spaced so that there is no question of tiring the voice by keeping it uncomfortably high for any length of time. Some whole pages could be sung without undue discomfort by a baritone, and indeed it is notable that when baritones turn tenor (Giovanni Zenatello, Renato Zanelli, Paolo Silveri and Ramon Vinay are examples), they often turn towards Otello. The suggestion therefore seems to be that the Otello voice is one where a certain baritonal thickness may help to give his utterances additional weight and mature authority. These utterances, however, do some-times have to penetrate some formidable masses of sound from the orchestra. This is especially true of the duet at the close of Act II, which comes after the strenuous 'farewell' solo ('Ora e per sempre addio') and some feverish declamation also over a heavy orchestra. For this there must be that kind of cleaving, sharp-edged tone more characteristic of the tenor voice than the baritone. The requirements are beginning to add up.

This is still only part. Giovanni Martinelli, who sang Otello without having any of the baritonal admixture, said that he had thought it beyond his scope till Maestro Serafin pointed out that at least three-quarters of the writing was lyrical (no doubt such considerations encouraged Pavarotti too when he came to add the part to his repertoire). Most of the love duet is lyrical, and the central passage of the great monologue; there are phrases of smooth if painful sweetness in Act II, and in Act III blandishments better suited to a Rossinian tenore di grazia but put to purposes of terrible irony. There are also times when the singing voice must be sacrificed in fierce declamation or in a suffocated intensity of emotion. It also comes back to the sheer matter of matter, for the role's effectiveness is jeopardised if the entrance is not impressive, and Verdi has set an almost superhuman task here, giving the solo voice just twelve bars in which to assert his power over all the forces of fortissimo chorus and orchestra that have been unleashed from the start of the opera. This is what the tenor is taking on, purely as a singer (quite apart from the demands of the drama): no wonder the role is commonly seen as the final challenge to the robusto quality which has developed beyond the lyric-dramatic or the 'pushed' voice of the spinto.

The original Otello of 1887 was the astounding Francesco Tamagno. To remind myself, for one can never be certain that memory has not played tricks, I have just taken down three of his records: it is an amazing sound, coming through from 1903 with massive power and absolute clarity. The recordings were made after he had virtually retired from the stage, suffering from a heart condition, and all of them are with piano accompaniment. Unbelievably (and no wonder he used to hug the machine in incredulous delight at the sound of his own voice played back to him) out comes the legendary trumpet quality in the opening 'Esultate', a broad timbre, immensely powerful and solid. The second solo, 'Ora e per sempre addio', is sung slowly, with a fine care for the evenness of line; and the Death scene, 'Niun mi tema', opens with a beautifully softened, rounded tone which was also a feature of his singing remembered by many who heard him in his prime. What concerns us here, considering him as perhaps the archetype of the heroic tenor, is the special nature of the voice – which is not simply that it is very loud but that it is all *one*. As you listen to Tamagno going up step by step in the climax of the 'farewell' (at the words 'della gloria d'Otello e questo il fin') you hear the high notes of the scale produced in apparently the very same way as the lower notes at the start; it is not that the point of change in vocal register has been smoothed over, as with any well-trained tenor, but rather as though there *is* no change. It seems that part of the heroic quality comes from this ability to support a breadth of tone in the notes around A flat and B flat such as would normally (and wisely) be restricted to the E flat to F area of the voice. Readers who have formed a sound-picture of this in their minds can perhaps go further and add another to help point up the contrast. Take, for example, Jussi Björling as a tenor who is of the lyric-dramatic type, just short of the robusto or heroic tenor who finds it natural to add Otello after his success as Radamès in *Aida*. The sound-picture here is drawn within narrower lines, like reducing the waist-line, and the high notes, shining and ringing as they are, do not emerge from the same open position as we find the upper part of the middle register. The extra weight that the true heroic tenor brings to bear has to do with the breadth of timbre and the openness of high notes at a point where the lyric-dramatic type will start to 'cover'.

So where have we, in postwar years, heard a voice that answers at all fully to this description? Not taking the comparison with Tamagno further than it ought to go (for a great deal could be written about the differences), we have to name Jon Vickers. Over the many years since his house debut in 1957 we have been able to sit in Covent Garden listening to this massive sound, that can be reduced to the most gentle, almost

20. Jon Vickers

76

whispered pianissimo and still reach the furthest corners with a rare, face-to-face immediacy, and marvel precisely at the way this particular area of the voice is produced. In *Otello*, continually striking was the breadth of tone, the feeling that the lie, the tessitura, of this role was exactly right for that voice. Casting an eye over the other roles most associated with Vickers, one gets a fair conspectus of the heroic repertoire. Peter Grimes clearly becomes part of it. Peter Pears, the original Grimes, sang the role in such a way that everything he did came straight through to the audience and was intensely memorable; yet at the same time, in Covent Garden at least, there was often a sense of a singer willing to give a greater volume of tone than he could produce. For all the loneliness and aspiration of this troubled soul, there is a rough and frightening power in Grimes that needs a big voice to make it effective. 'To hell with all your mercies; to hell with your revenge': one can hear Vickers' great house-filling voice in the phrases now, and without the reserves of an Otello-voice the more robust and formidable side of Grimes can be no more than suggested.

Grimes is not yet in the repertoire of Placido Domingo; Otello, of course, is. He himself is inclined to play down the achievement, or at

21. Placido Domingo

22. Renato Zanelli as Otello

least to put it into a different perspective. Everyone marvels and looks concerned when they hear he is to sing Otello, but no one seems to care one way or another when it is *I vespri siciliani*; and that, he says, is the real killer. It must be partly a matter of tessitura: Arrigo's music lies relatively high in the voice (no doubt a reason why it suited Helge Roswaenge, who sang in the early German revivals), and it could well be more arduous than Otello in that respect. The baritonal tinge in Domingo suits Otello and leads us to consider this very different kind of heroic tenor. Tamagno and Vickers in their differing ways both have warrior-voices; Domingo's is a lover's voice. My caricature at the start of this discussion depicted the robusto, sword in hand. Domingo's is a distinctly less militant timbre: one might wonder whether robusto is the term for him at all. Yet here he is, an Otello whose occupation is not gone yet, after some thirteen years 'i' the imminent deadly breach'.

Searching back in memory (but with notes made at the time to support it), I find that the phrases which come to mind most vividly from Domingo's Otello in the theatre are the opening of the love duet, the middle section of the monologue, the whole of the death scene, which lies (as Kathleen Ferrier used to say in another context) 'in the fat of the voice'. These are all middle-register, medium-volume passages, and in this type of sound the associations are with Renato Zanelli and Ramon Vinay – both from Chile, both beginning as baritones – recalling that Spanish-born Domingo began as a baritone too, singing in Mexico. In Zanelli's Otello (heard at Covent Garden in 1928 and 1930) the beauty of tone, depth of feeling and tall, dignified stage presence made amends for a lack of hard edge to cut a way through the orchestral hurly-burly. Domingo must have reckoned with this problem, for he has deliberately sharpened the edge of his voice. As one remembers him in early days, as Cavaradossi, Rodolfo and Radamès, the unworn surface of the voice made one say, in the inadequate vocabulary we have to employ, 'golden', 'velvet': those were his days as pure lyric-dramatic tenor. With Manrico in *Il trovatore* and with Otello he encouraged the metal to show through; phrases like the bitter 'anima mia' in *Otello* acquired a ruthless edge, of the sort one would hardly have thought he could produce. To some extent the sheer beauty of the voice has suffered, the purest 'gold' of earlier times being heard intermittently. The wonder is that it has suffered so little.

In the normal course of nature, Domingo has a good many singing years left to him. Caruso died at forty-eight, and he died without having sung Otello. So where in this classification of voices does he stand? In youth, Turiddu, Alfredo, the Duke of Mantua, Faust and Edgardo were the foundation-roles of his repertoire. Canio in *Pagliacci* was added as early as 1896, and Radamès in 1900, but the balance was still lyrical,

79

tipping towards the dramatic-heroic in 1908 when he sang in *Il trovatore* for the first time. 1915 brought Samson in Saint-Saëns' opera, 1918 Jean in *Le Prophète*, and his last new role was Eléazar in Halévy's *La Juive*. The voice darkened, as we hear on records, and the style became more strenuous. He never sang Otello, though he recorded published excerpts in 1910 and 1914, and the role was included in plans for the future.

That future, tragically hypothetical as it is, most surely have taken Caruso further and ever more exclusively into the 'heroic' category. Again the nearest likely modern parallel is with Vickers. As vocal personalities (a compound of timbre and humanity) the two differ from each other profoundly, but there are affinities. Reviewing a recital record by Vickers in the *Gramophone* magazine of June 1964, Andrew Porter wrote: 'This is marvellous – perhaps the most Caruso-like singing that has been put on disc since the death of Caruso.' He was making a precise point here: that Vickers was now developing a tone 'fuller, firmer, more even and thrilling just as sound, than ever before – in a word more Caruso-like'. The key-word there is probably 'fuller'. Caruso's late recordings, say those made in his last five years, have quite astonishing fullness. In these, he has not lost the thrilling top notes, but the middle ones are so full-bodied and kingly that one almost wishes him to stay within the middle and upper-middle part of the voice throughout. Vocally at least, he would have made a magnificent Siegmund. To take the point one stage further, by those last years Caruso had become, if not in repertoire then nevertheless in voice-type, a true Heldentenor. Vickers, whose voice came to have the most house-filling breadth of any tenor I have heard in almost forty years at Covent Garden, similarly belongs to this category, and it is only by thinking of the Heldentenor as essentially the singer of Siegfried that we fail to see this.

It is perhaps more useful to think of Siegfried as a part for the robusto. The tessitura, especially in *Siegfried* itself, is higher than that of Tannhäuser, Siegmund, Tristan and Parsifal, and, while the role certainly needs an exceptionally powerful voice to do it justice, the demand for power is not as daunting or distinctive a feature as the demand for energy. Energy can hardly be thought of as characterising any one particular voice-type – unless it be the 'robusto'.

It comes back, then, to the point raised earlier: whether there is a real distinction between the robusto and the heroic tenor (the Manrico as opposed to the Otello) in terms of anything other than volume, and whether there is any essential difference between the robusto/heroic tenor and the Heldentenor (the Siegfried and Tristan) except in terms of repertoire.

In fact there is probably a need for a different term altogether. A special type of voice does exist that can (if its owner so desires) undertake heroic roles in both the Italian and German reportoire, and its main characteristic is that it has weight, the notes of the upper 'passage' (the top of the middle register and the lower notes of the top) having unusual breadth. It is the Vickers-voice or the voice Caruso's was becoming. It is also a particularly dangerous voice, and tenors who encourage this kind of breadth in their tone do so at their peril unless their natural endowment is something quite special. It is very probably what Caruso had in mind when he earnestly warned the tenor Romeo Berti (later a singing-teacher in London): 'Je ne suis pas tenor à copier.'

6.   Baritone

ꙮ   Dramatic   ꙮ

By name, and often by nature, the baritone is opera's heavy-man. The 'tone' in his name speaks for itself; the 'bari' part, Greek in origin (and in Italian accentuated on the second syllable, 'barítono'), means 'weighty, heavy', as in 'barycentric' ('of, or pertaining to, the centre of gravity') and 'baric' ('of, or pertaining to, weight esp. that of the air cf. "barometer" '). Here endeth the first lesson.

The second should perhaps start with the observation that the name is not 'mezzo-tenore'. We normally think of the mezzo-soprano and baritone as being much the same thing but for the small difference of sex. Names and dates suggest otherwise. The mezzo-soprano is a species comparatively recent in evolution: the dictionary (*OED*, and probably not the best source of information here but we will accept it as a guide) gives 1753. The baritone (old spelling 'barytone' still preferred) goes back to 1609. That also is modern compared with 'treble' (1440), 'tenor' (1475) and 'bass' (1450), which were voice-parts in medieval choral writing. Mezzo-soprano, and indeed soprano itself (the dictionary cites 1830 for use in English), exist only after the emergence of women as professional artistic performers. The baritone is an invention of the Renaissance and coincides very closely with the birth of opera: he is, one might conclude, a dramatic necessity rather than a musical one.

But, granted opera's need for a 'heavy' voice, it might still be a question why the voice that we know today as the baritone (without thinking specially of its heaviness) should have been that voice. After all, tenors can be the noisiest creatures, and basses are not normally lightweights. I am not sure that Act I of *La Bohème* doesn't suggest an answer to this. There are on stage, till shortly before Mimì's entrance, four men (for a while five, with Benoit), of whom one is a tenor, one a bass, and two (three with Benoit) are baritones. In a good many performances I have been surprised to find that the tenor carries comparatively little weight. On records it is different; there the tenor often seems to be the most prominent. But on stage with famous tenors such as Björling (admittedly not a well man), Di Stefano, Bergonzi and

6. Baritone

Domingo (but not Pavarotti, whose timbre has focused attention), the voice one expected to dominate has not done so, and has sometimes even seemed small by comparison with his less celebrated colleagues. Nor has the bass, the Colline, normally come through with deep sonority. No, the big sound – and there has been plenty of it, and there needs to be to compete with the orchestration – has seemed to come predominantly from the baritones, the Marcel and Schaunard.

And that, one might object, may possibly demonstrate something, but it doesn't explain it. I can only hazard a guess, along these lines. The normal male singing voice (amateur, untrained but not unpractised) produces its fullest, most resonant tone in the area of middle A upwards to D. The bass will descend, solid and powerful, and probably arrive at another particularly resonant area around the low A. The tenor will rise and ring out on the high G or even top A. But the tenor's high notes ... if he is wise (and musical), he will cover (he won't make the sound a newspaper seller, football supporter or rock vocalist will produce at that pitch); and if he is to guard the tenor quality of his upper range he must, in general, forgo something of that rounder, deeper fullness in the middle notes. Similarly the bass knows, by instinct and experience, that the low notes will tend to lose something of their deep bass quality (or even become foggy and unreliable) if he lets himself go too often and too freely in what, for him, is the upper part of the voice. It is the baritone's special province, then, to have those 'central' resonance-notes (the middle A to D) as the very heart of his territory and to be able to strengthen what nature has made strong in the first place. Perhaps one should say that for the professional baritone the area is almost immediately extended; even so, with many fine and famous singers (Gobbi, for instance) the greatest resonance is heard in the theatre not on the high notes, but on the D and E flat. With his depth of timbre added to such fullness and power, the baritone lives up to his name: a man of weighty sound.

The epitome here is Titta Ruffo. He has been dead these many years, and the mighty voice was silent many years before that, but his name is still heard wherever the great voices are being discussed. His was the one voice that worried Caruso when up against his own. A 'once-in-a-lifetime experience' Rosa Ponselle called it, and she made it clear that it was the beauty, subtlety, and expressiveness of the singing, not simply its power, that made him unmatchable among baritones. 'The idol of the public' is such a cliché that we shrug our shoulders and pass on, but in his best years it seems to have been the sober (and heady) truth. Walter Legge heard him in London in the 1920s and was so impressed that for the rest of his life (as Beecham's assistant at Covent Garden and as impresario and producer for EMI) he went about looking

83

for someone who might at least resemble Ruffo in kind, if not match him in degree, but in vain. 'Manly, broad, sympathetic, of unsurpassed richness', Legge wrote, remembering a Queen's Hall concert in 1922; 'of gigantic proportions' and 'of pure baritone timbre' he added, describing the voice that can be heard on records. 'The legendary' is for once a justified epithet.

This is not the place to discuss the validity of that reputation (there is matter for debate); what concerns us is the *kind* of voice, of which Ruffo's was such a striking example. For one thing, though its glory (according to Ponselle and the evidence of records) lay in the middle and upper registers, its timbre had depth; Venceslao Persichini, his teacher in Rome and a specialist in the production of baritones, had believed him to be a bass. It was a 'dark' voice, and yet also a brilliant one: burnished in the forest of the night, like Blake's tiger. A listener to his records will also come away with another impression, hard to describe but rather as though, up to the climaxes, the sound is coming out through only a half-opened mouth. The vowels, particularly the 'ah' vowels, do not impress as open: there is a kind of snarl. One might expect this to constrict the tone, but on the contrary it seems to fortify it. It also affects the personality of the voice so that as an instrument it becomes still more dramatic, more appropriate to tragedy than to comedy, lending itself well to the expression of ruthlessness, malevolence, determination. Then there is the vibrancy. In Ruffo's day, particularly among his countrymen, a fast or reiterative vibrato was much more commonly found and widely admired than in singers today; several of the early Italian baritones whom we hear on record (Pasquale Amato, for instance, and, a little later, Benvenuto Franci) had it as a marked characteristic. By comparison with them, Ruffo's tone is 'straight'. But compared with others of his own race and time, his voice is reverberant: we are more aware of vibrancy in his singing than in that of Battistini, Scotti, Sammarco, or de Luca. Now, this fine difference in the 'pulse' of voices is as eloquent as the fine tuning of an actor's voice, the flicker of expression across a face which transforms its character and by which hearts and fortunes may be won and lost. The 'dark' baritone is identified, finally, by the vibrations of a split second.

Coming closer to our own time, we can recognise the vibrancy and the colouring, if not the sheer weight, in the voices of two Italian baritones born in the same year, indeed, in the same month. Gino Bechi was born in Florence on 16 October 1913, Tito Gobbi in Bassano del Grappa in the Veneto eight days later. Both made records early in their career, which had limited (if any) circulation outside Italy, but which we can now hear on LP and compact disc, and note, for one thing, the similarities. These are vibrant, unmistakably Italian voices but quite

23. Tito Gobbi

distinct from those of, say, Renato Bruson and Piero Cappuccilli who have been the leading Italian baritones of recent years. Like Ruffo, Bechi and Gobbi had a way of colouring their vowels, so that even if 'snarl' is not quite the word it will serve as an indication. There is depth, and there is brilliance on high; and both have, particularly in the rich middle of their voices, a modified version of the quick vibrato of their vocal ancestors.

Where are they now, we may ask, these dark baritones? Among the Italians, to whom we look in the first place, there is a vestigial flicker of the tradition in the singing of Giorgio Zancanaro. We in Britain have ourselves had such a voice, and not taken best advantage of the fact, in Neil Howlett. But it is rare. In the general homogenising processes of modern times, the distinctive quality of a fast vibrato has been ironed out: it attracts adverse comment when heard on records, and increasingly we listen even to live performances with record-tuned ears. The United States, the great melting-pot of national characteristics, has produced many fine baritones, but only the first of his line, Lawrence Tibbett, had (in his prime, that is) something of the special kind of vibrancy we have been discussing. Germany has never bred the type, nor is it characteristic of the French. From Russia recently have come two of the finest baritones I have heard in my life: Sergei Leiferkus and Dmitri Hvorostovsky, both with a thrillingly dramatic quality in their voice. Hvorostovsky especially has a quite remarkable depth of tone, which is undeniably 'dark'; yet one would hardly expect to trace its lineage through Gobbi and Bechi to Ruffo and Amato.

Still, I suppose that in the broader view, or at least the view that seems to prevail in the opera houses, all these 'heavy-tones', whatever their timbre, exist to sing certain roles. Certain roles, that is, require powerful voices with the recognised baritone range, and as long as there is a sufficient supply of them the operas can go into production. Central to their repertoire is Verdi; in fact we frequently hear of 'the Verdi baritone', and in the broad view, the term no doubt means something, even if it lumps together Ruffo and de Luca, Gobbi and Merrill, Wixell and Fischer-Dieskau, who if not chalk and cheese are at any rate gruyère and gorgonzola. Verdi was indeed responsible for some remarkable developments in the history of the baritone voice. Take the writing for Count di Luna in *Il trovatore*: much is required. Act I establishes him as a dramatic baritone, whose robust quality must stand up to the combined forces of soprano and tenor with some highly competitive orchestration. Then in his solo scene the demands go well beyond those made by the earlier operatic composers. His aria, 'Il balen del suo sorriso', starting low in the voice, generally lies high. There are many baritone solos – the Toreador's Song in *Carmen*, the Evening Star in *Tannhäuser*, even, at a pinch and without its optional high notes, the Prologue to *Pagliacci* – which can be sung by a bass-baritone, but 'Il balen' is another matter. In itself it suits the light high baritone who is halfway to tenor, but he will be no use in the cabaletta, 'Per me ora fatale', which follows shortly afterwards. In this the strings and trumpet do their darnedest to silence the baritone altogether. Here, the Ruffo-voice is not a luxury but a necessity, and I cannot recall in the theatre ever having been able to hear the voice in the way that records enable it to be heard. We tend to think of the baritone as a comfortable voice, an easy, normal, nothing-too-much voice. But 'the Verdi baritone' is a far cry from the local singer with the lovely voice who would sing Roger Quilter in the drawing-room and Stainer's *Crucifixion* in church. Verdi invites disaster: *Rigoletto*, so tempting because such a triumph, if successful, needs 'dangerous', 'pericoloso', stamped on the score. For different reasons, *Falstaff* has its perils too: singers tend to leave this till late on in their career so that one cannot be entirely sure about cause and effect, but it generally seems to me that the fat man leaves his impression on the voice and its production, and not to the benefit of either.

Despite this, the riches of the repertoire lie in these scores. Rodrigo in

86

6. Baritone

Don Carlos, Don Carlo in *La forza del destino*, Renato (or what the producer decides to call him) in *Un ballo in maschera*: they are all magnificent roles, particularly satisfying in their integration of drama and pure singing. Simon Boccanegra is perhaps the best of all. And then of course there is Iago: infinite variety here, from *ff* to *pppppp*, from emphatic declamation to the most suave cantabile, and his characterisation (and therefore vocal colour) ranges from the good chap of the Drinking Song to the naked demi-devil of the Credo. Deep-dyed villainy is all too often the 'dark' baritone's lot. Like Iago, Barnaba in *La Gioconda* can sing a jolly song with the lads and do the deeds of darkness with scorn and cynicism in his heart. His monologue, 'O monumento', with its jeering reference to that 'vecchio scheletro', the Doge, and its inspired vision of the spy and informer as real ruler of Venice, is tailor-made for the 'dark' baritone with his special resonances and his snarl. Then in Puccini, with the music so humanising the characters of Baron Scarpia and Sheriff Rance, the dark baritone is again in his kingdom, the power of the voice so allied to the power of the will and ambition that drive him.

Beyond Italian opera the pickings are not so rich. There is the Dutchman. Otherwise, Telramund in *Lohengrin* is the best of the Wagnerian roles for our baritone (Ruffo graduated to the part from the Herald in which he made a sensational début). In French opera, Thomas's *Hamlet* and Meyerbeer's Nelusko in *L'Africaine* were other Ruffo triumphs. In 'modern' opera there is Wozzeck to think about: I sometimes long to hear how Gobbi sang it. In the British renaissance, Tarquinius in *The Rape of Lucretia* may come to mind, and, with more urgency, Charles Strickland in John Gardner's neglected masterpiece, *The Moon and Sixpence*. Others, the 'dark' baritone may leave to his 'light' brother.

∽ Lyric ৩৵

The lyric baritone – 'light' as opposed to dark in timbre, and not necessarily light in volume – is the most commonly found and perhaps the most versatile of male voice-types. His Prize Song is Germont père's 'Di Provenza' in *La traviata*. The nimble pace and brilliant roulades of Rossini will be within his scope and he will (or should) rejoice in the elegant lines and flourishes of Donizetti. He can turn equally well to Bach and Handel, to Lied, mélodie and canzone, or to English song from Dowland to Finzi. The French repertoire will be his particular delight, and he will envy the baritones of the Opéra-Comique in Paris, who, especially throughout the latter half of the last century and the first of this, had such a regular supply of music pleasing to audience and singer alike, a good proportion of it new, the rest part of an affectionately shared culture.

In those days the French baritone was of a special type. We still hear sometimes of the baryton-Martin and catch a general connotation, though its origin has become obscure. Jean-Blaise Martin flourished as a leading Parisian baritone in the first three decades of the nineteenth century, famous for the quality and range of his voice which extended with ease to the high A. That is all a goodish time ago, and it is rather extraordinary that his name should be preserved in this way when there are plenty of later singers whose recorded voices would be of more practical use for such purposes of reference: I can't help suspecting that the term owes its longevity at least partly to the happy knack such things have of making their users feel knowledgeable. We certainly ought not to begrudge Jean-Blaise his survival as a ploy in the deadly game of operatic oneupmanship, but it might make more accessible sense if the term 'Pelléas-baritone' were substituted.

The role of Pelléas, of course, is quite often sung by a tenor, but the original, Jean Périer, was a baritone (also the creator of Ramiro in *L'heure espagnole*), and probably the best outcome is when a high baritone can – as it were – *think* himself a tenor for the time being. The role, and indeed all the vocal writing in the opera, is as French as the language itself. Its Frenchness, moreover, has much to do with language, the notes being written so as to produce music out of the rise and fall of speech. It is this very French characteristic that has made the light, high, lyric baritone something of a national speciality. Long before Debussy, the baritone in French opera was expected to take with a certain light familiarity passages that, to his Italian or German counterpart, would mean something quite different. The baritone's high notes in Verdi and Puccini are normally there to serve a full-voiced, resonant climax: in Gounod and Massenet they are much more to be addressed as part of the melody and of melodic speech. The result is characteristically a raising, freeing and thinning of the tone. French baritones have rarely produced the richly resonant sound associated with the Italians; and, as with tenors, this has been their loss. The gains have been a sense of freedom from the throat, and with it an impression of lightness, grace, intelligence.

Even so, although there is a distinctively French school here, the high lyric baritone is a thoroughly international type. In an illustrated talk on the subject, one would probably turn first not to a French example but to the records of an Italian, a German, and then a Russian. The Italian would be the great Battistini. He was forty-seven when he made his first recordings, the famous (and sometimes overrated) Warsaw 1902s, and though the full range of his voice was kept in an exceptionally fine state of preservation well into old age, its surpassing beauty lies within quite a limited area, roughly from middle B flat to the F above it. Below that the notes can be lacking somewhat in body and colour, while above F, though frequently impressive, they have less easy resonance and are more 'pushed', more of a special tour de force. But within that upper-middle compass, where much of the music lies, this was one of the loveliest of all voices on record, and its usage was that of a master.

Turn then, in the interwar years, to the prolific output on records of Heinrich Schlusnus, and you find something similar. Though he sings most of his Italian operas in German, the Italian ideal of pure bel canto is before him, and he too has a voice which starts to be beautiful with the upper-middle notes of his compass. When you listen to him for texture, as with Battistini, you find a perfect evenness: not as an *absence* of vibration (as in the modern old-music school) but with an assimilation of natural vibrancy into the main, perfectly even flow of tone.

Until recently the voice that in my own 'live' experience has come nearest to the sound of these two singers on record is that of Yuri Mazurok. He is sometimes described as a lazy tenor and it is quite possible that something of the sort was said at one time or another about the other baritones I have mentioned. But no: the voice as I recall it (and still more as it is heard on records) has a definite baritonal timbre but gains beauty and distinction in that same area of the upper-middle notes, where it acquires exceptional tonal purity and evenness of texture. He has been most familiar to audiences at Covent Garden as Eugene Onegin (which was also one of Battistini's favourite roles), but my most vivid aural memory of him derives from a relatively short solo in *Don Carlos*. Early in the opera Rodrigo (da Posa) tells Elisabeth of Carlos's wish to see her again: 'Carlo, ch'è sol il nostro amore'. The melody has a courtly grace and is entrusted to the singer, lightly accompanied, with the tessitura lying in exactly that part of the voice where such baritones are at their best. Here the extra weight, the darker colouring and latent snarl of the dramatic baritone would be no asset, and memory (as opposed to the recording) tells me nothing about the much more dramatic Tito Gobbi in this particular solo; nor for that matter does it recall the rounder, warmer tone of Renato Bruson. Mazurok's voice, of more slender cut and easy poise, is what lifted these two or three minutes of singing and made them treasurable. It was the first time – and the last but one – that I can ever recall thinking in the opera house that what I was hearing then bore some resemblance to how I fancy Battistini must have sounded.

A more recent example of the type is the Canadian baritone Gino Quilico. He also helps to extend the discussion in that he is the son of Louis. There was a too brief spell, in the early Sixties, when on a good night at Covent Garden you might hear, without guest artists but from the body of the company, as fine a baritone voice as you could wish for: these were occasions on which Louis Quilico was singing. One such was a performance ever glorious in the memory, a *Lucia di Lammermoor* in (I think) 1961, with Sutherland in finest form, Alain Vanzo on one of his rare excursions from Paris, and Quilico to complete the trio of principals. Everything worked, and the spirit of beauty was abroad in the house. When Pritchard allowed an encore of the sextet, it seemed no more than natural justice, and it spoilt the drama not a whit. Quilico's rich and evenly produced baritone gave depth to the casting, a full-bodied sound, perfectly steady in its resonance at that time, and in its nature *un*like the younger Quilico's voice, which is brighter, lighter and slimmer. From Gino Quilico we have heard a Rossini Figaro with a brilliant shine, a Valentin in *Faust* who had exactly the high clarity and freedom that we associate with the baryton-Martin, and most recently there has been a superb Rodrigo in *Don Carlos*, in which that first solo was sung with the ease and lucent purity of baritones in the line from Battistini. The immediate point is that both Quilicos, contrasted as they are in tonal character, would be placed under the general classification of lyric baritone.

Once again, as in so many of these discussions, we find that the broad generic term as defined by range and repertoire is only a beginning, and really the less interesting way of 'sorting' voices. In the baritone voice it is particularly so because there is a great deal of overlap. Many roles are open to both main types. Certainly the Italian lyric baritone will call a halt somewhere – Iago, Falstaff, Scarpia perhaps. The dramatic baritone, similarly, is unlikely to be found as (say) Malatesta in *Don Pasquale* (though as it happens, an outstanding Malatesta was Mariano Stabile who was also famous in all three of those dramatic roles). But neither the heaviest nor the lightest will be in a hurry to turn down Rossini's Figaro (unless on physical or temperamental grounds), and both types meet halfway in Rigoletto. Roles and range may coincide; the more interesting vocal difference between a Tito Gobbi and a Thomas Allen, a de Luca and Fischer-Dieskau, a Quilico and a Quilico, lies in timbre.

Let us briefly try this out in a few representative roles. The baryton-Martin (since we started with him) finds his specially made role, we might say, in Pelléas. Yet to many opera-goers of the present generation, particularly in London, Pelléas means Thomas Allen, and Allen's timbre is certainly not what we think of as 'Martin'. He sings the role so naturally that one might suppose it had been written for him, but his is not the usual French type of high baritone and he himself has said something about how he copes (H. Matheopoulos, *Bravo*, Gollancz,

24. Mariano Stabile as Iago in *Otello*

1989, p. 159). The part, he says, 'contains its own warming-up apparatus'; each scene prepares for the extension to the voice which the next will bring, and by the time the most taxing moments are reached, the singer has been exercised to meet them. So a lyric baritone of his type is enabled to deal with the role because of the composer's skill in writing for the voice – and (one might add) because this particular singer has the intelligence to perceive it.

Take, then, an opera with two baritone roles – one generally classified as dramatic, the other as lyric. *Pagliacci* opens with the baritone in the spotlight for the Prologue; his ten minutes of glory over, he then rejoins the rest of the cast as Tonio, the hunchback. It is an interesting character-role no doubt, but without the Prologue it might be considered inferior to the other baritone role of Silvio, the upstanding young lover who joins Nedda in a love duet which is the longest 'number' in the opera. In range and tessitura the Prologue and Silvio's part in the duet are not dissimilar, and if properly appreciated, both require grace and finesse (the Prologue in its 'Un nido di memorie' section, and the duet in the solo marked 'con garbo', 'with elegance'). But the two kinds of voice, the dramatic and lyric (or dark and light) come into play because of the contrasted voice-character or timbre required. The Prologue needs dark colouring for the quasi-melodramatic stuff about the

25. Giuseppe de Luca as Rigoletto

92

actor's cries of rage and bitter laughter; and it needs a voice of some breadth and majesty to give weight to the philosophical utterances later on. Silvio by contrast must sound young, and a higher, brighter timbre helps here; there is no snarl in his solos, and yet he has chances for expansion which the Tonio of the evening might envy. Of course a skilful singer can do much with coloration, and there must be many baritones who at some stage of their career could sing either part equally well, if necessary in the same performance (as with a little skulduggery might be managed and as Gobbi did in the film version). Nevertheless, there is a right timbre for each role, and that is a consideration which should be uppermost in the casting.

Then there is 'the Verdi baritone', in this instance the lyric kind, whose archetype is Giuseppe de Luca. De Luca was surely the lyric baritone *par excellence*: not a 'Martin', not ever incurring the suspicion of being 'a lazy tenor', but a finely rounded, beautifully produced voice, medium in all things – volume, tone-colour, range – except the superlative quality of his singing. He was a famous Rigoletto and, as records attest, was ideal in passages such as 'Ah, veglia, o donna', 'Piangi, fanciulla', and 'Miei signori'. But Rigoletto is also a dramatic role, and parts of it call for a Ruffo rather than a de Luca. Dangerous. Even a de Luca could be tempted away from the path of virtue, and in a pirated excerpt, the climactic 'Si, vendetta' duet, from a broadcast in the mid-1930s, we hear what we hoped not to: that is, this great stylist and model of good taste having recourse to the declamation of the 'ham' in order to compensate for the lack of sheer power.

Then, finally, we might look again at the solo mentioned at the outset as the lyric baritone's Prize Song: the Father's 'Di Provenza il mar, il suol' in *La traviata*. De Luca sings it to perfection. At least, so we think till we consult the score, and find that Verdi has written so many expression marks for emphasis, contrast, distinct articulation, that it almost seems as if he were saying that the last thing he wanted here was smooth, perfect, de Luca-type bel canto. It is very nearly as if he were giving that nod which is as good as a wink to suggest that if this is what the lyric baritone, the baritone of light, has to offer, then maybe the beguiling solo, together with the rest of the unpleasant character's role, should revert to the Iago of the company, the Tonio, the Scarpia, the man with the dark timbre, the baritone with the snarl. Very nearly, but perhaps not quite.

7. Bass-baritone

⁄⊙ Wagnerian ⊙⁄

In the old days it seemed that the bass-baritone owed his independent existence to Wagner and Peter Dawson. A strange dual identity had him entering Valhalla at the Opera House and proclaiming himself a gay and gallant bandolero in the drawing room. In his second capacity he aspired towards the manly style of the Australian, with songs about Devon and Somerset, Plymouth Ho and the Spanish Main. It took a bit of nerve to emulate the native cries and enthusiasm for 'tiny ball on end of string' in 'Waiata Poi', and 'Waltzing Matilda' was hearty enough for most of the company gathered there for a musical evening, where people generally felt more at home with 'The Floral Dance' and 'Old Father Thames'. Still, it was a relatively wholesome repertoire, irreproachably green, and it encouraged 'real singing', mollycoddling microphones and the whole ambience of modern pop belonging to a different world. If Peter Dawson was indeed the model, then it was one of impeccable voice-production, for Dawson, a pupil of Sir Charles Santley, had learnt the essentials of a singer's art with a thoroughness that is demonstrated in his singing of Handel: his recordings of Harapha's 'Honour and Arms' in *Samson* and Polyphemus' 'O ruddier than the cherry' in *Acis and Galatea* are splendid examples of a technical mastery which resorts to no second-best shortcut methods of articulating the runs, and which keeps the voice in training as a fine, evenly-tempered instrument over its wide range. If our bass-baritone's model is less accomplished, then there is the likelihood that his voice-quality will degenerate along with the style, and then we come upon a different phenomenon, the bass-barreltone of James Joyce's coinage. I wouldn't say that this is a type unknown at Bayreuth, but generally the Wagnerians inhabit a different plane, partly because of the character of their music (serious, noble, complex and so forth) and partly because of the sheer bulk of their voices.

Bulk is not a pretty word, and the Wagnerian bass-baritone is not usually remarkable either for the beauty of his voice or the refinement of its production. The pre-eminent exception among singers of this

94

century has been Friedrich Schorr. He and Rudolf Bockelmann were the two leading exponents during the interwar years, and to judge from contemporary accounts they gave performances of comparable merit in the theatre; on records, while Bockelmann can be heard as a sturdy singer with possibly the brighter, more keenly-edged tone, it is Schorr who lives in the memory by virtue of the sheer beauty of his singing. His voice had the power to fill Covent Garden and the Metropolitan, but that was not its special distinction. One of the English critics noted that while it sounded well at Covent Garden, in Bayreuth his voice was heard as a magnificent instrument. With the ideal acoustics for Wagner it was easier to appreciate quality, which of course is what comes to the fore in recordings. Fine in the strenuous passages where a singer needs all his reserves of power, Schorr's voice is at its most beautiful at quieter moments. The openings of Hans Sachs's 'Flieder' and 'Wahn' monologues in *Die Meistersinger* find in him the warm-timbred evenness of production that in itself creates character and expresses emotion. Like Frida Leider, the great soprano who was his partner in so many performances of the *Ring* operas, Schorr makes one realise how the first and most important interpretative act in operatic singing is to fashion the voice so that it has the right vocal character for the role. A bright and hard voice will not make a Hans Sachs, a Wotan, or a Dutchman, however powerful it is and however subtle the artistry with which it is used. Yet it is as rare an experience as any in the world of opera to find a singer of those roles whose voice has also the deep brown Rembrandtian softness of hue and texture that is needed for their complete realisation; and that pre-eminently is what Schorr did have.

When such a point is reached in conversation there follows a light sigh and a pause for the development of the 'Where are they now?' theme. There is no Friedrich Schorr today. No indeed; and, point sometimes overlooked, there was none before him. The great singers are never replaced. Anyone who in the mind's ear can summon up Schorr's voice christening the Prize Song ('die "selige Morgentraum-Deutweise" '), or observing how the splendour falls on castle walls ('Abendlich strahlt der Sonne Auge'), at the end of *Das Rheingold* cherishes that particular sound as an irreplaceable companion. But there are others who bring their own gifts, among them some which Schorr did not so very notably have to offer. The bass-baritone voice inhabits the isthmus of a middle state: like Pope's view of Man, 'created half to rise and half to fall'. Ideally it has a distinctively bass quality but with a baritonal freedom on high. Schorr, though never a bass, seems equally never to have been completely happy with the top Fs and so forth that Wagner requires from time to time. In pirated recordings from the Metropolitan in the late 1930s, the resonance has gone even if the note is still there in his voice; and even in the recordings made in his prime, when he was forty or just over, it is in the middle register and not the uppermost notes that the distinctive beauty resides.

At roughly the same age, the singer most identified with the role of Wotan today takes these notes with apparent ease, and with a baritonal lustre in their resonance. James Morris, though not resembling Schorr in timbre, shares with him the approach of a man who believes that the first, essential business of the singer, in Wagner as in Verdi, is to sing. Everybody (more or less) *says* this: that Wagner should be sung as a bel canto composer, and so forth. But not many of them do it, for part of the bel canto method is the preservation of an even line, without wobble, lumps or bulges. This is not commonly found among Wagnerian singers, but Schorr had it (his was a vibrant voice but it never loosened into the slow beat which is the usual affliction), and so in large measure does Morris. At just one point, in *Die Walküre* as heard recently at Covent Garden, Morris produces the soft, rounded tone that was associated with Schorr – in Wotan's repetition of the annihilating vision, 'das Ende'. And this is in the scene in Act II with Brünnhilde, where the narration of events in the murky past takes him down into a low tessitura, which a baritone Wotan must dread but where Morris is perfectly at home.

These Wagnerian roles still find few takers. They do make some formidable demands, though at the same time, as George Bernard Shaw was the first to point out, they also show remarkable consideration in rarely putting strain upon either extreme of the vocal range. By an odd quirk of history it is really the Italians, and most particularly Verdi, whose writing for the baritone voice places the music beyond the comfortable range of the average amateur. Yet, in terms of operatic repertoire, when we think of the baritone it is in precisely such roles as Rigoletto, Germont *père* or Iago. Seated at the piano, your home-made baritone can read through (say) Wotan's part of the scene with Mime in *Siegfried*, or the solos of Hans Sachs with quite gratifying results – at least as far as he himself is concerned; and yet these are the roles which are generally thought of as coming into a special category almost prohibitive in its strenuous use of the voice.

Of course part of the difficulty is the massive orchestration the singer has to contend with, and another is the sheer length of the opera. Let us look briefly at Hans Sachs as a singing-role. He is used sparingly in Act I, with several short solos not occupying more than a couple of pages in the vocal score. Their tone is fairly light, and a singer taking his first glance at the part might well conclude that it is meant for a high baritone after all. Much of it lies above the stave of the bass clef: its centre is around middle C, with one short high G and scarcely anything below the

D which even a tenor is likely to find in his part. Act II brings the Fliedermonolog, where the deeper part of the voice finds some scope. Even so, though important, the low notes are few. On into the scene with Eva, and Sachs sings quite lightly, almost conversationally, for much of the time, touching the low B flat and the high F, the music having a slightly lower 'centre' to it than Act I but still very moderate in its demands. Off-stage for the Eva-Walther duet, he returns to confront Beckmesser, and it is here that the singer really has to start producing big sound. 'Jerum', the cobbling song, is marked 'sehr stark' (very strong, i.e. loud), and though much is legato there is a declamatory element as well. Sachs is then busy to the end of the act, which is as yet a good way off. Again, Wagner asks nothing outrageous of him (except possibly a couple of trills!) at any one time, but by now the pressures of the role have become considerable and Act III is still ahead. Act III is about as long as the whole of *La Bohème*. Sachs is on stage as the curtain rises and there he remains, nearly always at the centre, with one break in which he will change costume in time to join the procession of mastersingers for the final scene. The 'Wahn' monologue again calls on his deeper tones, though there are no particularly deep notes written. The long scene with Walther is followed by the busy one with Beckmesser. Then comes a second duet with Eva, and the full-voiced address prefacing the Quintet. In another long solo he thanks the townspeople and introduces the prize-song competition. When it is all over he makes yet another public speech bringing the immense opera to its conclusion. His last bars involve a final, flat-out tutta forza, so he has to pace himself throughout the five-hour playing-time, knowing that he must keep sufficient in reserve to survive this final trial of strength.

It is this last feature that eliminates so many. Wagner demands not only a Hercules but one who is ready to perform the hardest of his labours last. It is so in *Die Meistersinger*, and also in *Die Walküre* (the Farewell requiring the greatest finesse as well as strong, house-filling volume at the end of the evening), and then again in *Siegfried* where, as James Morris has remarked, 'the last act is a killer'. Even in the role of the Dutchman this characteristic is noticeable, not so much in the part as a whole but in the writing of the first solo, 'Die Frist ist um', where one vocal climax is built on top of another, with the sustaining power of the bass-baritone voice tried to its uttermost in its highest register.

So, one might well ask, why should it be a bass-baritone at all in these roles? If Hans Sachs is in question, a good many baritones have taken the part, including some unexpected ones such as Caruso's friend and colleague, Antonio Scotti. (It nearly killed him to learn it, never mind the singing, for he did not read music and had to master the part while crossing from South America to Italy for the première at La Scala.)

What the baritone voice lacks, however, is not the notes but the character, or rather one important aspect of the character. When Fischer-Dieskau recorded Sachs he had character in plenty and more specific insight than any other singer I have heard either live or on records; but what is paternal, even patriarchal, in Sachs needs a voice with further reserves of depth and roundness. Yet something also goes wrong when a pushed-up bass takes the part. Karl Ridderbusch, an excellent Pogner, was disappointing as Sachs because though the voice-character was right, the tessitura is perilous for a bass voice and there is an inevitable loss of quality. Similarly with Wotan: a baritone or bass will sometimes bring it off, but generally the balance between the written notes and the voice-character calls for something in between, and to succeed fully the singer must be exceptionally full-bodied (a thinly penetrative tone is no use) and resilient.

In Kutsch and Riemens' *Dictionary of Singers* (German edition 1982), on my highly suspect count, 108 singers are named as bass-baritones. This compares with 171 basses and 520 baritones. The lists include some surprises. For instance, among the bass-baritones are Stafford Dean, Aage Haugland and Samuel Ramey whom I have always thought of as basses; also some, such as Raimund Herincx, Herman Uhde and Jess Walters whom I have classed as baritones. Among the basses are Sesto Bruscantini, Wladimiro Ganzarolli, Zoltan Kelemen and Bernhard Sönnerstedt, who surely belong with the bass-baritones; and, more surprising, listed with the baritones are Norman Bailey, Theodore Bertram, Rudolf Bockelmann, Ferdinand Frantz and … Friedrich Schorr. There is obviously and perhaps inevitably a good deal of uncertainty around the border-country. Similarly among the acknowledged bass-baritones one finds a wide range of differences, some of them national. Among the Germans is Otto Edelmann, a good example of the heavy type who maintain their steadiness of production though at some cost to the fluidity and grace of their tone. Hans Hotter, with warmer, rounder tone quality, also with a voice of exceptional amplitude, frequently forfeited steadiness, developing the wide beat to which many heavy Wagnerian voices are prone. The Austrian, Walter Berry, also listed as a bass-baritone, has sung a highly successful Wotan but has generally been less associated with Wagner than with Mozart and Strauss. He is one instance of a bass-baritone who has successfully preserved an exemplary style of voice-production, without coarsening of tone or loosening of vibrancy. José van Dam is another: an outstanding Dutchman, he has also maintained a wide repertoire outside Wagner, and in practically everything has been a model of good singing according to 'classical' standards, still to be heard in our time. Among the French are Jules Bastin and, from earlier times, Vanni Marcoux. In him we meet

26. Vanni Marcoux as Méphistophélès

with an extraordinary contrast to all the others. Though usually designated simply 'bass', his high-timbred voice is very French and hardly, to our ears, bass at all. He also leads us into the wider repertoire open to the bass-baritone.

∽ Beyond Wagner ∾

Success in Wagner can be costly, as much to the bass-baritone as to the heroic soprano and tenor. It is not just a matter of wear and tear on the voice but of a specialisation that threatens to exclude all else. Wotans are not two-a-penny, and those few who are deemed worthy to carry the spear must often wonder if there is life beyond Valhalla.

Hans Hotter's biography brings reassurance. Hotter sang his first

Wotan (the Wanderer in *Siegfried*) in 1930 and his last (*Die Walküre*) in 1972, when he was sixty-three. For at least twenty-five of those forty-two years he was in demand wherever Wagner was sung; any house looking for a Wotan would have Hotter at the top of the wanted-list, if it was at all realistic to do so. He could have lived on this and a handful of other Wagnerian roles alone, as Lauritz Melchior very largely did for so many years among the tenors. But in fact his repertoire, as listed in Penelope Turing's book about him (*Hans Hotter, Man and Artist*, John Calder 1983), numbers 118 roles in eighty-two operas. There were also oratorios, a large song repertoire and three operettas. His example gives an indication of the vast area open to the bass-baritone, even to one who, as Miss Turing says, for a quarter of a century, 'strode the international operatic stage as the definitive Wotan'.

Perhaps before looking at the formidable repertoire-list we should ask a few questions about the bass-baritone voice itself. The name sounds like a bonus, two for the price of one, but is it not perhaps a sort of apology for being neither one thing nor the other? Does the voice have a distinctive character of its own? What use is it?

So we'll take a further step back and ask a larger question first. What

27. Hans Hotter

is it that allies these voice-types with a particular kind of operatic role? If the answer had simply to do with the music it would be easy to find, for one could say, for example, 'Oh, the role goes to the tenor because it is written with a high tessitura,' to which the supplementary question would be, 'But why should it have a high tessitura anyway?', and the answer looms like a philosopher's nightmare, 'Because it is written for a tenor.' But what governs the composer's choice of a particular voice-type in the first place, assuming that it is not the accidental availability of some particular singer or a mere bowing to popular prejudice? The answer comes with appalling simplicity that, in the general concept, the height of the male voice varies in inverse proportion to the character's age and in direct proportion to his sexuality. This, it has to be said, does not extend to countertenors, despite Jochen Kowalski, or to the comic comprimario tenor. Let's put it speculatively. Chaucer's Canterbury pilgrims are commonly said to number among them all sorts and conditions of men ('Here is God's foison', said Dryden); there are saints and sinners, old and young, and most mixtures in between. If we were writing an opera, which pilgrims would go to which voices?

We know the Pardoner would be a countertenor, alto, falsetto or castrato, and his mate, the Summoner, who 'bar to him a stif bordoun', would be a bass: Chaucer tells us so. But there is no doubt, surely, that the Squire, the young man who sleeps at night 'namore than dooth a nightingale' and who is devoted to the service of love, would be a lyric tenor. This is the voice of youth and romance. The Knight might be an heroic tenor as he has fought 'in listes thryes, and ay slayn his fo', but further consideration raises his age, reduces his sexuality and begins to suggest that he might be a baritone (these speculations, I hasten to add, have no reference to the baritone, or any other voice, in real life and off-stage). The Knight, we remember, is a father, has a patriarchal air in company with the other pilgrims, does everything very correctly and in fact is a bit of a bore: he is, I fear (and with apologies), a baritone. The Monk, who follows the Knight in the social hierarchy, is surely a bass, a buffo bass, like Osmin in *Die Entführung*, for as 'a lord ful fat and in good point' what else could he be? So where does your bass-baritone come among this goodly company? I suppose in one of his guises he might be the Miller ('a stout carl, for the nones') or in another the Franklyn ('St Julian he was in his contree'), but essentially, I would say, he is the Parson. To make the Parson a tenor would be to have him light and romantic or loud and pugnacious, which would be wrong; as a bass, he would put on weight and solemnity, equally foreign to his austere, modest nature. As a baritone he would be too earthy, more like his brother the Ploughman. In short, he needs the common humanity of the baritone crossed with the deeper reserves and authority of the bass: he is a bass-baritone, José van Dam I wouldn't be surprised.

This is the bass-baritone's allotted span. He is not young, but no Methuselah either. He is not a sex-symbol, yet desire and performance may still concern him. He is not the High Priest, the blind prophet, the aged monarch or the Devil himself, for these generally go to the bass. But he does have an additional authority about him, some standing, depth and maturity. This is a picture of Hans Sachs and the Dutchman, of course; but it applies outside Wagner too. And such principles governing the casting of voices extend to most of European opera. Think for instance, of *Pelléas et Mélisande* (the young and attractive Pelléas a tenor or high-baritone, the older and less romantic Golaud a bass-baritone, the old king Arkel a bass), or of Tippett's *Midsummer Marriage* (tenors for the young lovers Mark and Jack, bass-baritone for the man of power and business, King Fisher, and bass for the Male Ancient).

Very much to the point here is the role of Boris Godunov. Though it is so inextricably associated with the bass voice, it is essentially a bass-baritone role. It never extends deep into the bass range and at certain climactic moments has exposed notes that (as Nicolai Ghiaurov has remarked) are as daunting for the bass as a high C for the tenor. At the end of his opening solo in the Coronation scene, Boris has to summon up all his nerve and vocal resources for the unprepared and unsupported high phrase in which any failure of the voice would constitute one of those catastrophic events that just mustn't happen; the sense of anticlimax (with this majestic figure the subject of so much expectancy and the sole focus of attention on a crowded stage) would be unthinkable. In the Monologue too, especially in the Rimsky-Korsakov version where the voice follows the upward sweep of the melody, it is the ringing high notes of a full-voiced baritone that seem to be called for. Yet baritones rarely yield to whatever temptation they might feel to undertake the part (Paolo Silveri was one who did), and basses rarely resist. The bass voice certainly adds to the sense of authority: when Boris Christoff sang it, part of the excitement and richness of his singing lay in the way in which he would take certain notes so that they were like a spring rising from a source of unfathomable depth. So, with these requirements for a bass's reserves of depth in the tone combined with a baritone's upward range, the role clearly calls for a bass-baritone with the acting ability and stage-presence that are perhaps still more essential to the part.

Boris Godunov is duly listed in Hans Hotter's repertoire: he sang it first in 1935, at the age of twenty-six. Others who have sung it as a bass-baritone part include Vanni Marcoux, who made some impressive records in French and with little that is distinctively bass-toned in the

28. Feodor Chaliapin as the Viking Guest in *Sadko*

voice, and George London, the first Westerner to sing the role at the Bolshoi, in Russian of course. Robert Lloyd, who is Covent Garden's resident Boris, also sings it with a bass-baritone timbre: it is interesting that whereas some singers whose voices are unequivocally bass in quality (Gottlob Frick, for instance) tend to lose some of the anticipated ease and solidity as they descend to the lowest notes, others whose timbre has something of the baritone in it (Ramey and Lloyd are examples) will be impeccably firm and ample in the depths. Interesting, too, that while most of the really deep basses who sing Boris seem to bring it off quite successfully, it is often hard to *imagine* them doing so. For instance, I cannot imagine how Norman Allin's Boris can have sounded, or in modern times Kurt Moll's, yet both have given admired performances. Mark Reizen and Nicolai Ghiaurov, the most lyrical interpreters of the part on records, temper their voices to the baritonal tessitura, and so also did the most famous Boris of them all, Feodor Chaliapin.

In press reviews Chaliapin's voice tended to receive less comment than his acting. To those who are familiar with his recordings 'live' from Covent Garden in 1926 and 1928, it will seem extraordinary that most of the critics' remarks on these performances are along the lines of 'not what it used to be', and that some even go so far as to say that there was hardly any voice left worth speaking of. Even when he first reappeared in England after the war at the Albert Hall in 1921 there was a consensus that this was not quite what people remembered from seven years back. One of the few who troubled to describe the voice was Herman Klein, writing in the *Musical Times*. Having noted 'the capacity for a mezza voce of infinite delicacy, a lovely fil de voix that can be attenuated and prolonged like a gossamer film of sound without losing continuity or charm', he noted some limitations: 'The power of the voice, like its compass, is not really remarkable ... [it has] none of the heavy reverberating timbre of the typical Russian bass but ... can mount to the loftier regions of a genuine baritone.' Klein's experience and memory went back a good many years, and he could bring out Edouard de Reszke and Pol Plançon for comparison; but the voice which Chaliapin's most resembled in his view, though it had less sheer power, was that of Anton van Rooy. Van Rooy was the favourite Wotan of the 1900s; Kutsch and Riemens in their encyclopaedia of singers wrongly, but significantly, list him as a baritone – but a bass-baritone is what he was, as, I would suggest, was Chaliapin.

A caveat is necessary here, because there is a tendency for basses to lose some of their bassness as they grow older. Chaliapin's earliest records show a voice of richer, darker hue, and a similar pattern can be traced in others, such as Marcel Journet, a near-contemporary, a magnificently solid bass through and through in his pre-electrical records, surviving with range intact but with a higher 'centre' to the tone in later years. A modern example of this may be Ruggero Raimondi, and I see that the first sentence of the chapter on him in Helena Matheopoulos's discussions with singers on their roles (*Bravo*, Gollancz, 1989) contains a reference to him as 'the Italian Chaliapin'. It becomes clear that the phrase is used principally with his physique and ability as a singing-actor in mind, but it has relevance in terms of voice as well. Raimondi was first heard in England some twenty years ago; even at that time the sound was at its most splendid in the upper register, but the timbre was unmistakably that of a bass. Since then the lower part of the voice has lost some colour and resonance while the 'centre' has shifted upwards. He sings higher roles, such as Don Giovanni, the Count in *Le nozze di Figaro* and, on records, Scarpia; also Boris Godunov, although according to Miss Matheopoulos, Raimondi lists this among 'his basso profondo roles'. He is, at any rate, now categorised as bass-baritone, and the development has been underlined recently by the reissue of his 1971 recording of *I Lombardi*, where his performance as Pagano, the soldier who turned hermit, includes some of the finest bass singing of its kind on records.

Those two Mozart roles, Don Giovanni and the Count, were also in Hans Hotter's repertoire, as was Scarpia. Scarpia, though essentially

29. Ruggero Raimondi

written for a baritone, and a high one at that, was also a favourite part with the Frenchman Vanni Marcoux (who gave Mary Garden an anxious moment or two on stage). Another baritone part that often goes to the bass-baritone is Escamillo in *Carmen*, understandably, perhaps, because in the Toreador's song the phrases sometimes descend to the low B flat in which the lighter type, French or Italian, may well be inaudible. Hotter was there too, as were Vanni Marcoux and Journet, and in recent times the best Escamillo in my memory, vocally at least, was van Dam. More surprising perhaps are Iago, Amonasro in *Aida* (Hotter again, and Friedrich Schorr) and Tonio in *Pagliacci*, where the inevitable Hotter is joined by Chaliapin: 'It suited the range of my voice', said the Russian (presumably excising the optional, but nowadays almost statutory, high notes in the Prologue), 'and I played the part quite well'.

There are plenty of other roles for the bass-baritone to look at in Hotter's repertoire, and several outside it, as varied as Wozzeck, Porgy, and Captain Balstrode in *Peter Grimes*. But still nagging away, and perhaps unanswerable, is the question of Don Giovanni. Baritones, bass-baritones and basses all seem to covet it, and I sometimes wonder why. They all agree that it exhausts them, and each tends to point out difficulties experienced by the others (basses in the Serenade, baritones in the final scene). Ruggero Raimondi makes an extremely good remark about it: Don Giovanni, he concludes, is 'a great hole'.

Freudian matters apart, there is a profound truth here, though not necessarily in the way in which Raimondo goes on to develop the view. The most important point about Giovanni in this respect is that he has no aria. He has some solos (a Serenade, a Drinking Song, and the one that everybody forgets because dramatically it is a kind of aside and musically it is the least distinctive in the opera); but whereas each of the women and Don Ottavio have arias in which their true selves are expressed, Giovanni is never known to us from the inside. The others all have a distinctive character in their music. Giovanni's two songs, both short and in a sense not necessarily his own (they are songs for an occasion) reveal no inward character: the nearest he comes to having a character at all is in the last scene with the bold, broad intervals of 'parla, parla, ascoltando ti sto'. It is quite in keeping that the part should be written so that it does not even define the voice-type needed for it: the bass-baritone *may* be right. Meanwhile we note that Tamino, the genuine lover in Mozart, is a tenor, and that there is nothing in the *music* of Don Giovanni (is there?) that tells of a genuine sexuality. As Raimondi says, there is a great ... void.

8. Bass

Foreign phrases have a way of conferring dignity upon the commonplace, musical terms being no exception. As a voice-category, 'singing-bass' looks more like a tautology than a concept, so basso cantante remains a generally accepted term, and it has its uses.

Like most of these descriptive terms, it indicates an emphasis rather than supplying a definition. The basso cantante is not quite the same as the basso profondo. He may have plenty of low notes at his command but may not make a special point of plumbing the depths. He may not *sound* particularly deep even when he gets right down there. Assuredly he will offer the role of Sarastro in *Die Zauberflöte*, but probably will not be mortally affronted to learn that in the house where he is a visiting artist it is customary to make a discreet upward transposition of either or both of the arias. Nor does he always reckon to be awesomely loud. The 'ample power to chasten and subdue', attributed by Wordsworth to an unseen presence, is a quality which the basso cantante would be happy to think attended his physical appearances on stage; but he will not covet the outsize tunic of the giant Fasolt in *Das Rheingold* or the speaking-tube through which the dragon Fafner issues his final ill-fated challenge in *Siegfried*. He will not want to blow the steerhorn and rally the vassals with Hagen's 'Hoiho's in *Götterdämmerung*; he is in fact something distinct from the black-toned 'giant voice', as the Germans call those basses who seem specially made for those parts. Nor does he necessarily – though here the qualities begin to overlap – possess the dramatic gift that goes towards making a satisfying Boris Godunov; and he will probably go out of his way to avoid the heavy garrulity of Baron Ochs in *Der Rosenkavalier*. He has been known to risk a few baritone roles, such as Scarpia in *Tosca* and Escamillo in *Carmen*. He may even earn a place (if of a somewhat different kind) in the catalogue of Don Giovanni's victims: many basses aspire to the role and find that they have to forfeit some of their bassness to do it. With an occasional exception, these roles are not home ground for the basso cantante, and they are not where we really want to find him.

107

He is to be found at his purest, the cantante element most to the fore, in Bellini's *La sonnambula*. Not that it is a particularly spectacular role, that of the Count Rodolfo who returns to his native village, casts a favourable eye on the maidens thereof, and finds himself involved, during one night, in mistakes which he rectifies to the general credit of himself and the aristocracy. But he has an aria, 'Vi ravviso, o luoghi ammeni', which expresses in smooth melodic flow the emotions of seeing again the loved places of his youth. This leaves the voice to itself, the accompaniment being little more than a quiet support, the singer having freedom to phrase and shade with all the imagination and elegance at his disposal. Essentially, he has his chance to do some real singing: the natural beauty of the voice can flower in this, and the cultivated employment of a truly even, well-bound legato tone can transform what in the printed score looks like a very ordinary piece of writing into something which in the opera house may be a moment of memorable loveliness.

In my own experience ('live', as opposed to recordings or broadcasts), I have known one such cherishable performance, and that was in 1960 at Covent Garden, when Count Rodolfo was sung by David Ward. He will be well remembered by opera-goers of the 1950s and 1960s: a Scot who came to London with a bass voice of unusual beauty, a massive and dignified stage presence and a genial, easygoing personality behind the scenes. From Sadler's Wells, he went on to Covent Garden and most of the world's leading opera houses, being widely regarded as a possible successor to Hans Hotter in the great Wagnerian roles. But the piece of singing I remember most happily was of this aria of Bellini's. The example is relevant in two respects to this matter of 'voice-category'. One point is that in practice the categories are far from distinct and exclusive (Count Rodolfo and Wotan seem as remote from each other as the little village and Valhalla). The other is that a singer's true category may be something different from the line in which a career develops. It would be rash to say, at this distance in time and with incomplete experience of his work, that Ward was a basso cantante whose true value could have been found in this school of Italian opera rather than in the Wagner for which he became best known. But, as I remember, there was a certain deception of the ear by the eye. You saw a big man; you seemed to hear a big voice. In fact it was a voice that sounded 'big' only when not covered by heavy orchestration. It was not another Hotter, or, in modern terms, a penetrative voice like John Tomlinson's. It was ample, warm and lyrical, produced with a seemingly natural legato singing-style: essentially a basso cantante, and it came into its own in the music written to suit best the qualities of this voice-category.

If that aria of Bellini's presents the voice in its purest form, the

108

leading bass parts in Verdi are its most rewarding. The role of Silva in *Ernani* preserves the true singing-line of Bellini, but extends the dramatic and emotional range. The recitative and aria 'Infelice' still focus the expressiveness of the music upon the voice, and there are opportunities to invest what again appears to be a simply-written vocal line with real subtlety and depth of feeling. In the Prologue to *Simon Boccanegra*, Fiesco the patrician expresses the sorrow of the wounded spirit '(Il lacerato spirito') in phrases of the purest legato. Their beauty is inseparable from the beauty of singing-tone, and when the part is given to a bass who may have impressive power and stage presence but does not have a beautiful voice, the miscasting is as patent as that of a Boris Godunov who cannot act. King Philip in *Don Carlos* is in many ways the summit for the basso cantante. The part certainly requires a powerful voice and a dramatic style, but the writing is still lyrical, and its details presuppose a singer who has kept his voice fluent and musical over a wide two-octave range.

Sampling a few recordings of these arias, we can hear differences immediately. In *La sonnambula*, Chaliapin is not the right bass for the aria: it is surprising, indeed, to find that he sang it at all, but it was one of the few bel canto pieces retained in his repertoire. He made two recordings, both of them in need of broader phrasing, smoother delivery and less of the curious 'w' that intrudes (like another man's 'h') from time to time. He could be an excellent singer (as opposed to singing actor, where of course he was supreme), but the appeal this aria had for him lay probably in its emotion, and his instinct would be to get through to this by means of the words rather than the melody. The true basso cantante puts his trust in the melodic line, as does Samuel Ramey. Here, however, we find a different sort of blockage, perhaps tonal, for his performance lacks sweetness and nuance. Nicolo Zaccaria, La Scala's resident bass for many years, comes closer to what is needed in the complete set recorded with Callas: his tone is warmer, his style more tender. But the old recording by Pol Plançon is in a different class altogether, for here is an artist whose voice was the perfect melodic instrument, and who had the taste and imagination to see exactly where the shading should fall and how the sentiment could be most eloquently expressed through the purest vocalism.

In Verdi, the model singer in modern times has often been Nicolai Ghiaurov. The *Ernani* aria, for instance, which he sings in the complete recording of the opera under Riccardo Muti, is one in which he binds the phrases evenly and commits himself to a testing run of notes on a single vowel in the cadenza instead of taking the easier and more common option of arranging it in words. Use of this device limits a little the achievement of the great interwar bass Ezio Pinza in his recording of the aria, and yet, overall, that performance reveals a still finer art. In fact this is a master-class in itself, for it shows how the richest natural provision of voice can work with the subtlest art and the deepest feeling: a close comparison of the two performances shows again and again Pinza's 1929 record (with a conductor not thought important enough to be named on the label) to have by far the more complete and complex feeling for the music and drama. Pinza also recorded the *Boccanegra* solo 'Il lacerato spirito', and magnificently too, though here it is his contemporary Alexander Kipnis who makes the deeper impression. Paata Burchuladze used this solo to open the recital recording which caused considerable excitement in Britain when it was released in 1985, and the sound certainly has massive authority and substance. But a comparison with Kipnis shows exactly how much of the complete art of the cantante still remained to be learnt by the young Russian; with Burchuladze you feel that the mezza voce is indeed only half the voice, and the duller half of it at that, whereas with Kipnis it was a feast in itself.

Often, in these arias, you long quite simply to hear an Italian voice. Burchuladze includes King Philip's solo from *Don Carlos* in his recital, and Kipnis also recorded it, twice. There are many good things about them all, but returning to Pinza the feeling is that, yes, this is the kind of voice Verdi had in mind after all: the singing-bass *par excellence*. Yet the great Philips of our time have been the Bulgarians Boris Christoff and Nicolai Ghiaurov, and when we come to look over the whole span of recordings in search of a master here, it is probably on the Frenchman Plançon, recorded in 1907, that we settle. Here is fastidious vocal elegance to match the royalty of the character, and with it a plasticity and depth of feeling needing nothing beyond the voice for their expression.

Plançon is the earliest of the singers on record mentioned here, but he leads us forward to Samuel Ramey, and to one of the brightest developments in modern times. For Plançon was also the master of the art of florid singing – his scales, arpeggios and trills (like those of his less famous contemporary Hippolyte Belhomme) are continually astonishing; scarcely more so, however, than the facility which Ramey has repeatedly displayed in his Handel and Rossini. The same solo recital that includes the *Sonnambula* aria also has solos from Handel's *Rinaldo* and Rossini's *Semiramide* that recapture a virtuosity almost lost to the basso cantante tradition in the intervening years. The revival of a liking for such operas has provided the spur, and several good artists have met the challenge (in Britain, it might be added, every professional bass has had to offer *Messiah*, and that meant the runs of 'The trumpet shall sound' and the rapid triplets of 'Why do the nations'). Ramey is distinguished largely because of the soundness of his method: he has used no short-cuts, but sings with concentrated tone and even production. Here is the other department in which the basso cantante should be working, that of the virtuoso. Plançon in the old days, and Ramey in our time, are the masters here. Pinza had not the same facility; the tastes of his time did not encourage its development. In other respects, for the arts and qualities of this kind of basso, he is the man.

✍ Profondo ✍

We think of the heavier type of bass singer as being also deeper, as sitting broodily on a rock, blessing or cursing somebody in his priest's robes, or dodging in and out of the green spotlight which is supposed not to let him out of its bilious beams. The curious thing is that, if he is indeed both heavy and deep, so little of his music seems specifically to call upon the depths.

One of the finest scenes in all Verdi is written entirely for two basses – the Grand Inquisitor and King Philip in *Don Carlos*. Philip has just concluded the great solo in which he reflects on his loveless isolation, and now the Inquisitor is announced. Aged and blind, he enters supported by a Dominican on either side. In the orchestra the double-basses lumber on with inexorable intent.

Now, we know this must be a deep bass. At first he need produce no great volume, but from the start there must be a sense of great power in reserve. And though the A flat at the end of his first phrase is as low as he will ever be required to sing, his tone must still suggest the cavernous depths.

But, we may ask, why 'must' this be so? We look at his music and, no, it is not particularly low-lying. In terms of sheer range, it is the King and not the Inquisitor who, at the very end of the scene, has the really deep notes. By contrast, when the Inquisitor has his two principal solo passages they contain nothing which could not quite comfortably be sung by a baritone.

So perhaps we have to conclude that this is one of those not unfamiliar instances where dramatic characterisation rather than the musical score is what determines the voice-type. The Inquisitor is to be a heavy and deep bass to differentiate him vocally from the King, but more particularly because he is an impressive man and an oppressive force.

Actually, the score is not quite so silent on the subject as at first it seems. After the restrained opening of the dialogue between king and priest, there comes a passage in which each has a sentence intoned for the most part on a single note. The note rises step by step as one character caps the argument of the other. Twice the Inquisitor pushes his reciting note up at the end of the phrase: that is his aggression, his affront to the throne. Each time, the King accepts the additional challenge but does not raise it further. The Inquisitor wins: their voices have been in combat here, and sheer weight is on his side. Later, in his one unrestrained outburst the vocal line is heavily marked with sforzando signs, so that the singing-style is clearly not to be that of the basso cantante, but a hard-hitting emphatic declamation, the brutal realities of power which the Church will use to enforce its will. So much for the black menace and weight that must lie in the Inquisitor's voice.

As for the depth his voice must possess, that is suggested by the double-basses which introduce him. They are him, and his voice must be like theirs: the depths of a primaeval darkness stir within it.

Where in opera, then, are we to find roles written specifically for the basso profondo? Why surely, we think, it must be in the Russian repertoire. The Russian bass is proverbial: we have visions of hundreds of white beards dimly lit as in some Eisenstein film, and all chanting away on a bottom C. 'Chaliapin!' some cry, as though they were invoking the deity of the deep notes, the human counterpart of the 32-foot organ stop which sends its reverberance through the pews and up the spine, there to tingle awesomely.

Fantasy, of course. Chaliapin was not a deep bass, and there is very little in Russian opera that openly acknowledges the existence of this proverbial type of Russian basso at all. It is true that there are many bass-parts. The score of *Khovanschina*, for instance, lists five of the fifteen soloists as bass, and two of these are among the leading characters in the opera. Prince Ivan Khovansky is the higher: the first pages of his score are baritonal in tessitura. The profondo is normally thought to be Dositheus, venerable head of the Old Believers and a mighty beard too. But again, when we look at his first solo we find a vocal line that spends most of its time near the top of the bass stave, and nowhere does it hint at the Russian bass of which legends tell.

And so this continues throughout the opera: bass-Khovansky sings in a baritonal range till cut down in his manly prime, and profondo-Dositheus does much the same even to his final 'Amen'. The main difference between the parts as far as the writing for voice is concerned is that Khovansky's music tends to be fast and Dositheus's slow.

One further example: *Boris Godunov*. The two certain bass parts among the leading roles are the monks Pimen and Varlaam. These are finely contrasted, the one venerable and saintly, the other a drunk. The general lines of casting are that Pimen should be the deep bass, Varlaam the brighter, penetrative type, and Boris a bass-baritone whose vocal assets may be reckoned less important than his stage-presence and acting ability.

112

The surprise is the writing for Pimen. By general consent this is the role for which a deep bass is sought, and countless audiences must have sat through the opening solo with perhaps a half-conscious feeling that something rather peculiar is toward. This is the 'chronicle' solo: the old monk has been working on a history of Russia and has now reached the final page. He sings quietly while the lamp burns low and the melancholy accompaniment flows evenly like the movement of his pen. The tone of the first sung notes, lying in the middle of the voice, makes a listener aware of the reserves of depth that lie below. But we are never to hear them.

Where the profondo does find himself in business is not in Russian opera but in German. When Mozart wrote Osmin in *Die Entführung* for Ludwig Fischer he gave basses throughout the ages an incentive for keeping their bottom Ds in working order. Not just the low Ds either, but the top ones, which are to be arrived at with no more than a breath between the two.

Of his most famous solos, 'Ha, wie will ich triumphieren' and 'Wer ein Liebchen hat gefunden', the first is the virtuoso piece, with triplets and trills as well as the two-octave range; yet a certain amount of comic bluster is permissible as being 'in character' and sometimes gets a singer through what otherwise he would not be well-equipped to manage. The other is in some respects more testing, for it needs smoothly polished singing, with full sonority on the low Gs and then an immediate transition to a light, gracefully placed note an octave and a half above. Hear Alexander Kipnis do this on an old record from 1930: there are some excellent Osmins on modern records but their conductors (or perhaps their own ideas) don't allow them time to expand and savour the notes as Kipnis does.

Even Mozart's writing for the deep bass begins to look moderate in its demands when one turns to see what Handel asked of his virtuosi, Giovanni Boschi and Antonio Montagnana. In operas such as *Ezio* and *Sosarme* he writes for a voice which takes brisk two-octave leaps, thinking nothing of the low F or the high, and is prepared to move down from the one, up from the other, riding in between on a string of semiquavers that would frighten the life out of any bass brought up on Verdi and Wagner. Yet in recent times these too have come out of the musuem, and on a compact disc devoted to Handel's arias for Montagnana they are sung with the greatest of ease by David Thomas, whose range is said to be even greater than that of the fabled original.

What we do not know with any certainty about these basses of the eighteenth century is how powerful they were by modern standards. They impressed their contemporaries as being very ample, but then both houses and orchestras were smaller.

30. Capiton Zaporojetz

The massive King-voice in *Lohengrin* and *Tannhäuser*, the giant 'black' voice of Hagen, Fafner and Fasolt in *The Ring* may be quite a different thing. Here the Germans have made a speciality and have been prepared to pay a price for it. The 'black' voice must sound bass through and through, and, since it is notable that the bass quality tends to compromise with the baritone in voices with a very extensive range, these 'black' voices are not encouraged to gain practised facility in the upper register.

Volume and weight are the prerequisites, but the blackness also derives from a method of tone-production that eliminates the more Italian quick vibrato. In its place is a kind of tonal solidity, a wall-like front, which may nevertheless prove susceptible to the other kind of vibrato, the slow beat or dreaded wobble.

In modern times we have done remarkably well for these big Wagnerian basses. Many of them have proved themselves adaptable both tonally and in repertoire. Kurt Moll is one with something of a warm quality, an almost velvety surface to the voice that is rare among Wagnerians. He has avoided the lumpy, uneven kind of production and gained his distinction from beauty of tone rather than penetrative force.

In the immediate postwar generation the supreme singer in this field was Gottlob Frick, not a profondo but certainly dark enough and absolutely rocklike in his firmness right to the end of his singing days at the age of seventy.

114

8. Bass

31. Malcolm McEachern

Where then, in all of this, is the real profondo, that deep, deep voice of the sort we can all hear in our heads and yet very rarely encounter on the operatic stage?

Sometimes one finds a Russian who answers to the description: Capiton Zaporojetz who sang Ludwig Fischer's song that in English we know as 'Drinking' made something of a best-seller of it on 78s.

But perhaps the archetypal profondo is another singer from those days, the Australian Malcolm McEachern who was the bass half of the once-famous Music-Hall duo 'Flotsam and Jetsam'. He also sang 'Drinking', and in a lower key still. As the eight letters of the title-word occupy their notes of the downward scale, each could be inspected and found to ring true.

There is one other aspect of the bass voice which should not go uncelebrated. To hear a bass *speak* is a treat in itself. They all seem to have it, this extraordinary richness and sonority – like the man in the chimney-corner in Hardy's *The Three Strangers* who spoke with a 'bass voice of musical relish … that if you heard it once you'd never mistake as long as you lived'.

British readers of a certain age will probably know who I mean if I

115

refer to 'Branny'. Owen Brannigan was a bass, perhaps not of the most polished and elegant kind, but one who always turned in a good performance (he was the original Bottom in Britten's *Midsummer Night's Dream*, Noah in *Noye's Fludde* and so forth). With a richly expressive Welsh-looking face (though in fact he came from up North, near Newcastle), he would have made a marvellous Glendower in *Henry IV*. And his speaking voice was a tonic. I remember not so much hearing as *feeling* it from the far end of the public bar in The Shakespeare, opposite old Sadler's Wells. The place was crowded and there was plenty of noise; but it was like an orchestra without a double-bass. And then it arrived. I was a long way from the door and could not see who had come in, but the sound, I swear, travelled under the floor and up through the soles of the feet. 'Who's that?' I asked. 'It's Branny,' they said. And a fine feeling of warmth and well-being spread throughout the bar.

116

Part II

Ten Singers

9. Elisabeth Schumann

In Hugo Wolf's song 'Wie glänzt der helle Mond', an old woman looks up at the distant moon and thinks about the star of her own youth, which seems more distant still. The accompaniment glimmers high over the voice, and the singer softly, serenely contemplates Paradise, where soon she will sit veiled in silver, gazing upon her white fingers, while St Peter by the gate cobbles away at some old shoes. As the years went by, Elisabeth Schumann became increasingly fond of this song. It was a memorable item in her programmes, and sometimes one felt she even chose her dress with it in mind. The cream silk, silvered on shoulder and pocket, set off the greying hair, with its white streak up from the forehead, the eyes adding a further sparkle, the smile another radiance. The voice never sounded beyond mezzo piano, and Schumann's tones were pure candlelit silver. They recalled with touchingly frail beauty the youth now glinting, light-years away, in the night sky.

Yet, aptly as she sang this song of age, one could hardly think of her as becoming old. Her voice seemed to inhabit a perpetual springtime. Even when its bloom faded and its shine became dim, it told only of a May day that had clouded over. Her personality remains vivid in the memory as a delicious breeze on a sunshiny day, full of gaiety and energy. One felt she might have said, along with Shakespeare's Beatrice, 'There was a star danced, and under that was I born.'

The danger for an artist who evokes such feelings and comparisons is that she will be thought of in the very terms Beatrice applies to herself, as one 'born to speak all mirth and no matter'. An English critic in 1926 characterised her as 'a mere fair-weather singer'. She shared with most – though not quite all – light sopranos a limitation of colour range: a darkening of tone was foreign to the nature of the voice, and even to experiment risked sullying the airy brightness so essential to its being. The critic no doubt meant that Schumann's emotional range, like the palette of her colours, was small compared with, say, that of Lotte Lehmann in opera and Elena Gerhardt in lieder. Even so, his criticism was mistaken. Her voice had tenderness and sorrow in its compass too, and the springtime gaiety was not just a passing prettiness but a strength. It was rather like G.K. Chesterton's discovery, as he drew with his piece

119

of chalk from the South Downs, that white is not an absence of colour but, when applied to a piece of brown paper, a positive, valiant affirmation.

Schumann is still a living memory, for she was active in concert work and teaching up to the time of her illness and death in 1952, not long before her sixty-fourth birthday. The time will come, however, when she has passed entirely into the musical encyclopaedias and the living history records of the gramophone. What the books will tell is that she was among the most admired singers of her age, enjoying a special success in the soprano leggiero opera roles of Mozart and the songs of Schubert and Richard Strauss, with whom she gave many recitals in Europe and the US, and who dedicated some of his songs to her. There: it will all go into a single sentence, carrying little more of the warm individuality than an epitaph cut in stone. Her name also will appear in the history of certain houses, notably the State Opera in Vienna and Covent Garden in London. Though she sang only in the 1914-15 season, she still has an entry in Robert J. Wayner's *What Did They Sing at the Met?* (She totals forty-five performances, with another five on tour, appearing, surprisingly perhaps, in as many as ten roles.)

In a library or secondhand bookshop, somebody from time to time will browsingly come upon a sentence that conveys an unusual warmth of feeling from the writer toward a singer. Victor Gollancz's *Journey Towards Music* tells of Schumann's Sophie in *Der Rosenkavalier*: 'No one will ever forget the soar and leap of her voice at the presentation of the rose. Imagine silver as pure as young happiness and as true as steel, and you have an idea of it.' Or maybe it will be an obituary piece by Philip Hope-Wallace in a posthumous collection of his occasional writings called *Words and Music*: 'A supreme artist, she had the demure simplicity of a child with the radiant wit of the most highly civilised society.' Or leafing over the biography of the conductor Otto Klemperer, somebody will read of the soprano with whom he fell in troubled love, and on whose account shots were fired in the Hamburg opera house one night in 1913. More likely a record will be playing, perhaps of 'Heidenröslein' or 'Deh vieni, non tardar', and something about it will catch the ear of one new listener, who will say, 'Now that's a singer for *me*! Who was she?' So a new love affair will begin, and the memory will survive.

Mind, it will depend on the record. I don't think the early, pre-electrical discs will work the spell. There are disappointments here, and they derive from faults that were not going to disappear in later years. For instance, the Baroness's song from *Der Wildschütz* has a jolly way of half-sounding a note, the other half being a scoop or a semi-staccato that makes a speech point rather than a proper singing note. It was this kind of practice, along with the slight build and playful

120

32. Elisabeth Schumann

manner, that prompted the judgment many will have found offensive in Michael Scott's *The Record of Singing*, Volume II. Throughout her records, he feels, 'We are all too conscious of the winsome ways of the soubrette.' Her achievement, he concludes, was one 'of personality, like that of a *diseuse*'. Admirers should not rise to the bait with instant apoplexy, for the art of the diseuse, 'a talent to amuse', is not altogether to be despised. Moreover, the judgment is supported by some acute technical analysis, as well as a number of quotations, which may on balance have a belittling effect, but which are taken from comments by contemporaries. There are also critical notes on the records, and these readily can be tested in the course of any Schumann recital to which we might treat ourselves.

For myself, the programme begins with the quintet from *Die Meistersinger*. This recording, so fine in nuance and detail (down to the incidental trill, beautifully turned where it is often not bothered with), derives its *strength* from Schumann. 'Hell und laut' (clear and loud) are among Eva's words, and in just such a way her voice rings out as the ensemble swells in volume. No doubt she is placed forward of the others, who include Lauritz Melchior and Friedrich Schorr, but Eva is the centre, the focal point of the group, and her prominence is justified. Even so, there is little sense in the recording that she needs any special consideration, for the voice seems to carry of itself. Reverting to the critical analysis of Schumann's method, one notes how finely sustained these notoriously testing phrases are – no suggestion of shallow breathing or unsupported tone here. Scott remarks that 'By the time she was forty, her voice was no more than a wisp of tone.' That would have been in 1928; but this recording was made in 1931, the sixth 'take' of the session. She also had sung the role at Covent Garden the previous year, when there were no complaints about a lack of carrying power. One remembers Gollancz's 'true as steel' comparison, and I also recall that one of the gallery habitués at Covent Garden in those years mentioned how small the voice of the accomplished Adele Kern sounded in 1933 to ears that had been accustomed to Elisabeth Schumann.

That, however, was in Schumann's famous role of Sophie. Our record programme would have to include 'Wie himmlische, nicht irdische', where the high B is so beautifully placed and the phrase, though deliciously floated, does not dissolve into some incorporeal loveliness but remains eager and impulsive. Marcel Prawy, historian of the Vienna Opera, wrote that 'For all its tenuousness ... it filled every corner of the house,' and this was true as late as 1937. No doubt we normally would be listening to it in the studio recording of 1933, but there is also one of those strange, erratically pitched, unreliably labelled records of fragments that found their way into Eddie Smith's EJS series.

This has been authenticated as a composite recording of excerpts from two performances at the Vienna State Opera, one in 1936, one in 1937, with differing casts but having Schumann as Sophie in both. Here, far from being a 'wisp' and a mere emanation of personality, the voice holds its own in trio and duet – if anything, finer than in the studios.

Sophie and Eva are substantial parts, as indeed are Ilia, Pamina, Marguerite and Mimì, also in her repertory. Still, a word that clung to her was 'miniaturist', and it is true that much of her best, most characteristic work was done in music that is light in style and in its physical demands on the voice. One of her roles at the Metropolitan was Humperdinck's Gretel, and the short extracts she recorded are worth turning up – miniatures each of them, but none the worse for that. The waking of Gretel ('Wo bin ich? Ist es ein Traum?') is among the best of the pre-electricals, whether on the Odeon of 1917 or the Polydor of 1920. The manner is *not* winsome, pert or coy, and the voice is even throughout its range and is not pallid (I am taking up some of the critical terms) or feeble in the lower register. In the better-known recording of 1935, with piano accompaniment, she sings Gretel's 'Ein Männlein steht im Walde', again with perfect firmness and without arch little-girlishness. This is followed by the Sandman's sleep song and the evening prayer, recorded as a duet with herself, in which she shows the accuracy of her ear as the two voices meet in unison on the last note. She also manages to throw in a sample of the Schumann whistle for good measure.

Central to her opera repertory was Mozart, and it is here that the criticisms in *The Record of Singing* become most severe: 'The incessant slithering and sliding, pecking and twittering, the lack of a solid legato, assume a greater prominence than they would have in the opera house or concert hall with the artist's physical presence to distract us.' Strong words, but the records are at hand, and we can judge for ourselves. 'L'amerò, sarò costante' from *Il Re Pastore*: an occasional slither, maybe a twitter or two. 'Venite, inginocchiatevi' from *Le nozze di Figaro*: yes, a slide and a peck every now and then. But 'incessant'? On the contrary, the majority of notes are taken cleanly and held firmly for their full value. As we move on to 'Voi che sapete', the complaints become absurd. Clear, bright tone, well-bound phrases, judicious shading, a sure feeling for rubato – enjoyment restores a sense of proportion.

Schumann was not without faults, and they show up in Mozart, as in Bach and Handel. For my own part, I would be content now to move on to lieder and perhaps end up with some operetta. But we'll take another Mozart record first – 'Vedrai, carino' from *Don Giovanni*. Not a slither, a slide, a peck, a twitter, but a tenderness that is never mawkish, expressed with an unaffected simplicity that is never insensitive. As for her physical presence, no, it is no longer there, alas, 'to distract us'. I fancy, though, that you do not need to have seen her in order to see her now. Voices with character carry a physical image. Glance at a photograph, as a record of Elisabeth Schumann is playing, and you see her clearly enough. The star of youth that had become so distant to the old woman of Hugo Wolf's song is quite close after all, and the voice shines with the radiance of its owner as it did when she was a loved, honoured figure in the musical life of her time.

10. Elisabeth Rethberg

'What Destinn was to the opera-goer of the first decade of the century, Rethberg is today: the lyric-dramatic soprano par excellence.' Thus spake the oracle of my youth: the anonymous prophet whose word was law (as far as I was concerned) and whose gospel was published in the old pre-war HMV catalogues. He also supported his own view of things by quotation from another authority. 'Elisabeth Rethberg is the greatest living soprano' was the pronouncement, and it was made by Maestro Toscanini himself.

Rethberg died, in America, on 6 June 1976, and I remember that it seemed sad to me at the time that the death of one who was once acclaimed 'the greatest living soprano' (and, by American teachers of singing, 'the most perfect of living singers') should have occasioned so little comment in England. Brief obituary notices appeared in the expected places, but that was all. And yet perhaps it is not so surprising, for Rethberg had retired in 1942 and sang last in this country in 1939. Although a familiar and welcome visitor to Covent Garden since 1934, she had been absent from the opera house for nine years since making her debut here in 1925. She was never at the centre of English musical life. Yet we knew her records. Many, like myself, must have been brought up with them, and through them we came to know certain standards, certain essential ways in which singing should be what it very often is not. She came uncommonly near to perfection, and that in itself is cause enough for us to honour her memory.

Strangely, no sooner has one said this word 'perfection' than it calls for a cautionary note, for the last years of her career were, according to some accounts and some recordings, years of at least a partial decline, and that at no very great age. Even as early as 1936, when she was forty-two, some critics would observe that her voice was not quite the lovely instrument of earlier days. By 1942 some who knew her as the most reliable of singers were saddened by a loss of focus and a change of quality. Opinions differ on the point; and certainly it would be a curious anomaly if a singer so well trained, an artist so musically schooled, should indeed have declined in what might well have been the years of most striking achievement.

125

33. Elisabeth Rethberg

Achievement of course there was, and that in plenty; and in great glory too. Gramophone records, limited as they are in number and in quality of recording, allow us to hear her in the years of her prime in music from her widely varied repertory. The voice itself can be heard unaccompanied and fully exposed, in the opening section of a solo from Meyerbeer's *L'Africaine*. The record shows very faithfully its purity and clarity. There is a bloom and freshness about it, a natural resonance in which the vibrations are true and regular, a definition of line in which nothing spills over or runs into fatness. There are also many delicacies of style, the voice responding as a well-trained servant to the demands made upon it by the artist. It will, for example, produce an echoing softened tone that is all of a piece with the rest: a homogeneous voice, not one in which the floated soft notes are separate 'effects', apart from the main body of the tone. It is also flexible, finely conditioned so that the singer can move confidently and cleanly over broad intervals with no misgivings about awkwardly changing registers. All is as such things should be: the instrument is beautiful by nature, by fashioning and by maintenance. And that is a singer's first and most essential concern.

One might then turn to Mozart, to see how the finely conditioned instrument served one of the greatest of composers. Rethberg recorded many of the most famous arias, but one not closely associated with her is Susanna's 'Deh, vieni, non tardar' from *Le nozze di Figaro*. She was, I am sure, a fine Countess in that opera, and the lighter, more vivacious character of Susanna was probably not hers by nature. But there is much to admire in her singing of this aria. It sounds like simplicity itself, all is so natural and so naturally right. But a few points are worth noting. The song does, in its modest way, call for a range of two octaves, from low to high A. Many sopranos in those days declined to take the low notes and sang them an octave higher; many in our day sing them as written but tonelessly. Rethberg neither shuns, skimps nor exaggerates, and the unity of tone is preserved. The high A is touched lightly and gracefully. The intervals, as in the opening phrase, are clean and exact, and yet there is enough well-judged portamento to avoid any suggestion of a musical machine. There is warmth of feeling, light and shade of nuance. And when the syllables of a word spread over more than one note, no little aspirates ease the way and spoil the legato.

Now this scrupulous evenness of line, the genuine legato so infrequently heard, is also a feature of Rethberg's singing of Italian opera. In the way of singing which she appears to have so faultlessly preserved during these years she makes even the stormiest of emotional outbursts newly moving by making them newly musical. We have all, I am sure, been stirred by the sweep and fervour of Maddalena's aria, 'La mamma morta' in *Andrea Chénier*. We know, for instance, Maria Callas's

127

passionate treatment of it in comparatively recent times, and Claudia Muzio's, as a great contemporary of Rethberg. The comparison of Muzio's and Rethberg's recordings is interesting, not so much by way of establishing a value-judgment as in pointing a difference. Muzio, with her marvellous way of exposing the nerve-centre, gives a performance where all the Latin qualities of timbre and temperament are brought to bear. First a deep brooding richness, and then a sharp-edged, furnace-heated passion of lyricism, in which the artist gives, if anything, more generously than she can afford. Though the voice is sorely under pressure in the last bars, the spirit is indomitable. But while Muzio's record was made near the end of her career, Rethberg's comes from early on. And her way with the music is very different. Something is lost, much is gained; but the aria becomes a different piece of music when sung as she sings it. The bold, broad melody is soothed rather than seized, affectionately held rather than passionately driven. No doubt the temperament of the two singers is reflected in the difference; something too of the difference in national, cultural backgrounds. There is much enjoyment in both. But Rethberg's is the way of the school we would call – if we used the wretchedly vague and abused term at all – the school of bel canto. It will not pressurise the tone so that it loses beauty or homogeneity; it will give all the notes full value so that they can be part of a lyrical flow; it will preserve the essential evenness of emission without which there is no true singing. Rethberg's use of the voice implies that as a first principle, an axiom, perhaps even a creed.

It would be wrong, though, to conclude that so much purity, perfection and evenness made Rethberg a passionless singer in Italian opera. She *could* be cold, and she could be wooden as an actress; many of her admirers will concede that this is true. Even so, recordings like the Love Duet from *Madama Butterfly* do not lack ardour. Some of her very earliest records (this being one of them) were made in or around the year 1920 with Richard Tauber, and they provide excellent illustrations of the way in which German singers were often doing the Italians' job for them: that is, catching the full fervour of the score but preserving a genuine care for bel canto. At the start of the second side of their recording (sung in German) we hear Tauber singing with a fine feeling for the urgency and forward pressing of Pinkerton's love-making, but locating it not in a general emotional huffing and puffing, but in a specific musical feature of the score – the dotted note rhythms. It is this that he uses rather than any kind of tonal disturbance to express the turbulence of the emotions. Responsively, Rethberg sings her part without stinting either the tone or the emotion. But certainly what distinguishes her is the sweetness of her vocal quality, particularly in the phrase 'O quanti occhi fisi attendi'. In both singers there is a sensitive and imaginative feeling for both music and drama.

In music such as this and the other recordings mentioned so far, Rethberg sings roles that are generally thought of as belonging to the repertoire of the lyric soprano. She was, however, regarded (as my oracle put it) as a lyric-dramatic. Aida was the role with which she came to be most identified, and that is generally considered to call for a more powerful, more heroic voice than the Countess, or Butterfly or Maddalena. It may also be that, from records alone, a listener would conclude that those (rather than anything heavier) were the roles for which her voice was fitted. Nevertheless she undertook a good many of the lyric-dramatic roles, including several of Wagner's. Elsa, Eva and Elisabeth were all in her repertoire, and in them she left memories that are deeply cherished by those who heard her (her way with the opening of the *Meistersinger* Quintet is cited as an example, and it is something I would love to have heard). She also sang Sieglinde (though 'not quite up to the climaxes' is the phrase which goes down into history through Rosenthal's book on Covent Garden), and eventually she sang (in one performance only) the *Siegfried* Brünnhilde. The wisdom of such an excursion was more than merely questionable. Still, it was a voice with considerable power behind it, and this is clear in the way in which it rings free of the orchestra in the opening and climax of Elisabeth's Greeting, 'Dich teure Halle', in *Tannhäuser*.

That is a record worth keeping in mind as one comes to view the whole span of her career. For the present, illustrating the variety and range of her work, we might pass to another part of her repertory, the song.

She had indeed a most impressively large repertoire of songs, whether the claim that it numbered over a thousand is true or not. She was, after all, a German musician. She sang in Bach cantatas, in the *Missa Solemnis*, in Brahms's *Requiem*, and the whole range of lieder composers; in many fields, in fact, inadequately represented by her recordings. There are a few worthwhile songs in her early Brunswick series, but a major opportunity came in 1934 when she was engaged to sing for the Hugo Wolf Society. The ten songs that were issued do very probably give a fair picture of her qualities as a lieder singer, but to me they do not seem to have for the most part any very great interpretative strength. Her programme includes, for instance, 'Wie lange schon', the song in which a girl complains of her violin-playing lover and where the pianist enacts the violinist's painstaking practice in the postlude. It is hard to believe that this is the song that comes so vividly to life when Elisabeth Schwarzkopf sings it; for Rethberg does not communicate the humour even if she feels it, and all is rather uncommitted and colourless. Yet in the intense and tormented song 'Mühvoll komm' ich und beladen' from

129

the Spanish Songbook she does sing with feeling, and does succeed in communicating the sense of a soul, a person, a spiritual condition.

There is much understanding and sympathy in this performance. The penitential poem prays for grace to kneel before Christ in sorrow, to anoint His feet with tears as did the woman whose sins Christ absolved. 'Gleich dem Weib, dem du verzieh'n': a quite moving tenderness comes into the voice at this point. The song is also well 'built': that is, there is a careful, finely judged gradation of volume and intensity, mounting to the strong fortissimo cry 'O nimm mich an', and then softening, with a rapt fading ecstasy in the last phrase, 'du Hort der Gnaden'. I rather fancy that the song is capable of more still – that there should be a change of colouring, for instance, as the sense and music modulate from sorrow and abasement to an assurance of Christ's power to heal ('Du nur schaffest, dass ich weiss wie das Vlies der Lämmer werde' – 'Thou alone canst make me white as the lamb's fleece'). And I must say that I do not lament the passing of that style of piano playing. Still, it is a fine record, and I think one might note also, in passing, how whole and firm Rethberg's voice is even at the strongest climax. There is not the slightest hint of wobble (the very idea is ludicrous and alien). Nor is there anything of that lumpiness of texture that seems to be such a common affliction that people (critics and others) seem almost to take it for granted.

But the full purity and soundness of Rethberg's way of singing (I want to say 'goodness', almost meaning something ethical by it) is probably most strikingly shown in her recording of Amelia's aria, 'Morrò, ma prima in grazia' from *Un ballo in maschera*. This is the classic Rethberg. The emotion finds completely adequate expression through the singer feeling the form of the phrases, letting the voice play like an instrument, imposing nothing, marring nothing through any flaw in its condition: doing in fact the work of the true singer. Hearing this record, we know just why Toscanini should have been so warm and so firm in his praise.

So far, we have been considering Rethberg in the years of her prime, singing at the top of her form. We can follow her career through its last decade in a different kind of recording: more primitive, less easy to listen to; sometimes and in some ways more exciting, and possibly (for all the technical inadequacies) more faithful. These records are from live performances, transcribed privately though by this time circulated widely among collectors. Of course the quality of sound varies a great deal, but normally we listen 'through' the extraneous noises, and capture sounds that otherwise would have been lost for ever. The lover of singing, and the historian too, can only bless the pirate.

Most of these recordings come from the United States, and most of those from the Metropolitan Opera House. A few are European, and they serve to remind us that though Rethberg became part of American musical life (and an American citizen), her training and upbringing were German. The fresh and precious years of her early career were centred on Dresden, and it is said by the authors of a biography published in 1928 that during her time there she sang altogether 106 roles. In an early number of *The Record Collector* (IV.11, V.1) Mr J.B. Richards summarised this rare book (he had to send to New York for a library copy) and listed the roles she sang in 1921 alone. They were: Agatha (*Der Freischütz*), Aida, Anna (*Hans Heiling*), Butterfly, Elisabeth (*Tannhäuser*), Elsa (*Lohengrin*), Euryanthe, Eva (*Meistersinger*), Countess (*Figaro*), Ilia (*Idomeneo*). Ines (*L'Africaine*), Empress (*Die Frau ohne Schatten*), Konstanze (*Die Entführung*), Leonora (*Trovatore*), Marie (*Bartered Bride*), Mimì (*La Bohème*), Micaëla (*Carmen*), Nedda (*Pagliacci*), Octavian (*Der Rosenkavalier*), Pamina (*Die Zauberflöte*), Saffi (*Zigeuner-baron*), Sophie (*Der Rosenkavalier*), Tosca.

We sometimes grumble at the ways in which young singers are thrown in at the deep end, too much demanded of them, too many big parts too often, and so forth. But there was Rethberg, at the age of twenty-six with everything from Konstanze to Aida, and so little fuss about 'Fach' that she could sing both Sophie and Octavian in the same year.

One of the finest of the pirated, 'live' performances is from Vienna, 1933. Agatha in *Der Freischütz* was always one of her best roles, and we can hear her sing the two arias, clearly enough, even though most of the consonants and much of the orchestra get lost. The orchestra is under Karl Böhm, and other artists in the cast, both performing particularly well, are Franz Völker and Michael Bohnen. In the long solo from Act II starting 'Wie nahte mir der Schlummer' much, most indeed, of the singing is surely ideal. There is finely supported quiet singing, ample in the breadth of phrasing, lovely in the purity of tone. The recitative is vivid (if not exactly *visible* as was Lotte Lehmann in her recording), and there is strength and radiance in the excited cries of 'Er ist's.' Then, in the fast section, the main tune (easy enough for the violins to play in the Overture, but not at all easy to sing) is done smoothly and instrumentally, crowned with a shining, full-voiced top B. And we hear the audience greet enthusiastically the conclusion of the long, testing solo. But, speaking for myself, I enjoy the concluding section least. The singer is just a little hard-pressed; a little inclined, herself, to press too hard. And though the degree of discomfort is very small, perhaps negligible, here in 1933, it was to increase in the following years.

There was, I would say, the very faintest warning that this might be so in the recording of Elisabeth's Greeting from *Tannhäuser*. It is an excellent performance, perfectly successful. But one felt that the voice had no more to give, and that more should not be asked of it. It had, one

131

felt, sufficient power, but that (if one can so put it) it was a *slim* power. Many truly dramatic sopranos have some touch of the mezzo about their timbre, which thickens the tone and strengthens it that way. Rethberg had nothing of this; she was a pure soprano, and in that lay an essential part of her charm. But press that soprano tone too far, in dramatic music, and where it cannot gain power through *body* it will aim to increase penetration and risk a loss of quality.

And if some features of her voice and repertoire pulled her towards the dramatic-soprano, others pointed in quite a different direction. The clear, high tones together with her exceptional fluency in florid work sometimes suggested the potential coloratura. Gatti-Casazza at the Metropolitan had plans for just such an extension of her work, though they were never to be realised. How fine and suitable she was in sheer terms of flexibility can be heard in several recordings; quite persuasively, for example, in Donna Anna's taxing aria 'Non mi dir' from *Don Giovanni*. There is a live recording from the Salzburg Festival of 1937, under Bruno Walter. I think that, as one listens to it, one may feel that this is not quite the beautiful voice heard in the earlier recordings, but there is no doubt that we are still hearing a master-singer, one who has been trained to the point where the technical difficulties of such an aria as this are looked upon not as obstacles but opportunities. There is the sense of a well-oiled voice, which will take the scale-passages with ease, clarity and smoothness; and when it comes to the reiterated high B flats and A naturals, then again one observes with some wonder the *boldness* of her way with these.

When Rethberg sang, people forgot the difficulties of the music. That was a comment made back in 1918 when she thrilled the Dresden audiences with her accomplishment and ease in the coloratura music of Konstanze in *Die Entführung*. It is still true of that 'Non mi dir' in 1937. But it is also probably worth noting that the role she was singing was Anna, with its strenuous 'Honour' aria, and its tradition of belonging to a strong, dramatic soprano. Rethberg, surely, was one of nature's Donna Elviras, and one wonders whether it is not with that role that she might best have stayed.

But several things are questionable about the direction her career took during those years. There were wise words spoken – notably by formidable old W.J. Henderson of the *New York Sun*. It sometimes seems that he, in his old age, had become a little grouchy, a little inclined to know that things weren't what they used to be even before the things in question had been heard. But he knew a good voice and technique when he heard them, and he knew when things were going right and going wrong. So when he gave a warning, it was worth taking notice. He had originally praised Rethberg highly (in his somewhat

132

severe terms). After her Sophie in *Der Rosenkavalier* at the Metropolitan in 1922 he predicted that with adherence to her schooling she would achieve 'a position of considerable importance in her profession'. That was high praise, coming from him. In 1924 after *Der Freischütz* he wrote of the 'lovely quality of voice which has given pleasure to so many audiences'. But the first warning came in 1931 when she sang Rachel in *La Juive* for the first time at the Met (she had sung it previously, with outstanding success, in Chicago): 'she had style and she showed feeling, but the effort to conquer the strenuous utterances so plentifully scattered through the score may not benefit her singularly captivating voice'. In 1937 Henderson was noting that her voice sounded tired, 'without the brilliant tone associated with the creation of its fame'. By 1940 (Henderson by then dead) Irving Kolodin commented on her performance in *Le nozze di Figaro*: 'Rethberg's fading Countess would have been a masterpiece ten years before, but was now merely stylish and rather breathy.' On 6 February 1942 came what Kolodin unsparingly called 'the *reductio ad absurdum* of her career ... a lamentable effort to sing the *Siegfried* Brünnhilde'. She parted from the Metropolitan not on the best of terms, feeling slighted, Kolodin says, by the contract offered her and in fact refusing it, singing there for the last time in *Aida*, the opera of her debut twenty years earlier.

Records and other critical accounts nevertheless show her still to have been a very fine singer during the late 1930s. There are, for instance, two 'live' recordings of her performances in *Otello* with Martinelli and Tibbett. From the performance of 12 February 1938, it is interesting to hear the 'Ave Maria'. The recording made for Victor in 1930 is well known and a very fine one. This performance in the opera house goes much more slowly, and the feeling is more tender, the shading more sensitive. Just occasionally intonation is uneasy, but she is still perfectly recognisable as 'the world's greatest soprano'. And the last A flat, taken so purely and cleanly, is held for its full duration of six slow beats; rarely heard in the theatre.

The second performance, on 24 February 1940, is useful for the illustration of another side of her work. Listening to the passage from the last Act, from Desdemona's awakening to the murder, it is clear that although she was no great actress she was by no means an inert interpreter. Rather interestingly, and in a way not uncommon in these privately made recordings, there is a change of sound about halfway through the scene, and we suddenly come as it were face to face with the two artists on the stage. There is no mistaking the dramatic tension here. Martinelli's Otello had of course a quite exceptional intensity, but Rethberg too gives a strongly acted performance. It takes no great effort on the listener's part to see the stage in the mind's eye: certainly this is the performance that I always hear inwardly when the music comes to mind. Also it is worth noting that a good deal of voice remains at Rethberg's command at the end of a strenuous evening at this late stage in her career.

Such records as this do indeed support a very different opinion on the quality of Rethberg's singing in these years. A musician who knew her work possibly better than any other has said this: 'What is important to me to record is the fact that Madame Rethberg is one of the very few singers whom I have known through the years who did retire from public life *before* she deteriorated in any way.' These are the words of Edwin McArthur who very kindly wrote to me answering queries I made about this particular point. He recalls, too, a charity concert at New York in 1942 when Rethberg was indisposed but nevertheless sang rather than disappoint the sponsors and the public. 'Unfortunately,' Mr McArthur writes, 'Madame Rethberg's indisposition was *not* announced to the public which attended that concert.' He adds: 'the public is all too ready to remember one performance from a *human being* which may be slightly less than what has been the usual order' (his underlining of the words 'human being' reminds us also that an artist has a private life and that its joys and sorrows may not be totally dissociated from the public art).

'The usual order' was, of course, of quite *un*usual distinction. There is a thoroughness about her, an adherence to standards, a sort of *centrality* in her position among all recorded sopranos. Listening (as I have just been doing) to some tapes of Beethoven's 'Ah! perfido' and the great aria from *Fidelio* – even though they come from a time when, to my ears, something *had* been lost in the beauty of the voice – one cannot fail to recognise the work of the unostentatious virtuoso. I do not believe that Rethberg ever did anything showy, and brilliance is not the first word that comes to mind in connection with her. But the 'Abscheulicher' is a fearfully difficult aria, and in the runs every note is distinct, without aspirates or other 'separating' devices, and they rise on a long breath to her finely preserved high notes with no anxiety about their arrival and no breaks of register. It is rare that the soprano voice remains 'whole' to this extent; in this respect there certainly does not appear to have been any deterioration. She sings her Beethoven, moreover, with full responsiveness to the changes of mood; the interpretation never goes to sleep or loses sensitivity. Yet it too is unostentatious. Its essential *rightness* draws no special attention to itself. Her distinction is of that dignity which exercises its mastery in the central places of her profession. It is often the eccentric who holds our fascinated attention. But it is to the centre, ultimately, that we look for the standards essential to the continuing tradition.

That is why we remember her now, and why it is to be hoped she will always be remembered by those who have the art of singing at heart. Sad to relate, there is no single example of her singing now listed in the current British record catalogues.[1] If a single disc had to be chosen, I think my own selection would be the aria from *Un ballo in maschera* mentioned earlier. But that would be to pass over the role with which she was most associated throughout her career. She was the most admired Aida of the inter-war years. The lovely purity of her voice, the evenness of its production, the scrupulousness of its placing: these must have been among the joys of her performance. All are present in a recording which takes us back right to the beginning of her international career. It shows how she sang 'O patria mia' when she first appeared at the Metropolitan in 1922. Old Giovanni Martinelli told how in later years she decided that the public should not be disappointed of the full-voiced top C which other singers of the role had taught them to expect. But when she came to the Met from Germany, he said, she originally sang that phrase *dolce* as is marked in the score, spanning it with superb breath control, as she does in the pre-electrical recording dating from 1924 or 1925. It was in that year and in that opera that Edwin McArthur heard her, singing with Martinelli: 'I could not believe,' he wrote, 'that such sounds could come from the human throat.' She was, he said, 'the most beautiful and perfect singer I have ever known in my long career'. Hearing such records as this, we can well believe it.

[1] Since this was written some of Rethberg's records, including *Otello* at the Metropolitan in 1938, have become available on compact disc, though at the time of writing there is still no collection of her solo recordings.

11.   Rosa Ponselle

Rosa Ponselle's debut was an astonishing affair. Here you had a twenty-two-year-old American girl chosen to sing the leading role opposite Caruso in the first performance ever given at the Metropolitan, the great national opera house, of *La forza del destino*, a major Verdi opera, and a première that had been deferred because in that golden age, as people sometimes call it, they couldn't find a soprano really suitable for the role. Ponselle got the job because the manager, Giulio Gatti-Casazza, with all his experience there and at La Scala, and the great tenor himself, believed in her. And they took quite a risk for she had never sung on an operatic stage in her life.

What Caruso and Gatti-Casazza heard was a voice of such beauty and power that Caruso, for instance, knew at once that it was right: 'You will sing with me at the Metropolitan' he said straight away. There was not only a rich and lustrous quality, but something inherently dark and nobly dramatic, that made it particularly appropriate for the heroine of this sombre, doom-laden opera. In an unpublished test-recording for the Columbia company made in 1918 just before her debut she sang the aria from the final act, 'Pace, pace, mio Dio', accompanied on the piano by a man whose influence on her career was one of the most decisive, a composer in his own right, Romano Romani. He taught her much but in a sense she had no teacher. And she was quite frank about this. Later on in life she did a good deal of teaching herself, but the methods were largely intuitive.

That is what Igor Chichagov feels. In her later years he worked with her as a pianist who, according to Ponselle, was the only man who really understood her methods. And yet, as he says, there *was* no method, certainly no intellectually formulated one:

> What her singing was, it was an unending, unlimited line. I'm quite sure she had that intuitively. And the wonderful phrasing which I'm sure … she never went to any school or anything, but that phrasing of hers was so wonderful because she *felt* it. She talked about, 'Keep the throat open.' She would say, 'Square throat.' She would say that Caruso used to use the words 'square throat' which, to me, I think don't quite make sense,

but to *her* it made sense. She was *thinking* 'square'. She meant by that really 'open throat'. But you ask ten – or a hundred people what 'open throat' means and you get a hundred different answers. (Igor Chichagov in interview)

34. Rosa Ponselle as La Gioconda

137

Sensible words, and words that, with their insistence on the intuitive element in Ponselle's art and voice-production – the phrasing that was so wonderful not because she'd worked it out on principle but because she felt it – make one wonder all the more at the artistic achievement that her career involved. For instance, one can sample the first note in that aria, the F natural of the held note on the word 'Pace', the first note she ever recorded, and then hear how it had developed by the time she came to record it again, in 1928. Much work has gone on in those ten years. The *messa di voce*, the swell and decrescendo heard so impressively in the later version, was one of the things spoken of years afterwards.

But how did the voice impress those who heard it in the flesh? Most will tell you that the records, fine as they are, give only a fraction of the truth about her. And when these people try to describe what they heard, they commonly have recourse to similes, to flowers, port wine, or in this instance:

> Her voice could only be compared to molten gold, pouring, pouring and pouring. That's what I think of Rosa Ponselle. And she certainly proved in any opera I was with her or was not with her the idea of continuously beautiful singing as violin and cello together. To me it was something altogether out of this world. (George Cehanovsky in interview)

That was the verdict of an old-timer of the Met, a bright-eyed ninety-year-old, George Cehanovsky, who the morning I met him had been rehearsing the Met chorus in their Russian for *Boris Godunov*. He sang with Ponselle in many performances, and recalls the first time he heard her voice, in a rehearsal of *Ernani* with Titta Ruffo:

> The aria she sang beautifully, exquisitely, but when Ruffo appeared with her and she sent him away in low chest notes I did not know which was Rosa Ponselle and which was Titta Ruffo – this is true. (ibid)

It was the chest notes, that lower register, that George Cehanovsky remembered there as being so amazing. Yet the phrase remembered specially by another colleague was one with a beautifully placed high B flat in it. Rose Bampton, later to take on some of Ponselle's roles, was then a mezzo, and she could listen, as it were, with two pairs of ears, her own and her husband's, Wilfred Pelletier, for many years conductor and repetiteur at the Met. Rose Bampton remembers Ponselle in *La Gioconda*:

> When she used to walk off singing 'Enzo adorato' it was the most heavenly high B flat pianissimo. And when she came off my husband would be standing in the wings and she'd say 'Was it all right?' And Pelly would be in tears and could hardly say, 'Yes, yes, it was glorious.' (Rose Bampton in interview)

Glorious, yes, but not quite in the normal way of the soprano voice. George Cehanovsky, you remember, spoke of it as 'violin and cello combined'. To Rose Bampton it was pure soprano, but to Cehanovsky there was a strong element of the mezzo, or even of the contralto:

> Rosa was absolutely dramatic soprano of them all, because partly she was like mezzo soprano. That's why I said when she sang 'Che vuol il re da me'[1] I almost thought it was Titta Ruffo ... It's a known fact that Rosa is a mezzo-soprano. But, with her diligent study, continuously, continuously, she was able to become a real soprano. The high tones of her were not there, because she was born mezzo-soprano. I mean, mezzo-sopranos go to high C, but sustained tessitura of soprano and then come to high C, that's another story. (Cehanovsky, ibid)

Cehanovsky's belief that the mastery of soprano roles came only through hard work is supported by probably the best of authorities, Ponselle herself. After her retirement she spoke in a radio interview about the envy she used to feel for the mezzos. She stresses too the weight of responsibility she felt when eventually she took on the role of Bellini's Norma. The waggish interviewer compliments her on her magnificent success and she acknowledges it fairly enough:

> Yes, I finally mastered Norma, but at what a price. Gatti-Casazza and Tullio Serafin, the conductor, and my coach Romano Romani would tell me to practise those big arias as vocal exercises. They would say, 'Work on this opera and maybe you'll do it years from now.' Then one day they broke the news. They were going to revive *Norma* the following season. That was in 1927. I had mastered it vocally but, I assure you, the whole idea of this opera on stage made me tremble.
> *Interviewer*: It must have. Quite a responsibility.
> *Ponselle*: It wasn't only *Norma* that gave me that feeling of responsibility,

---

[1] There is a confusion here for the scene in *Ernani* has no words similar to these, which are sung by the Grand Inquisitor in *Don Carlos*.

Mr Goldovsky. Almost everything I did or had to sing had that same sense of urgency. That's why I envied the mezzo-sopranos. I used to stand in the wings and how I wanted to sing Amneris and Laura and Dalila. My voice was dark enough you know in colour, low enough in register, and I could have let myself go dramatically without having to worry about the next high C coming up.

Interviewer: Do you mean to say you worried about high Cs? It never sounded that way out front.

Ponselle: It didn't because I worked on it, and I had a technique that always stood by me, thank God. (Ponselle in interview with Boris Goldovsky)

Although the obliging Mr Goldovsky says that the high Cs never sounded a problem, Ponselle herself found them alarming. Transpositions were common in *Norma* and *Traviata*. And although we associate Aida with her, through recordings, she sang the part only twice at the Met, with twelve performances on tour; and according to her own account it was chiefly because of a dread about the high C in 'O patria mia'.

To some extent her Victor recording of that aria shows why she had reason to fear the aria in stage-performance – it is a good solid note but not comfortable in its resonance, whereas other, lower parts of the aria, and still more the Tomb Scene, show exactly the voice that George Cehanovsky described, 'violin and cello together'.

For the people who were producing her records in those early days she must have posed a problem. It's always said of Ponselle that recording never did her justice. The experience described by Ida Cook, a devoted admirer of Ponselle, is probably typical:

We had heard one or two [of her records] and were expecting a great deal, but while she was here in that first season at Covent Garden they put out a record of the *Ernani* aria and on the back the 'Pace, pace', and we played it on our gramophone and we put it away and said we'll never play it again now we know what she's really like. One's terribly glad to have the records; they are something for one. But my distinct memory is that when we played the records as they were then and we could have her in real life we couldn't bear it: it was just a faint echo, you know. (Ida Cook in interview)

Ponselle's recordings, of course, didn't end with that rather boxy series made by Victor in the late 1920s and early 1930s. There was a remarkable and rather exciting appendage to it when after she had retired the RCA company arranged for recordings to be made in her home, at Villa Pace near Stevenson, Maryland. Her accompanist in these sessions was Igor Chichagov:

People heard in New York that she was singing and was in great voice so RCA sent people here and said, 'Why don't you come to New York and make a record?' She said, 'No, no, no, I couldn't go to New York' – at that time she wouldn't go to Washington, the furthest she would go from here was Baltimore. And then someone had a brilliant idea. They said, 'Rosa, if we sent our people down here would you be willing to record?' and she said, 'I might do it.' So what RCA did, they sent all the equipment and an engineer here, and we set up here in the foyer and the piano we pushed all the way to the exit of the music room. And what would happen, she would go through her old repertory and say, 'Yes, let's record this song.' So that's put in front of me, and we sang it through once and then we recorded it. And now when I hear some of these things back I think, 'My goodness, how terrible I played that thing,' because I'm not with her, and some places she has surprised me, because she never sang the same way twice. (Igor Chichagov in interview)

These recordings were made in October 1954, when Ponselle was 57. Her public career as a singer had virtually come to an end in 1937, seventeen years earlier.

Just why it ended so early is still an open question. But to understand at all one must probably go back once more to the beginning, to that extraordinary debut and even before.

The Ponzillo family was Neapolitan, not from the city itself but from the Province. They came to America in 1885, eventually settling in Meriden, Connecticut, where Rosa and her elder sister Carmela were brought up. It was Carmela who first became the singer, with Rosa playing the piano and so getting some sort of musical education. Then they found that she too had a voice, and the two sisters went on the stage, singing together:

My sister was in vaudeville at the time, and there the sister-act was much in vogue and her manager suggested, 'Carmela, why do a single act? Haven't you got a sister?' And she said, 'I sure have. I've got a kid-sister singing at Cafe Malone's', a very conservative, fashionable eating-place. I was singing there at the time, and I was only sixteen years old. Mr Hughes said, 'Well, get her down here.' And she got me down that weekend and I sang. And he said, 'Wow, she sure can sing, but she's got to get some fat off.' And so she bought me this book, *You can go thin*, and I got the thirty pounds off, and we went into vaudeville, and we stopped the show every week, the Ponzillo sisters, three thousand dollars a week. (Rosa Ponselle in interview)

And so she goes on, chattering about the past with tremendous energy and pace. There was an enormous fund of energy in the woman, much of it no doubt what we call 'nervous energy'. And no doubt that had much to do with the drive towards a great career and then the sudden withdrawal from it.

Anyway, the vaudeville act obviously was no common one. Both of the voices were quite exceptional and both girls were given an audition for the Metropolitan. But Rosa's was the voice they were looking for, and so came the famous debut opposite Caruso in the first performance of *La forza del destino*, and all at the age of twenty-two.

The success was genuine and spontaneous, and without preliminary publicity. The story took the headlines and made national news in a way it is now hard for us to visualise. Over the next seventeen years Ponselle became one of the great ladies of the United States. And the reputation was international, even though she hardly ever sang outside the States, just the three seasons at Covent Garden and one at the Maggio Musicale in Florence, 1933. In December 1936 she married, and this seems to have been the dividing point in her life:

> Her life was divided into two halves, the first forty years when she was the great artist, the great public figure, in what was then an incredibly extravagant scene. It was really the time of big names in the theatre, films, opera and everything else, and she became one of the great figures in the United States. Then at forty she retired. There are various accounts of why she retired – I believe that in the new book they give what might possibly be the real account, I don't know. But then she married and she retired to Baltimore in the Greenspring Valley, where at that time they really weren't interested at all in music and art – it was horses and whisky. And it took some time for them to realise what they had among them. Then of course they began to adore her, and she became a figure that was again a star, in retirement. It was an extraordinary situation. (Ida Cook in interview)

The book which Ida Cook refers to there is Ponselle's biography, written by James Drake in close collaboration with the singer, who, unhappily, did not live to see it finished. The question of the retirement is discussed in it, as are the years following. Part of the reason was a clash with the Metropolitan management over roles, but Dr Drake clearly believes that the causes went much deeper:

> Gatti got her in the stable, developed the racehorse, but, as happens to all racehorses, comes a time when they can't do it any more. And then what? In her case it wasn't the analogous matter of the legs giving out, so to speak, or the body not being able to do it. It was the mind. The mind rebelled, at the endless seasons, the endless scheduling, the lack of personal life. That's what began to influence that decision. And yet we have to be careful and say that Rosa Ponselle never *decided* to retire. She

142

was unable to confront key decisions at all and would instead do what a lot of self-destructive people do and let events make decisions instead of people, and she became the victim of circumstances, I think.

I do believe that Rosa Ponselle was in classical terms, Shakespearean and Greek terms, a tragic figure, that the element of her own destruction, careerwise at least, was there from the beginning, and that in the end it made itself evident in classical fashion, and a complicated personal life ensued. At the Met there was a change of management from the fatherly Gatti-Casazza to Edward Johnson, with whom she had a very indifferent relationship, one as a senior artist to a junior one, frankly, and having no longer the luxury of Gatti to rely on, no personal life – her mother had gone, her mother was the key figure who I think held her together, mentally too, and then emerging troubles in the family with her brother and sister, and then, one by one, you begin to see her destroying her circle of friends. It may be that 'destroy' is too active a verb, but the relationships died out one by one, and pretty soon the lady who had been everything to New York was isolated in Baltimore by her own doing if not her own choosing.

She rose phoenixlike really from the mess she found herself in in 1947 ... Here was a woman who ended up in an asylum for four months, receiving electric-shock therapy daily for one of those months. This was no passing illness that she found herself in the midst of. And as a result she sang not at all. She kept saying, 'My career did this to me, my sensitive nature, and look what this career did to me.' It was only after a round of parties in which she was reunited with de Luca and Martinelli and sang through at their insistence part of the Nile Scene, and people found her voice absolutely unimpaired. Robert Merrill sang with her about a week later and told me the same thing. 'Believe me,' he said, 'nobody could believe that Rosa Ponselle had been retired. The voice was just as fresh and lovely as what we hear on the recordings.' (James Drake in interview)

When James Drake says that she 'rose phoenixlike', he is referring to the new life she found, partly in this rediscovery of her voice, and partly in her work with the Baltimore Civic Opera. From 1947, when she was invited to a rehearsal of *La traviata* till sometime before her resignation in 1979 she worked with the artists, rehearsing, teaching, loving all the renewed contact with operatic life and a new generation of singers. She became again the centre of a world, loved as a teacher and simply for herself. At her eightieth birthday she had messages of congratulation from more than one US President, from the Met and all the musical world of the present as well as a vast company of friends. At that time she was still vigorous, would still swim underwater the length of her sixty-foot swimming-pool, would still sing. When she died, four years later, in 1981, she left behind her a considerable fortune for the foundation of scholarships for young singers.

Though something still eludes us in the boxy old recordings, enough of the glory is caught for us to see why (for instance) Serafin spoke of 'a vocal miracle' and Walter Legge of 'the supreme alchemist', why old George Cehanovsky called her 'the dramatic soprano of the century', and why to the Cook sisters she was 'the greatest artistic experience of our lives'. The crisis in mid-life and the tensions which prepared for it are of course saddening. Yet in another sense they are reassuring. The smiling photographs tell us little about the artist; the tragic element which James Drake discerned in her life and character surely fed her art even while it destroyed her peace. As we think of her now (we of this later generation who never heard her in the flesh) it is perhaps primarily as voice, the 'molten gold' or whatever other simile seems right. But the voice comes with phrases of music and in a certain dramatic colouring, and in this there is more than beautiful sound. At best, her art was ennobled by a feeling that is very close akin in spirit to the theme of the opera of her debut, and it was this in conjunction with the sheer quality of voice that gave to her audiences the sense of something quite special, of unique time.

Ida Cook had a story which she told often but which brings the point home. She was present at the Maggio Musicale in 1933 when Ponselle sang *La vestale*. After the Prayer aria there was an extraordinary rush of emotion in the audience and the demand for an encore was almost irresistible. But the conductor resisted. He signalled that he was about to continue, then suddenly he stopped and the encore was given. Years later Ida Cook met him in the gardens at Glyndebourne – it was Vittorio Gui, who conducted there in most of the postwar seasons up to 1965 – and recalled the occasion in Florence all those years ago. 'Do you know why I let them have the encore?' he said. 'I heard a poor little voice behind me say "Who knows if we shall ever hear anything like that again?" And I thought, "Who knows? And they shall have it!" '

12.   Claudia Muzio

In the Museum of the Teatro alla Scala, Milan, hangs a portrait of a smiling woman with a fan in one hand and a camellia in the other. The visitor reads that this is Claudia Muzio (1889-1936), which may of course signify nothing at all; but if it does mean something, through records perhaps, hearsay maybe or just possibly, even at this date, memories, the visitor looks again at the portrait and assimilates the mild shock which its identification has caused. For depicted here is, you might say, the embodiment of youth, health and happiness, while silently, in the mind of the onlooker, an old gramophone record plays and the voice which sings through it is infinitely sad. One walks away from the portrait, on to the next exhibit, and out into the street. But the picture remains vivid, as does the sound-picture of the voice. Clearly the lady with the camellia is the heroine of Verdi's *La traviata*, and it is the Violetta of Act I who is represented here: the pose is deliberate, 'artistic', but the smile is lively and spontaneous, the eyebrows are slightly, almost questioningly raised, and there is something spirited, courageous even, in the tilt of the head. This, one reflects, is the young woman whose tragedy is to unfold. The voice of a sick woman who reads a letter bringing hope that comes too late also steals into the mind: this too is Muzio, a voice of sighs and tears as one of her colleagues called it. Aware of 'the personal heresy' in criticism, of the fallacies inherent in confusing art with biography, one still feels that the song, Violetta's 'Addio del passato', and the singer are associated with an unusual closeness. The mournful events on stage echo in the life of the singer, and that too is why the smiling portrait comes as a mild shock and remains to haunt the walk home.

Muzio was one of the great operatic artists of her time. In Italy it was the Romans rather than the Milanese who took her to their hearts, and the scene of many of her greatest triumphs was the Teatro Colón in Buenos Aires. She sang at the Metropolitan, New York, and regularly throughout the years of her prime in Chicago and San Francisco. Paris and London, Sao Paolo and Rio de Janeiro also heard her, but she appears never to have sung in Germany or further east. Her repertoire was largely the standard one of the Italian lyric-dramatic soprano, with

145

35. Claudia Muzio as Norma

an occasional *Lohengrin* and *Walküre* (Sieglinde), and a single
Rosenkavalier (Marschallin) at Rio in 1920. *Le Prophète* and *Eugene
Onegin* were other operas she was introduced to at the Metropolitan,
where she also sang as Giorgetta in *Il tabarro* in the world première of
Puccini's *Trittico*. The operas of her other 'creation' roles have mostly
disappeared from the lists: Mulé's *Baronessa di Carini* and Zandonai's
Melenis (Milan, 1912), Smareglia's *L'abisso* (Milan, 1914) and Refice's
Cecilia (Rome, 1934), which was written specially for her and of which

146

she became increasingly fond. The most strenuous role she undertook, in its demands upon the voice, was probably that of Turandot, but having introduced it to the Colón in 1926, the year of its arrival on the world's stages, she, no doubt wisely, abandoned it. *Norma* and *Aida* remained with her for many years (her final Norma was given in her last Rome season, 1934-5). The opera which occurs throughout her career with the greatest regularity is *Tosca*, and the one with which, from the mid-1920s onwards, she was most personally identified was *La traviata*.

Although her public appearances in England were confined to the 1914 summer season at Covent Garden, London did have a special place in her life. Born in Pavia on 7 February 1888, she came to London at the age of two. Her father had been appointed assistant stage-manager at the Royal Opera House, where he was still working at the time of her debut. In an interview with the *Daily Mail* she claimed that she first sang in public when six years old at her school in Tottenham: 'It was a pupils' concert and how it was that such a little thing as I was admitted to take part among the others who were young ladies I cannot now remember.' The reporter does not manage to simper a compliment at this point, but no doubt it was implied. The young Claudia remained at school here till she was 16. She then studied music (harp and piano) at Turin, and voice at Milan. Her Italian debut in 1910 led her in three years to La Scala, thence to Paris where she was heard by Covent Garden's Harry Higgins in a rehearsal of *Otello*. Her English debut as Puccini's Manon Lescaut won some thoughtful reviews, the most detailed and appreciative of which appeared in the *Morning Post* (7 May 1914):

> Her voice is a legitimate dramatic soprano of most musical quality throughout its range, and capable of meeting all the varied demands modern Italian opera makes upon it. Its timbre is usually charming. There is complete freedom from tremolo, and there is in it the natural vibrato of a perfectly produced voice. No unpleasant quality mars it even when used in the most dramatic way, and it can be made to express a great deal since its owner understands the art of vocal gesture ... Manon's coquetry, her passion and her final despair were all vividly expressed by means of her voice. Its warmth and colour made up for some restraint in bearing that was shown in the earlier scenes; but there is no question that Signora Muzio is well equipped as an actress, for her struggles with those who attempted to put her on the ship were very real, and the pathos of her dying moments was very touching. She is a most welcome addition to the list of artists at the opera, and her next appearance is looked forward to with the keenest interest.

There followed an admired Tosca, with Caruso and Scotti ('the most promising dramatic soprano that Italy has sent us for a long time';

'Passion, pathos, horror – all was there – in fact, her frenzied, fervid acting was quite disturbing'), then Desdemona to the Otello of Paul Franz. Here the *Evening Standard* summed up the state of critical opinion: 'With every fresh appearance in public the clever young artist deepens the impression her acting and singing made when she first took opera-goers by surprise. She is certainly one of the greatest acquisitions the Syndicate have secured for years ... Her versatility is remarkable, and though it is perhaps early days to speak of the place she is likely to occupy in operatic history, it may at least be said with confidence that she will never do anything badly. Last night she sang and acted with real charm and pathos, while in the more dramatic moments of the opera she never failed to rise to the occasion.' There were some adverse criticisms: the *Daily Telegraph* warned against 'anticipating the essential note by a kind of vocal appoggiatura', and *The Times* observed that, as Desdemona, 'the expression of a perfectly even tone and of legato phrasing is a thing she might learn from her predecessor' – who was Nellie Melba. But *The Times*, like the others, found her 'the most promising of the newcomers' and the *Musical Times* – not given to extravagant praise of opera singers – went so far as to call her 'one of the greatest artists' to step on the stage at Covent Garden. She added Mimì in *La Bohème*, Margherita in Boito's *Mefistofele* and Mistress Ford in *Falstaff* before the season was over; and the *Evening Standard*, after praising the humour of her part in *Falstaff*, reported that 'She will be with us next season, I am glad to say'.

'Next season' was as ill-fated as any operatic heroine. When it eventually arrived the year was 1919, and it did not bring the return of Muzio. She was by then well established in both the Americas. Father also being an assistant stage manager in Manhattan (though he died shortly after her arrival), she soon came to feel at home in New York and was worshipped in Brazil. Rather than follow her career in detail from this point, it might be interesting to listen to her, as far as this can be done collaboratively through the printed word. What we have of her now, after all, is her voice on records, and there are a good many of them.

We can hear her first in a recording from 1911, when she was 22. In Milan she had what might be regarded as a trial run for the Gramophone Company, and the item to be published immediately was Mimì's solo from Act I of *La Bohème*. She is an eager, frank narrator, with a fresh, well-defined voice that has an Italianate hardness on some of the top As. To an English listener a striking feature that adds to the impression of *naïveté* is the openness of the 'ah' sounds (as in a northerner's pronunciation of 'last' compared with the southerner's 'larst'). The style is inclined to be syllabic rather than flowing. Quite

148

possibly the record would pass without notice except that the singer's development sends one back to it with curiosity. Where, perhaps with the provision of hindsight, one might identify the artist-to-be is at that crucial place where the narrative becomes more overtly emotional. At 'ma quando vien lo sgelo' the heart opens, and here the young Muzio's pretty, smiling lightness of manner changes: this now is a moment of deeply felt personal accounting, and there is some pathos in the consumptive girl's pleasure in the early sunshine ('il primo sole è mio'). Then, with the return of the music's earlier mode her own mood reverts to the lighter, ingenuous tone of the opening. Thus on reflection, this *is* an artist, though she has doubtless much to learn.

Her first full-length catalogue of recordings was compiled with Pathé Frères in New York around 1917-18. There are still limitations, some of them technical: for instance, in the slow arpeggio which takes Desdemona up to the high A flat at the end of the 'Ave, Maria' Muzio sings 'Ave, ave' so that each note is a separate syllable and there is a chance to breathe again on the way up. One wonders whether this remained a permanent feature of her performances. More pervasive in this series is the lack of detailed shading, so that in 'Ernani, involami' the sotto voce markings go for little. Yet both of these negative observations are countered by a real advance on both fronts, technical and interpretative. This is a testing aria with a wide range that has to be readily at command; the difficult groups of six notes and the cadenza show a voice that has been kept supple with regular exercise (she was punctilious in this), and it is also remarkably even, free from register-breaks throughout the two-octave compass. As to expression, there is, if not subtlety, then at least authority and a sense of concentration, of which the recitative gets as big a share as the aria.

Next came a long list of recordings for Edison. These began in 1920 and continued until 1925, covering what may well have been the years of her vocal prime. Another Verdi aria, Leonora's 'Pace, pace, mio Dio' from *La forza del destino*, again shows a voice that has been kept in good trim, and the advance in expressiveness is considerable. The lower notes, without breaking away from the main body of the voice, have gained in depth and resonance; phrasing and nuance receive much more attention. But it is in a different part of the repertoire that she becomes most herself, and at the same time most clearly a great singer in all respects. An aria from Catalani's *Loreley* (a role she sang at the Metropolitan and in South America) shows both what command she had over her voice in those years and what a subtly expressive instrument it had already become. Her high notes are full, free and thrilling, the florid work is brilliantly done, and always we are aware – even without knowing much about the dramatic context – that this is a genuine actress with the voice.

This is what became known to the world at large (for the Pathé and

Edison recordings had limited circulation) through Muzio's final series of recordings, on Columbia, in 1934 and 1935. It will be noted that there is a gap of nine years, which is in fact virtually ten, since only a single song was issued in 1925. A great deal had happened in the meantime, and the likelihood is that at least the first half of this silent period in the recording studios was the very time when her gifts, vocal and interpretative, were most in equilibrium. Certainly when we hear her again in 1934 the depth of tragic utterance has increased so that her singing has a quite unforgettable intensity. It is also clear that she no longer has the stamina for strenuous passages lying high in the voice. The breath still supports steady tone – we never feel a 'beat', let alone a wobble threatening the firmness of the notes – but it does not allow any great breadth of phrasing. As a result, the 'Casta diva' from *Norma*, exquisite in many ways, lacks resources for the climax of the verses, and in the duet from Act III of *Otello* she needs to breathe between noun and adjective in 'le prime lagrime'.

The beauty of spirit, artistry and indeed of sheer voice in this series still touches the heart whenever one returns to these recordings. There is some most beautiful lyric singing in the *Otello* duets, and a noble revulsion in the phrase 'ciò che esprime quella parola orrenda.' Exquisite is the impulsive 'Bada' in Mimì's farewell, the face lighting up, and then an incomparable veiling of the 'senza rancor'. Marvellous, and utterly characteristic, are the baleful, tragic tones of the solo from Cilea's *L'arlesiana*, the passionate commitment of Maddalena's aria in *Andrea Chénier*, the light and shade, the fine phrasing and the vivid suffering of 'Poveri fiori' from *Adriana Lecouvreur*. The sighs of Boito's Margherita in 'L'altra notte in fondo al mare' become inseparable from the music and the record in one's memory, and as one *lives* through the *Traviata* solo with her ('Addio del passato', recorded on the same day as the *Mefistofele*) that performance becomes equally unforgettable. There were some songs too, most notably the elegiac 'O del mio amato ben', a tender, very personally inflected performance of Reger's 'Maria Wiegenlied', and, showing that the smile of the Scala portrait was not quite lost, a charmingly concluded 'Bonjour, Suzon'.

But these were the recordings of a sick woman. A heart condition had been diagnosed some years previously, her personal life developed unhappily, she lost her fortune in the Depression, and on 24 March 1936 she died. The 'restrained interior fire' of her singing (as the tenor Lauri-Volpi memorably described it) no doubt fed upon her own heart; and yet, withdrawn and reserved as she became in these later years, she seemed utterly devoted to her art and indeed to have little life beyond it. All of this is why the visitor stands in front of her smiling portrait in the Museum, hears an old gramophone record playing in the silence of the mind, and walks back to the hotel a little thoughtfully.

13. Four Faces of Maria Callas

᎒᎒ Elvira (I puritani) ᎒᎒

It not infrequently happens that the music in which one first hears a great singer becomes almost totally identified in the mind with that voice and that art. For many record-collectors it must have been so when they bought, in the last years of the old 78s, an aria from *I puritani*, itself something of a rarity in those days, sung by a soprano whose name meant nothing unless through remote hearsay. It was also a long name, and at first one could not be sure of having it right. What become abundantly clear on first listening to the record was that this was a name that simply *had* to be remembered, and a more attentive look at the label afterwards established its syllables in correct order. Maria Meneghini Callas: new to us then, and never to be forgotten.

The aria was Elvira's 'Qui la voce' in Act II. Even before that began, however, a special quality was apparent, for the phrases which introduce it ('O rendetemi la speme, o lasciatemi morir') lived a new life, like fine Carrara stone in the hands of a master sculptor, and they went straight to the heart. The aria itself gained emotional strength from the fullness of tone, which was that of a lyric-dramatic soprano rather than what was normally thought of as a 'coloratura'. Here too was what one little thought to hear in a modern singer, an imaginative and instinctively musical use of portamento and rubato, carrying the note over affectionately and creatively, letting the music linger when it wanted to and regain tempo with grace and good judgment. On the second side (marked 'Conclusion') came the cabaletta: 'Vien, diletto, e in ciel la luna'. This was still more exclusively, in our experience, the sphere of the 'coloratura', and I doubt whether many of us had really considered it as anything more than a lively tune and an opportunity for Tetrazzini (for instance) to be brilliant. Callas again drew on the tone-colours of a quite different type of soprano, and her inflections had a gentle pathos which brought out something different in the music. When we looked into it a little further, the dramatic situation became real rather than nominal; those descending chromatic scales were the haunted sighs of a clouded mind. Nor was the technical brilliance in any way dimmed, and

151

the high E flat arose astonishingly through this voice which also had such depth within it.

That early recording was made in 1949, and Callas had only very recently sung the role for the first time. This was in Venice, where she was called at six days' notice to substitute for the indisposed Margherita Carosio. By 1953 when the complete recording of the opera was made, she had become world-famous, and her Elvira had been heard in Rome and Mexico City. Ahead were remarkable performances in Chicago, the first of which opened the 1955 season. Later in her career she gave up the complete role but retained some of the arias in her concert repertoire. 'Oh vieni al tempio' from the Wedding Scene was a solo for which she had a special affection; and in 1958 we read in *Opera* magazine of Covent Garden's Centenary Gala, where the enthusiasm 'reached its peak in the enormous ovation accorded to Mme. Callas after her performance of the Mad Scene from *Puritani*, an example of consummate operatic singing and acting which held the audience spellbound.'

Covent Garden audiences never heard more of Callas's Elvira than that, while the opera itself, which had been a favourite with the great nineteenth-century sopranos such as Grisi, Patti, Albani and Sembrich, was not given at the house between 1887 and the revival with Joan Sutherland as Elvira in 1964. That it was heard in the 1950s at Chicago and the other cities mentioned here was largely due to the impact which this extraordinary singer had in so short a time upon the operatic world. Nor had the complete opera been previously recorded, though individual arias and a few duets had had a rather glamorous recording history. Many of the great names of the past were involved: Tetrazzini, Kurz, Galli-Curci and Hempel among the sopranos, Bonci, De Lucia and Lauri-Volpi among the tenors, and Battistini and de Luca prominent among the baritones. The arrival of Callas upon the scene came at a time when the general thirst for a revival of great singing had become almost desperate. It also coincided with a demand, particularly on the part of younger enthusiasts, that they should have a chance of hearing and judging for themselves these operas which the older generation had very largely written off as naive and inept. The demand had regularly been countered by the answer that there were no longer the singers for such roles, and indeed it seemed all too likely that this was true. Yet here, in Callas, despite some pertinent misgivings, was a singer who pre-eminently could undertake them. Moreover, she invested them with a depth of feeling for which most listeners, now hearing these things for the first time, were quite unprepared. The recording of *I puritani* and *Lucia di Lammermoor*, the latter made in the previous month, played an important part in one of the most notable extensions of musical appreciation in recent times.

꧂ Fiorella (Il Turco in Italia) ꧁

Callas-and-comedy is a phrase that trips off the tongue more readily than it appeals to the imagination. The clown who wants to play Hamlet will often make a better job of it than the tragedy-queen turned comedienne. Yet Garbo had her *Ninotchka*, and Callas her *Turco*. She was not by nature an amusing woman: so, at least, we are told by two of the men who produced her in comedy, Walter Legge on records and Franco Zeffirelli on stage. Looking back, Zeffirelli said, 'Maria was not a very funny lady. She always took herself so damn seriously.' To stimulate the spirit of comedy at La Scala he devised stage-business which he knew would arouse her interest, loading the Turk with jewels so that when he offered her his hand she would examine it with comic zest. Legge felt that 'her lack of humour and comedy were handicaps she rarely overcame'. He remembered her Rosina in *Il barbiere di Siviglia* at La Scala, which 'woefully lacked humanity', and only in the London recording of that opera 'did comedy brush her with his wings'. Possibly he had forgotten this *Turco in Italia*, and perhaps Zeffirelli had momentarily forgotten that she had enjoyed a brilliant success in the opera before he himself produced her in it. For us at this later date it becomes easier to visualise Callas in comedy if we have seen the filmed performance of a concert in which she sang Carmen's Habanera. Not that that of itself was comic, but the smile had such radiance it illuminated the whole being, and those large eyes that opened so wide in happy wonder at the spell they were casting irradiated the whole scene. Shown that, with no other evidence, one might well guess that here must have been a personality ideally made to sparkle in the comedies of Rossini. Hearing the two Rossini recordings, the *Barbiere di Siviglia* and the *Turco in Italia*, one would be convinced of it.

As ever, she excels in recitative. Even when in one phrase she hands the Turk his coffee and in the next enquires whether he has enough sugar, the personality works its magic. In the lightest of conversational passages, as in the duet 'Siete Turchi', she has a sure touch, utterly charming and genuinely comic because she also hints in occasional phrases at the hard centre of the sweet little miss. In the duet with Geronio, which ends the second scene, she almost guys her own tragic self: as Fiorella sings 'No, mia vita' and 'Voi crudele' we hear faintly parodied overtones of Lucia and Elvira. Then in the final solo of the opera, 'Si mi è forza partir', the sentiment is real; the tragic accent now marks a genuine development and the character gains a new warmth and depth in a way which perhaps only an artist with Callas's skills and experience could bring out. It is a remarkably complete portrayal.

In the pattern of her career, while *Il barbiere di Siviglia* is incidental, *Il*

Turco in Italia is woven into the design. When she sang it first she was at a decisive turning-point. As the *Opera* critic, T. de Bebeducci, wrote of the opening night in Rome, it was 'extremely difficult to believe that she can be the perfect interpreter of both Turandot and Isolde'. But that was the reputation she had at that time. Both of those roles were now to be put aside, and with a single broadcast performance of *Parsifal*, a few months after the Rossini triumph, she bade a permanent farewell to Wagner. As usual, there was a major influence behind the decision. First it had been the conductor Tullio Serafin: now it was the producer Visconti. He and his friends of the 'Anfiparnasso' intellectual circle mounted *Turco* in the Teatro Eliseo, a suitably intimate theatre in Rome. Gavazzeni conducted and the famous Stabile was in his recorded role of the Poet. Visconti opened the horizons for Callas, giving a view of a more sophisticated world of ideas, and it was a part of that process that he should submit her first to the completely different art of comedy. This was in 1950. The recording was made in 1954, and the five performances at La Scala followed in the next year. These too were seminal, for they introduced her to Zeffirelli, who was the second producer of genius to be associated with her. Again these were a revelation to all who were present, for here was the great Norma, the great Lady Macbeth, lightening her voice miraculously, yet lifting the part well beyond the familar concept of the soubrette and re-establishing it in the proud tradition of the dramatic coloratura. Then came the unhappy *Barbiere* of 1956, with which Callas's stage career in comedy came to its premature close. At least the recording of that opera in the following year provided the association with a happy ending, and together with the *Turco in Italia* provides posterity with a happy view of Callas too infrequently caught in her lifetime.

⋙ Norma ⋘

The role of Norma has a special place in the repertoire of the dramatic soprano, rather comparable to Otello in that of the heroic tenor. One notable difference is that Otello does not have to sing scales and semiquaver runs as though he were Rossini's Count Almaviva in disguise. Nor does his part take him above the stave too often; and, while it is highly desirable for him to have a sound legato style at command, he can still make a considerable effect without it. A successful Norma has to cope with further difficulties. The voice itself is constantly exposed, the whole range tested, the sheer beauty of timbre being no less requisite than the power. Without orchestral covering, it has to carry a responsibility seldom required of it in later Verdi and still more rarely in Wagner. All of this, moreover, is in a sense no more than the preliminary

36. Maria Callas as Norma

qualifying ground. It is a great role for the singing-actress, both in its details and in the sum of its tragic grandeur. A fine discrimination of shades is involved in recitative, and the depths of the tragedy have to be sounded through notes which, to a casual reader of the score, may suggest little beyond charmingly melodious sadness.

Not surprisingly, great Normas are rare. In the first decades of the present century the shadow of Lilli Lehmann fell across the role: formidable authority there, with the style of a practised Mozart singer and the power of a Brünnhilde. It needed Rosa Ponselle, probably the greatest soprano of her time, to restore the opera to the repertoire in New York and London. And after the Second World War came Callas: a brief period of splendour, during which the singer and the role conferred glory upon each other. For Callas, *Norma* was the opera in which her greatness was most completely exercised; for the opera itself, Callas was the artist who regained for it an honourable and central place in the schedules of the great houses.

The earlier of her two recordings of the opera preserves her performance as it was in the years of her vocal prime. It was made in Milan in the spring of 1954, at the end of a triumphant season at La

155

Scala, where her roles had included those of Medea, Lucia, Alceste and Elisabeth de Valois. In the last of these operas, *Don Carlos*, she sang with Ebe Stignani, the Adalgisa of this recording, who had made her debut at La Scala, also in *Don Carlos*, as long ago as 1926. In spite of the disparity in age and the difference of timbre, the voices blend remarkably well, and one feels a sympathy and mutual understanding not always evident in the duets for the two women. The later recording, from 1960, has Christa Ludwig in the role, a singer with a very different background and with a tone-quality unlike either Stignani or Callas herself, yet again achieving a fine blend of voices, showing, for one thing, how Callas could discipline her unmistakable individuality and match voices equally well with quite different partners. In the six intervening years, her voice had perceptibly deteriorated in fullness, beauty and ease of production. Her feeling for the part had matured, and yet in comparing the two versions it is frequently the depth and intensity already achieved in the earlier one that impresses most strongly.

Whatever the respective merits of the two recordings, the 1954 version is the one which will recall for British, as for Italian listeners, the performance as they knew it in the theatre. Callas sang Norma at Covent Garden in 1952 and 1957 with Stignani as her Adalgisa (there was a revival in 1953, when the mezzo was Giulietta Simionato). Her debut, a great event in itself, also marked the introduction of the opera to a new generation. As Harold Rosenthal, certainly not overstating in his *Two Centuries of Opera at Covent Garden*, puts it: 'The occasion was one to remember.' *Opera* magazine's reviewer was Cecil Smith, who attended four of the five performances, and whose previous Normas had included Ponselle, Raisa, Cigna and Milanov. He found Callas 'a singer of grand format'. He noted that she 'sings with two voices', the chest notes and upper tones being clean and strongly edged, the middle register 'heavily covered'. His marvel was that 'by some mysterious alchemy ... these two voices coalesced into one as the evening progressed'. He made a special point of the glissandi in the cadenza of 'Casta diva' and of the stupendous long-held high D in the second-act trio. After that, he said, she rewarded her audience by 'never letting them down, and by reaching a peak of eloquence in the infinitely moving closing pages of the opera'. On her last appearances as Norma at Covent Garden, the verdict of *Opera*'s Editor was that Callas 'despite the vocal imperfections, is a creative genius of the first order, whose personal magnetism is such, as was the case with Pasta [creator of the role in 1831], that the critic forgets these vocal imperfections'. Perhaps it might be added that the present writer, no critic in those days, confesses to having forgotten both the imperfections and most of the finer points of the performance he attended in 1952: perhaps, the repeated hearing of recordings has dimmed the memory. What he does recall, with almost painful clarity, is the glimpse, half an hour or so after the performance, out in the street beyond the stage door, of a woman with a white face, wide-eyed and anxious, and very, very tired.

⁓ Madama Butterfly ⁓

For an actor it can be advantageous to have a face that is not instantly recognisable. Nose and brow otherwise tend to proclaim the inescapable identity of the player beneath the make-up. Similarly, one would think an opera singer might benefit from the possession of a voice that, of its own kind, is 'standard', not too manifestly individual. But what we find is that some of the most adaptable voices are also the most idiosyncratic. Chaliapin's voice was unmistakable; Lotte Lehmann's was always her own. Yet Boris and Varlaam, Prince Igor and Khan Konchak are distinct characters in Chaliapin's records, as are Lehmann's Marschallin, Sieglinde or Frau Fluth in hers. The voices least susceptible to the art of make-up somehow belong to the artists who are best at it.

In our time the prime exponents of this art of vocal make-up have been Maria Callas and Tito Gobbi. The immediately distinctive timbre of both voices was itself a feature of their greatness. Yet Gobbi's Michele and Gianni Schicchi (for instance) presented not merely different faces; they had different voices. Callas's Tosca and Mimì, as we have them on records, are utterly separate creations; and on records the voice is *all* we have. It is reported that Toscanini was asked about the voice of the tenor Aureliano Pertile. He objected that he could not think of any such thing: Radamès, Lohengrin, Canio, Nero, there was a voice for each of them. The remark certainly applies to Callas, and to none of her roles more aptly than to her Butterfly.

The transformation is not so complete that one is denied the thrill of recognition at the first sound of her voice off-stage in the entrance music. The single word 'Aspetta' is entirely characteristic, yet, equally, it could not be the Callas of *Norma* or *Tosca*, and when she arrives ('Siam giunte') it is, miraculously, the fifteen-year-old girl and not the great Callas who stands before us. Utterly childlike are the introduction to Pinkerton and the direction to the relatives: 'Uno, due, tre, e tutti giù'. We are to see the child develop into a woman: but not all at once. Just as something of the child remains even in the last scene (the excitement and cruel disappointment), so the woman emerges occasionally in the first. As she tells how poverty has touched her family, how the hurricane shakes the strongest oak, the voice fills out to acknowledge life's harshness. The child is there again in the quick, tight little word 'Morto' in answer to Sharpless's enquiry about her father; it is a child who has a

37. Maria Callas as Butterfly

private sorrow associated with a deep pride which she will carry to her death. Callas's portrayal is so moving partly because it creates, in these early episodes, a girl capable of tragic dignity, and then in the second half of the opera, when experience more than years has brought maturity, she still mingles the adult's voice with the tones of the girl. Her imaginative grasp of the part is marvellously complete.

The whole performance is rich in detail. Perhaps more consistently than in any of her other recordings, each phrase here seems to have something special about it, and a whole essay could be written, with its emphasis on what we categorise as 'interpretation'. In a sense, we do Callas less than justice by the process. Her art was still that of the singer, and behind the mass of interpretative points the singer is sometimes lost to view. At this time, in 1955, her voice could still be an instrument of very special beauty. In the *Madama Butterfly* recording a few high notes have a raw edge, a wayward pulse – the D flat concluding the Entrance is the prime example. But generally her singing is fine as 'pure' singing, and sometimes exquisite. A lovely example is the broad melody ('Io seguo il mio destino') in Act I, where she tells of her newly adopted religion. Equally in the second act, the solo starting 'Che tua madre' is the work of a great *singer*. But of course when she was at her best, as here, there was no separating the singer from the interpretative artist. Everything in that solo as in 'Un bel dì' is beautifully sung and has also some special insight within it that enriches the beauty. And the final solo ('Tu, tu, piccolo Iddio') is doubly moving because not only is it fine in itself but it is only now, at the moment of death, that this Butterfly becomes the complete woman, alone on stage for the only time in the opera and only now abandoning the restraints within which she has suffered, and it is only now that we hear Maria Callas as herself.

Surprisingly, perhaps, Butterfly is a role that she sang on stage, in Chicago for three performances in the November of 1955. She worked hard to ensure authenticity in her movements. The deeper authenticity of character had been achieved three months earlier, in the recording studio.

14.   Elisabeth Schwarzkopf

After the Second World War (very much as after the First) the word went round that ours was not to be an age of great singing. A certain pleasing mournfulness attended the declaration, which events such as the visit of the San Carlo Opera from Naples in 1946 and the first season by Covent Garden's resident company in 1947 did nothing to counter. In the September of that year, however, the Viennese arrived in London. During their short season at Covent Garden the Vienna State Opera gave several good reasons for thinking that the art of singing might be alive after all, and on the opening night in *Don Giovanni* most striking evidence of this was found in the performance of the new Donna Elvira. Among the other singers introduced to London in these weeks were Hilde Gueden, Sena Jurinac, Irmgard Seefried, Ljuba Welitsch, Anton Dermota and Erich Kunz. It was a distinguished company; but the artist who was to develop most steadily and surely over the longest period was that Donna Elvira, Elisabeth Schwarzkopf. In the thirty years that followed her Covent Garden debut, Schwarzkopf's appearances in London became a regular and special feature of the musical year; indeed, in all the main centres of civilisation throughout the world her presence came to be valued as a token of culture, the representative of a high European tradition of art in word and music. She brought along with her voice and musicianship a radiance and as it were a renewal of standards. In our time she provided for many listeners their best understanding of what an age of great singing might mean.

For those three decades in which she was one of the world's leading singers there were something like fifteen years of preparation, and they drew richly on the best musical traditions of her country. Music had always been part of her life. She learnt the piano at an early age, sang in the school choir and took the lead in a Haydn opera at Magdeburg. Becoming a full-time music student, she played the organ and viola as well as the piano, and soon her voice showed promise enough for her to be accepted as a pupil of Lula Mysz-Gmeiner at the Berlin School of Music. Mysz-Gmeiner, one of the most respected lieder specialists of her time, was herself a highly trained singer having studied under Gustav Walter, Etelka Gerster and Lilli Lehmann. She had plenty to

38. Elisabeth Schwarzkopf

teach, as she did with much success as Professor at Berlin from 1920 to 1945. But she appears to have gone widely astray with Schwarzkopf. Herself a contralto, she trained her pupil to be one too. Schwarzkopf found it a strain and her mother found it intolerable so she took her away. This was 1935, Elisabeth being just twenty. She had made one false start, and not for several years did the voice settle properly into its true *Fach*, its natural repertoire. At one time she studied Sieglinde in *Die Walküre*, at another Zerbinetta in *Ariadne auf Naxos*, eventually to be the role of her debut in Vienna. The high notes were quite securely there, and that no doubt encouraged the notion that her future lay as a coloratura soprano. No doubt too the fact that her second celebrated teacher was one of the great coloratura sopranos of the century gave further encouragement. This was Maria Ivogün, whose voice was delicate as the finest porcelain and whose art Richard Strauss described as that of a genius: 'an Ariel of the opera world' one critic called her. She took immense pains over Schwarzkopf, reconstructing the voice virtually note by note. What she accomplished was surely the work of a great teacher. Yet here too all was not well. For one thing, Schwarzkopf found when working with her husband in later years that they would have trouble over intonation in music that she had studied at this time, and for another, this was still not the repertoire which suited her best. Schwarzkopf was really to be an Ariadne rather than a Zerbinetta, a lyric soprano rather than a leggiero. It says much for the material these teachers found in her voice that one of them could hear a contralto in the making, the other a high 'coloratura'. It says something too that she should have come home at last, the voice unimpaired and ready to serve as such a fine and durable instrument over such a long career.

The career began in 1938 with an appearance in Berlin as one of the Flower Maidens in *Parsifal* (a part learnt overnight) and continued with a Page in *Tannhäuser*. In wartime, programmes of her concerts appear to have offered the Ivogün repertoire of famous coloratura arias and arrangements of Strauss waltzes. She was auditioned in 1942 by Böhm for the Vienna State Opera but a period of illness delayed her debut there till 1944. New roles included Adele in *Die Fledermaus*, Nedda in *Pagliacci*, Liù in *Turandot*, Rosina in *Il barbiere di Siviglia*. And it was in that role, at the Theater an der Wien, in January 1946, that she was first heard by Walter Legge.

Legge was of course the greatest influence in Schwarzkopf's work, and both could have spoken of their marriage as Legge himself did when he called it 'the longest and happiest association of my life'. He remained her fellow-worker, teacher, critic and inspiration from the time of their first meeting till the day of his death, 22 March 1979. He was a challenging sort of man with no time for mediocrity: there must be many still alive who have known the sting of his tongue or pen. Conversely there will be those who can hold some appreciative remark of his in their little store of that rare commodity, the compliment that helps to justify a lifetime. As a thorough-going, hard-working woman with quite fiercely self-critical artistic standards, she must have recognised in him a man whose standards she could trust and respect. There would be work and more work, but the reward would be that if he was satisfied she would know that something had actually been achieved.

In an article for the American *Opera News* (May 1975), reprinted in *Opera* of April 1976, Legge described his first impression of Schwarzkopf as he heard her in Vienna singing Rosina: 'a brilliant, fresh voice shot with laughter, not large but admirably projected, with enchanting high pianissimi'. He admired too what he called the 'hair-raising agility' of her Constanze in *Die Entführung*, and this he took care to catch in the first recording session that year (1946) in Vienna. He could also see clearly enough where the future lay: 'The voice was by nature a lyric soprano. At my urging she was soon singing Agathe in *Der Freischütz* and the Countess in *Le nozze di Figaro*: the younger Rosina was a girl of the past.' Even so, the list of her roles as a member of the Covent Garden Company, which she became from 1948 to 1951, makes surprising reading today: in those years she was Susanna rather than the Countess, Sophie not the Marschallin; she sang Gilda in the 1948-49 season (learning the part in English in twenty-four hours) and again in 1950-51; Violetta, Ciò-Ciò-Sàn, Mimì and Manon (in Massenet's opera) were other roles in this period. The happiest memories are probably those of her Pamina (an exquisite performance), Marzelline in *Fidelio* (a role she also took in some great performances of the opera at Salzburg), and Eva in *Die Meistersinger* which she was to sing gloriously in the Bayreuth Festival of 1951.

1947 was the year of the break-through, Schwarzkopf being now a principal soprano of the Vienna State Opera. She had made a powerful impression in London ('Madame Schwarzkopf once more showed that the human voice can be as fine an instrument of phrasing as the violin', wrote *The Times* after a concert in which she had sung with Tauber and the Vienna Philharmonic under Krips). At Salzburg she sang her Countess under Karajan, and in Lucerne there was a Brahms *Requiem* conducted by Furtwängler. That was the year too of Karajan's recording of the *Requiem* in which Schwarzkopf's singing of 'Ihr nun habt Traurigkeit' was admired as something close to perfection by Toscanini. Moreover the records of the Vienna sessions were now becoming known, and the Schubert coupling ('Seligkeit' and 'Die Forelle') made something of a best-seller. She was also approached by the management of La Scala Milan where she had a substantial and interesting career. By

1951 it could be said that the world knew about her. Hers was a brilliant part in a brilliant occasion at the première of Stravinsky's *Rake's Progress* at La Fenice, Venice, and a few days before that, she – a German – was chosen to sing in an otherwise all-Italian performance of the Verdi *Requiem*, as part of the celebrations that year in honour of the fiftieth anniversary of Verdi's death. All was set now for her to become truly and fully herself, choosing the operatic roles that were right for her and steadily developing her capacity to become one of the greatest of concert artists.

Although her recitals took up an ever-increasing proportion of working time, Schwarzkopf's operatic career continued up to 1972. It was skilfully directed, at first with an expanding repertoire, and then a contraction and concentration on half-a-dozen roles. The house which saw most of the expansion was La Scala. Her first Marschallin was given there in 1952; she also sang Elsa and Elisabeth, Marguerite and Mélisande, collector's pieces all of them, doubly so in that the last two remained unrepresented in her recordings. The invisible stage of the recording studio was in a sense another opera house for her, in that she had a wonderful ability to give a performance that would be almost as vivid to the mind's eye as anything seen on stage. Thus we have her Ariadne, her Giulietta in *Les Contes d'Hoffmann*, her Gretel, and memorable excerpts from *Arabella* and Walton's *Troilus and Cressida*. As her American career opened up she became more and more identified with Mozart and Strauss. *Così fan tutte* was 'the success of all the successes' in San Francisco, as Albert Frankenstein wrote in *Opera* (December 1956): 'The entire production was as fresh and sparkling, as clear of routine and cliché, as if the Mozart masterpiece were a new discovery'. She appeared at the Chicago Opera in 1959 and at the Metropolitan in 1964, when Irving Kolodin wrote: 'Faultless in manner as well as manners, Schwarzkopf's Marschallin was the first truly great one the Metropolitan had seen since Lehmann's'. There was also a gala evening later that year in which Schwarzkopf sang Act I of *Rosenkavalier*, Tebaldi Act I of *Bohème* and Sutherland Act I of *Traviata*. At about this time the process of contraction began, leaving an operatic repertoire comprising Fiordiligi, the Countess, Elvira, the Marschallin, the Countess in *Capriccio*, and Mistress Ford in *Falstaff*. Her final stage appearance was given at the Théâtre de la Monnaie in Brussels in the first act of *Rosenkavalier*, a performance 'full of fine detail and still hauntingly sung' (*Opera*, February 1972). Happily too, it was in this theatre that having taken her farewell as an opera singer she made her debut as a producer, in May 1981, with another *Rosenkavalier*: 'meticulous' was John Higgins's word for it in *The Times*, and, he added, 'notably unflashy'.

Her concerts continued right up to the time of Walter Legge's death, when she herself was sixty-three. In the very last years I believe she sang essentially for him, though the voice remained firm and beautiful within its more limited range, and it was always managed with consummate skill. A Schwarzkopf concert was an occasion. From the earliest years of the 1950s onwards, singer and impresario brought care and creativity to every aspect. The programme itself would be a special creation, never thrown together or merely following convention. Work with the pianist would be painstakingly thorough. The singer's dress and personal appearance were also part of the occasion: nothing was left to be second-rate. It was through her concerts that the largest number of people came to know her (in New York, for instance, her Town Hall and Carnegie concerts brought her fame and a large following long before her debut at the Metropolitan). Through her concerts, too, audiences came to know a wealth of previously unfamiliar German songs, and at the Festival Hall in London, as elsewhere, even came to recognise certain Wolf songs as 'pops'. There grew up a marvellous responsiveness in these audiences, who learnt the emotional depths of the songs as never before and who also came through to the exhilarating discovery that so many of them were for smiles and even laughter. Schwarzkopf herself is quoted on the matter of her audiences at the end of Edward Greenfield's valuable articles on her in *The Gramophone* (October and November 1976): 'If you ask me what the magic is, I think it is that people *really listen* to my singing.'

That people 'really listen' no doubt owes much to the sheer beauty of her voice, but it has more to do with the way in which this singing specifically engages the intelligence. One can think of many good and famous singers whom it is quite possible to hear in German song without feeling impelled to gain anything more than the most general idea of what it is about; but with Schwarzkopf one has to *know*. Songs like Mozart's 'Abendempfindung' and Wolf's 'Wiegenlied im Sommer' can wash over the mind very pleasantly, creating a sense of beauty that may be thought sufficient; but there is the difference between listening and '*really* listening', and it is essentially through a more alert responsiveness to the singer's own intelligence that one comes to know the songs for what they specifically are. Many of them tell a tale, crack a joke, are sung in character or even in dialogue. With Schwarzkopf none of these things can be ignored, for as she enters the song so thoroughly the listener who does not 'really listen' is left like an idiot grinning at a joke he does not understand or a dreamer who only half hears an urgent tale of human joy or sorrow.

It also has to be acknowledged that Schwarzkopf by the very nature of her art challenges critical analysis more insistently than do the vast majority. Like most of the really interesting singers of our day and of earlier times, she is controversial. It is not unknown, indeed, to find criticism levelled against her in a manner which to call ungenerous would itself be an act of generosity. The adjective 'mannered', too blunt an instrument for proper critical use, is repeatedly offered, and It essentially serves as a means of discrediting the expressiveness of her singing. The perceptions and insights accruing from years of study and performance are dispatched with the charge of affectation. But affectation means insincerity, and insincerity is betrayed by lack of care or sensitivity towards the supposed object of attention; and as one tests Schwarzkopf at any point it is to find her deeply sensitive to all that is going on in the music, such as orchestral harmonies and colours which more often than not singers show no signs of being aware of at all.

Even so, such criticisms, whether just or not, must, if they have been honestly formed, have some point of origin. I fancy that it is the price exacted by the particular nature of the success. With Schwarzkopf, especially on records, one is always aware of a *face* with the voice, and it is exceptionally vivid and mobile. It changes from one operatic role to another: as, for instance, the Countess Almaviva suddenly disappears and in her place stands the smiling, playful Susanna, and as we turn to the *Rosenkavalier* and *Hansel and Gretel* excerpts, so the thirty-year-old woman becomes a girl and then a mere child. A single character will change, too, as does Constanze, from her elegiac mood in the first solo to the resolute defiance of the second. In the songs, it is one person who tells of the enchanter ('Der Zauberer') and quite another in the next item, who prays in Schubert's 'Litanei'. The face within the song is ever-changing and is as vivid as in spoken dialogue. Sometimes, and very rarely, the face is wrong (as, to my mind, in the start of 'Depuis le jour' from *Louise*, which then becomes a lovely performance with the phrase 'l'âme encore grisée de ton premier baiser'). Again, if listeners have both earlier and later recordings by Schwarzkopf of songs such as 'Die Forelle' or 'Der Nussbaum' they will find the face changed again, for each performance of a song was for her a separate event, seen and felt differently.

All these changes may well be found disconcertingly various where so many singers are reassuringly the same. They are indeed a kind of magic, and of course a sorceress meets with some suspicion. But Schwarzkopf knew her magician's business – which was art and not artifice, for what we have been speaking of as 'face' is part of the means of expressing character, and that in turn involves heart and soul.

15.   Tito Schipa

Raffaele Attilio Amedeo Schipa was officially admitted to life on 2 January 1889. The reference books share a conviction that it happened twelve months earlier, but the City of Lecce's *Atto di Nascita* confutes them. Schipa's biographer, Renzo d'Andrea, believes the singer was born toward the end of December, and that his father thought military service, when the time came, might be deferred if he postponed recording the birth till the New Year. The date doesn't matter; the name does.

In a cast list or on a record label, 'Tito Schipa' has such an immediate identity that the sound of his voice comes unbidden to the mind with all the clarity of a photograph. But how would we feel about Raffaele, etc.? 'A good name,' says Ecclesiastes, 'is better than a precious ointment.' Singers' names have a way of *becoming* their voices. Melba could not possibly be Mitchell. It would be an affront to the mighty voice to refer to Titta Ruffo as Ruffo Titta (which he was). 'Rosa Ponselle' is a rich fabric woven with two strands of deep crimson to one and a half of a lighter shade, perfectly proportioned, perfectly apt. By contrast, the 'illo' part of the original 'Ponzillo' introduces a garish brightness. A Tito Schipa by any other name, you might say, would have been no less himself. But no: the name is the voice. The vowels have the lightness, the consonants the sharp definition, and the balance of syllables has the grace.

His grace is what we hope and yearn for, in vain for the most part, when in the opera house we sit to the end of *Lucia di Lammermoor* and the tenor starts up his 'Tu che a Dio spiegasti l'ali'; we knew he would not have the grace, because there was no sign of it in Act I with 'Verranno a te'. Or in *La traviata* our Alfredo for the evening sings 'Un dì, felice', and an old record runs in the mind simultaneously; and then still more insistently near the end, when 'Parigi, o cara' sounds coarse by comparison with that private, mentally recaptured performance in which Schipa partnered Amelita Galli-Curci. Or perhaps a tenor recitalist will give as an encore one of those Neapolitan songs that used to be so popular. The tenor may invest them with all the fervour of his being and all the voice at his command, but somewhere another voice is calling: it

39. Tito Schipa as Des Grieux in *Manon*

sings 'Mandulinata a Napule' or 'Marechiare' with an individuality and instinctive rightness that work their magic even in memory, even while our modern tenor approaches his climactic phrase, which surely will bring the house down.

If Schipa himself ever brought down houses, it certainly was not by the feats of a vocal Samson. He was careful to see that the specification 'lyric tenor' would remove him from the league that, willingly or not, was seen as competing for the throne left vacant by Caruso's death in 1921. He stood on his own ground and never stepped beyond it. His repertory was fairly small, though it contained a number of surprises, such as Tamino in *Die Zauberflöte* and Vladimir in *Prince Igor*, both of which he sang at La Scala. Generally it was an alternation of *Il barbiere di Siviglia*, *Don Pasquale*, *L'elisir d'amore*, *La traviata*, *Rigoletto*, *Manon*, *Werther*. In America he was an admired Ottavio in *Don Giovanni*; at Monte Carlo in 1917 he sang Ruggero in the world premier of *La rondine*; and late in life he unexpectedly turned up in *Il matrimonio segreto*. The list is not complete by any means, but it suggests the area. On records we find that his first session in 1913 included 'Cielo e mar' from *La Gioconda*, and that among the last opera arias was Chénier's 'Come un bel dì di maggio', but both are sung as pure lyric solos, which in themselves they are. Similarly, when he recorded the Siciliana from *Cavalleria rusticana* (an opera in which he did appear onstage), his performance had neither the ring of Caruso, the vibrancy of Corelli nor the intensity and broad phrasing of Martinelli, but within its own lyrical terms – that is, in grace, clarity and poise – it is ideal. One also can sense from such records that it was a good *carrying* sound, well projected and free of the throat.

In the song repertory too he was generally careful not to go outside himself. To judge from remarks by the critics, he was not so successful with the Schubert and Brahms that sometimes had a place in his programmes; but he seems to have been aware of this himself, and though he knew and was fond of Hugo Wolf (as I believe his pupils will testify), he never would sing Wolf's songs in public, because he considered his German inadequate. The usual *arie antiche* would be at hand to open his recitals, but there is no doubt that what he really enjoyed were the Italian café songs, of which he seems to have had an inexhaustible supply. These often would monopolise the second half of his programme, and many felt this to be more than enough.

It is a curious anomaly that this elegant singer, so fastidious and stylish in his own sphere, should have shown such doubtful taste in the music he chose for recitals. We must beware of musical snobbery, of which I think there was an element among the section of his London audiences who found his inclusion of 'Amapola' to be particularly infra dig. It is no doubt a facile little melody (though the facility for writing such things is not all that common), but it is shapely and graceful; moreover, it suited Schipa's voice particularly well, and as he sang it, it became a thing of affection and charm. There were, however, tunes less memorable and more banal, among them some mildly deplorable tangos that sought to suggest a passion they did not contain.

The anomaly runs a little deeper when his posthumous reputation comes to mind. One rarely sees nowadays a reference to his singing that is not profoundly respectful: Schipa is not only pre-eminent among the lyric tenors of the century but also, it is felt, artistically an aristocrat among the vigorous plebs to which the majority of Italian tenors belong. The best of him amply justifies such a view, but it needs qualifying. On the one hand, he could show the most exquisite taste in phrasing and shading a Donizetti air, such as 'Sogno soave e casto' in *Don Pasquale*, yet he also could associate himself with tawdry, even rather gross music. He had a weakness – and I think it *is* a weakness – for the popular music of his time, with its saxophones and 'beat'.

When his 1962 Town Hall recital was announced, he gave an interview to the *New York Times* in which he was engagingly frank: 'Some of my friends want me to be upset about modern music, especially about the way American popular songs are taking over in Italy. Why get upset? When music is done the way it is supposed to be done, it is always beautiful. I learned the twist last year. It seems to be good for my leg.' Well, this is a liberal attitude, and perhaps it shows old gentlemen how to stay young. It is a strand that runs through his career. In Chicago he had a jazz band of some kind. I don't know what his operetta *Principessa Liana* is like, but the songs of his own composition that he recorded do little to raise expectations. He wrote the theme song for an early Janet Gaynor movie, and he appeared in several films himself. The most successful of the musical scores seems to have been Bixio's for *Vivere*, the brash title song of which is so much of its period (1937) that even at this distance its recipe of life, laughter and youth has a distastefully bitter flavour.

Again, as with so many artists who have become touchstones of excellence for us in the present, it can come as something of a surprise to read the irreverent reviews meted out when they were alive and in their prime. Schipa did not appear in London until 1928, when he was a gramophone celebrity with a reputation for being something different among Italian tenors. But the *Musical Times* was not impressed. 'The makings of a pleasing if probably not a musicianly singer' was the best the critic could find to say of his Albert Hall recital:

> He was uncertain of his technique in all but the lightest of Italian and Spanish pieces of a popular nature. In more exacting music we noticed his upper-chest breathing, and although he did not sing throatily, the whole

170

of his thought was obviously directed to avoiding throatiness. He hardly dared pronounce a single consonant all the afternoon, and he took breath without thought of anything but vocal convenience ... His tone was pretty; but if one's command of an open throat is so uncertain, one is not a technician.

A huffy, stuffy review perhaps, but the man has listened and can give chapter and verse – the separation of adjective and noun ('und die einsame/Träne') in Brahms's 'Die Mainacht', intrusive aspirates in an English song. It is perhaps some comfort to read Ernest Newman, who could be devastating, particularly where Italians were concerned. Schipa, he said,

> ...has one of those captivating voices that seem only to call for the mouth to be opened to sing of their own accord ... [He sang] beautifully in tune, with never a suspicion of tremolo. But the ostensible absence of effort is really a manifestation of considered art, as was clear when he passed from the smooth legato of arias by Gluck and Scarlatti to the light staccato of an Italian song, 'The Butterfly', arranged by himself. And much lies behind his vocalisation: his power of emotional suggestion made itself felt in 'Le rêve de Des Grieux' from Massenet's *Manon*. In fact the effect of light and colour was cumulative in a programme that well illustrated his versatility.

And Newman clearly has listened too.

My own memories of Schipa's concerts come from the twilight years, the 'farewell' recitals of the early 1950s. Both were at the Royal Festival Hall in London, and the first was one of those fraught occasions where anything – or indeed nothing – might have happened. *Expectans expectavi* – we waited. Then came the dreaded announcement that Signor Schipa had laryngitis. We groaned. 'But seeing the wonderful audience he has here tonight' – we brightened – 'he is willing to come out and try his voice.' We cheered. Out he came, almost at a run, and as the legend stood before us we did all that was possible to promote confidence. I remember trying to think whom he reminded me of, and could come up only with the indispensable Italian of the old gangster films, Eduardo Ciannelli. There was nothing sinister here, but a nervous flickering of eyes that did not quite seem to be looking at anything. When he started to sing, the sound was small but clear, and I was told later that it reached the back of the hall perfectly. He himself seemed dissatisfied, and a microphone was brought out, which seemed to make him happier. 'That must be the first time he's done that,' said the man behind me, who had brought his young son to learn what real singing was about.

And one could still learn: there was still, for instance, surprising

171

power and resonance in the upper notes, plus a freedom throughout, which became impaired only on low notes, and he generally found some way of avoiding those. At the end, when we thought he had come through remarkably well, he apologised. The little speech was touching but painful. 'I am sorry,' he said, in a husky, rather high tone, with of course an endearingly strong accent – 'It is all my fault.' 'No, no!' we assured him. But with a wan smile he concluded. 'For you see ... I can sing – no more.' Unbearable. It brought tears to the eyes, for it was both true and untrue. Under the circumstances, he had sung magnificently; yet quite possibly, under the circumstances, he should not have been still singing at all.

The other concert, a year or so later, went through without trouble, except for the unfortunate pianist, who had to cope with disintegrating sheet music, with bits added here and taken away there, and all to be transposed at sight. I listened to part of the programme from a more distant place in the hall, in a doorway, where the sound of that voice I had known since childhood, now singing the romance from *Martha*, was so *exactly* the voice I knew that it produced one of those strange sensations where dream and reality contend and neither seems quite to gain the victory. The voice *was* the same, despite the years, despite the transposition – firm, pure and poised. The last programmed song was 'Chi se ne scorda 'cchiu', in which he would sing the first half of the last refrain on a thread of sound and a single breath. To conserve the air, he seemed to hunch in, but it was accomplished – again just as on the record from the golden days of the 1920s.

Those were indeed the days. As we go back to the lovely records of that time – the *Mignon, Lakmé, Werther*, the duets with De Gogorza, the *Bohème* scene with Lucrezia Bori – it is to hear an art that remains unequalled. More, it is to hear 'Tito Schipa', a compound of voice, art, character and idiosyncrasy. And what, one may wonder, became of Raffaele Attilio Amedeo?

16. Giovanni Martinelli

Martinelli is a very personal singer, by which I suppose I mean two things: the voice and style are very individual (I shouldn't think he could ever be mistaken for anyone else), and (the other point) a taste for his singing, certainly as recorded, is also a personal matter in that people react very differently.

For myself, Martinelli's records have been, almost from first acquaintance, an irreplaceably precious 'inner' possession – because one 'learns' his records, hears them vividly in one's head, as with few other artists. But when I said '*almost* from first acquaintance' I have to think back to the month of June and the year 1941. A ten-inch record of Martinelli singing two Italian songs was on the dreadful deletions list of that year. I ordered the record, looked forward to its arrival, bought it, played it, and was dismayed. To my young ears it registered as a kind of affront, a strangely concentrated series of offences. But I played it again. And throughout that summer, this voice, which had at first repelled, drew me back; and the record began to show bad signs of wear.

One of the songs was the famous 'Torna a Sorrento', and Martinelli's way with it seemed to me then, and indeed still does, to *concentrate* its feelings and to raise the simple, possibly facile melody to the point where it becomes almost noble. The next year or so brought several newly acquired records of Martinelli in which the reactions followed a similar pattern. It was so, for instance, with the 'Improvviso' from *Andrea Chénier*, an intensely personal performance, with much subtlety in its changing tones, the interchange of lyrical and declamatory styles, the feeling for the shape both of phrase and of overall form. This was so, I found, quite reliably with all his records of that period – from *Aida, La forza del destino, Pagliacci*. The trouble was that they were all too few.

Then one day the record shop had a pile of old things, throw-outs from another branch, and among them were some pre-electrical recordings of Martinelli. And now one heard an appreciably younger voice, handled even then, in 1915, with mature mastery and individuality, but with an art which was clearly that of a singer trained in the classic bel canto method of his country.

Then came another moment of dismay, almost comparable with the first one: another trial of faith through ordeal. This was the issue of a set of excerpts from *Otello* made in America in 1939. Again, if I can recall my own experience, the first impulse was one of straight rejection. No, the voice was too old, the dryness of timbre (helped not one jot by the closely boxed acoustic of the recording), the sense of a voice driven well beyond its natural limits. And yet, and yet … One returned to those records and played them again. And once more, in spite of everything, they became an infinitely treasured possession. And *all* of Otello's utterances, learnt through this intense medium, came to bear permanently the impress of this voice and art.

＆ II ⑇

If *Otello* was the crown of Martinelli's career, it was certainly not a crown made to measure. He lacked the sheer size of voice and physique, and when he won his audiences it was in spite of quite clear limitations. But we have his Otello on records, in several complete performances from the stage of the Metropolitan, and records can be marvellous distillers. That is, they can eliminate contingent matter and reveal pure essential. Martinelli's Otello *sounds* tall. The absence of a baritonal weight or (at the other extreme) of a shrill brightness places his Otello tonally in an aristocracy of pure, defined tenor. On records, bulk does not necessarily affect us; concentration does, and everything in Martinelli's Otello was concentrated. The tone was concentrated, so that never a suspicion of loosening, let alone wobble, comes into mind. The total performance was concentrated in that, as you come to know this Otello, every phrase in his music bears the stamp of Martinelli's intensity indelibly upon it.

He never, I imagine, had the satisfaction of thrilling the house immediately with a massive effect of power in those twelve bars of the 'Esultate', formidable not merely in themselves but because they have to give a sense of personal dominance over the combined fortissimo of orchestra and chorus in all that has gone before. On records, however, one listens *through*, to the firmness of line, the fine clean definition of the high A ('dopo l'armi'), and to the fervour and authority within the soul of the singing.

Otello's return to the stage, stopping the fight between Cassio and Montano, again calls for a physical power which it was not in Martinelli to give (the effect should be comparable to Shakespeare's 'Put up your bright swords or the dew will rust them', important because it shows the apparent solidity of character which is so soon to disentegrate). Even so,

174

40. Giovanni Martinelli as Otello

the fire of the declamation compensates for much – the scorn, for example, of 'da sbranarvi l'un l'altro'. Still more effective is the change of tone as he turns trustingly to 'onesto Iago'. Then the sudden spurt of temper as he finds Montano wounded ('ferito') catches exactly the quick unthinking anger which is to prove so ruinous as the blood begins to rule the judgment. But it is an ever-changing, ever-responsive performance, so that, as he turns to see his young wife ('la mia dolce Desdemona'), affection enters the voice, only to exacerbate irritation and induce the rashness of Cassio's dismissal from office.

The opening page of the Love Duet is a touchingly *scrupulous* piece of singing. Breadth of phrase was always one of Martinelli's distinctions, and the whole of the first line is taken as one, unbroken, which of itself is uncommon. Surprisingly rare in observation, too, is that of a detail in the score, the accentuation deliberately marked over the second syllable of 'amplesso'. And in fact very closely observed are all the dynamic markings and contrasts of tone to the end of the solo. Has there ever, one wonders, been an Otello who has so beautifully filed down the voice to the pianissimo of that last phrase: there again is the aristocrat among stylists. In the later phrases of the duet, and especially in the earlier of the recordings, the tone sometimes comes nearer to the lyrico-spinto of his vocal prime, when the sheer beauty of sound could be ravishing. 'Ingentilià di lacrime la storia il tuo bel viso' will sometimes bring this out in an exquisite lyrical span of phrasing. How well, too, he catches the 'dying' ecstasy (marked 'morendo') of 'e il labbro di sospir'. But everything here deserves its own comment. The expansion of the strong A flat on 'paradiso', for instance, or the indrawn silvery tone of 'E tu m'amavi' and the exact feeling for Verdi's markings of crescendo and decrescendo. The shudder of an almost unbearable happiness at 'tale è il gaudio dell'anima', the reality of the well-founded fear in 'temo che più non mi sarà concesso', and the smooth, broad phrasing of the passage 'l'ignoto avvenir del mio destino': all of this is the work of a great artist.

The *pain* of that fear ('for I fear that my soul hath her content so absolute that not another moment like unto this succeeds in unknown fate') presages the tragedy. Martinelli's tone always had a remarkable capacity for expressing pain (I am not one for prying into the private lives of artists, but I am sure that there must have been in Martinelli's life a self that was quite different from the jolly Giovanni he seems to have been so much in public – the emotional sensibility is that of a man who knows about suffering). As we come to the second act, the pain begins to gnaw through the anger which is half-stimulant, half-solace. Shakespeare's Othello responds to Iago's promptings readily enough; in Verdi he is quicker still, and from the frank, courteous invitation to Iago to speak his mind to the 'Ah!' scored without musical notation, the psychological revolution is effected in two minutes. The later recordings bring us very close to Martinelli's Otello at the cry of pain 'miseria mia!', and the rise to the high B natural has about it the instinctive desperation of a wounded animal.

He was remarkably sensitive to the need for contrasting tone. After the strain and bitterness of that outburst comes the sound of Desdemona's voice from offstage and Martinelli catches the heartbreaking sweetness that Verdi himself must have had in mind when he wrote the direction, 'soavement commosso', 'sweetly moved'. Then he brings out the touching, almost childlike dignity of his inward speculations about himself (black and 'declined into the vale of years') in the Quartet. In the so-called temptation scene he feels intuitively the agony in the chromatic descent of 'lo non sentivo sul suo corpo divin' and follows it with the sweet-toned nostalgia of 'che m'innamora'. The Oath Duet itself, like the 'Esultate', calls for bigger sound; even so, the incisiveness tells and the stamina impresses.

Perhaps for any Otello, but certainly for this one, the great act is the third. Otello's greeting of Desdemona ('Dio ti giocondi') is sung with a courtliness in which a terrible bitterness and irony are always lying just below the surface. Increasingly with Martinelli we are aware of the tension within, the false elegance of the manner just managing to contain the furious misery which is soon to burst free of its restraints. He observes, again more scrupulously than most, the *pianissimo* markings in the phrases which give a fearful potency to Otello's continual references to the handkerchief, and, more important, the purpose of them is understood: the menace is all the more bewildering to Desdemona for being something she can only fearfully glimpse through a veiled wrapping. The warnings, 'Bada!', 'smarirlo' are then rapped out with intimidating clarity. Again the rage mounts and is controlled, till Desdemona uses the grace he has now come to see as diabolical, to revert to her pleas for Cassio. Vivid now and terrifyingly real is the snapping of controls: 'Pel cielo! L'anima mia si desta', with growing menace till the last demand of 'il fazzoletto' towers (no matter now about physical stature). The open vowel in 'condanna' ('corri alla tua condanna') concentrates the ferocity, and the 'Giura e ti danna' crescendo overwhelms with the intensity of the vocal gesture. At the end comes the most terrible moment. Otello changes suddenly and resumes his manner of ironic courtliness. The music returns to the false smoothness of the start till the fury breaks through, and then the score directs 'cupo e terribile' and 'voce soffocata'. Verdi writes an alternative version of the phrase 'quella vil cortigiana' which shoots the voice up on the last syllable to a staccato high C. I think he wanted it to be taken, and

177

in early performances Martinelli did so: potentially (for he does not quite secure it) the effect is like the crack of a whip or the smack of a hand.

The monologue ('Dio, mi potevi scagliar') takes us to the heart of Otello, his *de profundis*. Again it is Martinelli's tragic sensibility, his capacity for creating a tone which is an actual embodiment of the suffering, not just an expression of it, that etches his performance upon the memory. A great sadness, a suffocated bitterness, a terrible sweetness, all are there in those first phrases, sung within the scored discipline of the monotone. In the live performances (as opposed to the fine studio recording) the slow tempo makes formidable demands on the singer, but all the customary breadth is maintained. The quiet pity in 'che mi fa lieto' prepares for the majestic breadth of the rising phrase ('spento è quel sol') to the long-held B flat: all the dignity and noble tradition of classic tragedy lie within it.

17. Richard Tauber

Ever-rolling streams, as well as bearing things away, are also good at giving them a wash. Time has done this for Richard Tauber, who in the latter years of his life was in some senses too popular. Fitzgerald makes old Khayyám say that he sold his reputation for a song, and Tauber came very close to doing just that. The song was tied round his neck like an identity disc. When he gave a concert he was invariably expected to sing it. When he went into a restaurant the band would strike up with it as soon as he was recognised. When he sang in opera fashionable women arriving fashionably late would enquire anxiously whether they had missed it. 'Dein ist mein ganzes Herz' became synonymous with Tauber for perhaps a few hundreds of thousands, and in its English translation as 'You are my heart's delight' it became the Tauber-song for millions. 'Serious' musicians would say this was all very well but would recall that he had been a fine operatic and concert singer, and in particular one of the very best Mozart tenors of the century. Then they mostly stopped recalling this and in their view he became essentially an emigré to the land of smiles, increasingly associated with second-rate musicals and third-rate films. Occasionally a gramophone record or reappearance on the operatic stage reminded the public and the critics of his musical origins, but such occasions were comparatively rare. After his death he suffered the further indignity of popular artists whose private life is posthumously made public. Reissues of his records continued to sell, and the song still shadowed him in death as in life. Gradually, however, the shadow has dimmed; or rather, it has merged into something altogether larger.

Tauber's ghost is in fact returning to the musical world to which he originally belonged. When his name is recalled now it is usually in musical company which honours him for his years with the Vienna Opera, with Dresden and Berlin, and for his gallant final appearance in *Don Giovanni* at Covent Garden only months before his death. Increasingly his early recordings are sought out, not for their rarity but for their musical value. The other side of his work was not worthless by any means, and when the obituary columns said that he brought charm and melody and the gift of his voice and art to millions who would never

179

41. Richard Tauber

have gone to the opera house to hear him, that also was perfectly true and just. But time, which can play tricks with reputation, can also be a great rinser, and Tauber's musical reputation has emerged with a new freshness and strength.

The full extent of his repertoire was never really known in Britain or the States, or indeed by his world-public in general. He appeared in as many as sixty-four operas altogether, all of them learned between 1913, the year of his debut, and 1926. The foundations of his repertoire were the Mozart operas, *Don Giovanni*, *Die Zauberflöte* and *Die Entführung*. Max in *Der Freischütz*, Matthias in *Der Evangelimann*, and Paul in *Die tote Stadt* were also important, with Bacchus in *Ariadne auf Naxos* and Florestan in *Fidelio*. It was a good, broad-based international repertoire he had in those years: *Carmen*, *Faust* and *Mignon* were among the French operas; *Traviata*, *Falstaff* and *Cavalleria rusticana* among the Italian; *The Bartered Bride* and *Eugene Onegin* among the rest. The 'bel canto' operas included *La Fille du Régiment* and *Il barbiere di Siviglia*; Puccini figured prominently, with *La Bohème*, *Madama Butterfly*, *Tosca* and *Turandot*; there were even secondary roles in five Wagner operas – and what a start it would give to a performance of *Tristan und Isolde* to hear Tauber's voice, unaccompanied, singing 'Frisch weht der Wind der Heimat zu'.

His career is a remarkable story of persistence. He was the illegitimate son of a provincial singer of very limited means; his physical disabilities included lameness and defective sight; he developed arthritis and was unable to move his wrists; and at the height of his career he had an illness which might well have proved fatal. Luckily his parents had their share of persistence too. Tauber was born at Linz on 16 May 1891, taking his mother's name of Seiffert. When he was six, and she could support him no longer, she wrote to the father, who was in Prague. He was an actor and his career had prospered reasonably well; he was also delighted to learn of his son's existence. He saw to it that the boy was properly educated, and when at the age of sixteen Richard announced that he wanted to become a singer, he responded like a sensible father, urging caution but also providing practical assistance. An audition with Leopold Demuth, principal baritone at the Vienna Opera, ended in flat discouragement, but again the persistence of both father and son came into play. He entered the Frankfurt Conservatory, worked hard at piano, composition and conducting, and then, at Freiburg, had an audition with Professor Carl Beines. This was the first turning-point, for the teacher was a remarkable one. He recognised a great potential through a very limited and in fact distorted achievement, and he trained Tauber scupulously in daily exercises, exacting a promise that he would not sing in public for eighteen months. The lad who came along forcing his voice in Wagner learned the art of bel canto and made his debut in Mozart.

Zauberflöte (2 March 1913 at Chemnitz) was followed a few days later by *Der Freischütz*, and this resulted in a contract for the Dresden Opera. These were the great years for experience and development; happy years too, shared with colleagues such as Elisabeth Rethberg and Tino Pattiera. They brought guest appearances at the Berlin State Opera, the Volksoper at Vienna and in 1922 a contract with the Vienna State Opera itself. Already his association with light opera and operetta had begun. *Fledermaus* and *Zigeunerbaron* were in his repertoire and very shortly he sang his first Lehár operetta, *Frasquita*, at the Theater an der Wien. He enjoyed such a success in this, transforming what had been a dying show, and clearly having such a natural affinity with the style, that a new line in his career opened up from that time on.

For some years he was able to run his careers in opera and operetta simultaneously, though it was thought to be somewhat beneath the dignity of a Vienna State Opera artist to be associated with what was considered a lower kind of art. Tauber refused to see it as in any way beneath him, and he was still proving himself indispensable to the operatic world, as was instanced by the German première of *Turandot*. This took place at Dresden on 4 July 1926, and Tauber had three days to prepare for the event, substituting with resounding success for the indisposed Curt Taucher. Then later that year came another demonstration of the Tauber magic. Lehár himself was fully aware that he had found a singer who might make all the difference to his own future fortunes, and he wrote his next operetta, *Paganini*, specifically with him in mind. When the show opened in Vienna, Tauber was singing in Sweden. It duly failed and the impresario who had booked it for Berlin did all he could to cancel the contract. Lehár insisted, Tauber was now available, and *Paganini* became one of those sensations of which the legends are made. It virtually inaugurated a new career for the composer, who rapidly followed up these successes with *Der Zarewitsch* in 1927 and *Friederike* in 1928. Each of these operettas was equipped with its 'Tauberlied', and they culminated in *Das Land des Lächelns* which had its world première at The Metropol Theatre in Berlin on 10 October 1929. That Tauber was able to sing in this, his greatest personal triumph, was something of a miracle, for he had suffered from virtual paralysis for four months.

With the new decade, Tauber's career followed the popular path more resolutely. Films, *The Land of Smiles* in English, a first American tour, and *Lilac Time* all diverted him from opera, and when Germany and then Austria became closed to him because of the Jewish part of his ancestry his operatic career might well have been ended for good. In fact, there were some notable appearances in opera during these years, and perhaps one should include the film of *Pagliacci* among them. This had its première in London in 1937 when it won some critical esteem as well as the enthusiastic response of the audience, which applauded as though in a theatre. Covent Garden at last invited him to sing there; in the 1938 season he appeared in *Die Zauberflöte* and *Die Entführung*, followed by *The Bartered Bride* and *Don Giovanni* in 1939. There were also tours to South America and Australia and he enjoyed an ever-growing popularity in the States and Canada.

While he was in South Africa, war was declared. He sang some performances of *Bohème* in Switzerland, then returned to England where, throughout the war and in the first years of the peace, he appeared in a number of musicals and conducted some concerts with the London Philharmonic Orchestra. Gradually the musicals sadly lost their appeal; a generally bad press greeted him on his return to America; his vocal condition, closely related to his health, showed some deterioration. In 1947 cancer of the lung was diagnosed and the end of his career was in sight.

182

It came, however, with a final burst of glory, for in the September of that year the Vienna State Opera gave a short season at Covent Garden and Tauber was able to sing with the company of which he had been such a famous member, joining them on their last night, in *Don Giovanni*. This was on 27 September. The next night he made what was to be his final broadcast, 'live' of course, and successfully despite intense anxiety in the studio. On 4 October his left lung was removed in Guy's Hospital, but the disease was too far advanced and he died in the new year on 8 January. The *Don Giovanni* performance provided his career with the happiest and most honourable finale he could have wished for. After seven years away from the operatic stage he went into the performance without a rehearsal and with virtually a single lung, and he sang magnificently. It was the ultimate triumph of the persistence which had driven and supported him all his life.

Among his colleagues on that last night was Elisabeth Schwarzkopf, and her testimony is of particular interest because Tauber clearly impressed her as a singer who was utterly special, different in kind rather than degree. His technique, particularly his breathing, and the individuality of his style and tone ('not an arid voice', she said, and the negative description has an unusually positive force) combined to make him 'the greatest tenor I had the fortune to hear'. Against this, one has to note that, in the English press, reviews of his concerts and operatic performances were quite frequently critical. In opera, Ernest Newman found himself irritated by the consciousness induced, as he felt, by the singer himself, that the character on stage was Tauber rather than Tamino or Belmonte, and in concerts he would say that while he enjoyed an effective diminuendo as much as the next man you could have too much of a good thing, and with Tauber you did. And there is no doubt that Tauber could irritate. *Musical Opinion's* 'Figaro' (A.P. Hatton, an old hand but no old fogey and quite capable of enjoying a musical and a famous tenor singing in one) took himself to *Lilac Time* at the Aldwych in 1933 and wrote as follows:

> The pity of it! Tauber's light baritone [*sic*] voice is as accomplished as ever in technical difficulties: he can bewitch even old Covent Garden hands by the almost insolent ease with which he walks, or waltzes or slides, tiptoes or whirls, somersaults on his melodic tight-rope without the smallest sacrifice of insinuating (yes, that is the word) charm; but turning Schubert insideout to put an extra gloss on his purely physical pranks – bah! Now is this singing?

To the *Observer's* drama critic, Ivor Brown, visiting *The Land of Smiles* in 1931, it was an extraordinary piece of stage magic that 'a singer with a presence so little romantic ... impersonating, if you please, a Chinese diplomat ... should be able to magnetise his audience to the top of adoration's bent'. The stage-production was nothing to look at ('starved' was his word), but Tauber's voice 'can do all Vienna's business without benefit of other aids ... he smiles and chants, flourishes an arm as though he were leading the orchestra of the world's desires, and chants again'.

And now, of course, he chants from beyond the grave and through the gramophone record. His legacy of recordings is probably the largest of all comparable singers of his time. From 1919 to 1946 he was constantly in demand with the German Odeon or the British Parlophone companies, and his discography numbers well over seven hundred items. The trend of his career was reflected by his recordings, so that in the later years, say from 1934 onwards, popular songs and excerpts from operettas and musicals predominated; but at any point in the list, songs by Cole Porter, Haydn Wood or Rudolf Friml might be followed by Schumann or Grieg or even by a Mozart aria. In the earlier years the proportions were reversed, and he could be heard in some surprising operatic pieces outside his normal repertoire: excerpts from *Trovatore* and *Aida*, for instance, or *Walküre* and *Die Meistersinger*. In all of them, I think without exception, Schwarzkopf's negative phrase fits: 'It was not an *arid* voice'. Limited in some ways it clearly was. The upward range was short, extending happily to the high A, more effortfully to the B flat where a tense rapid vibrato appears, and perilously if at all beyond that. Audiences tended to find that records had led them to expect more sheer volume than he actually possessed, while recording at close range probably exaggerated the nagging effect, increasing over the years, of certain characteristic vowel distortions. But 'arid' is exactly what he was not.

Listening to the recordings he made in the first session of all, we hear first how free and forthright his production was. In 'Zueignung', for example, the tone is full-bodied and manly, and in 'Ruhe, meine Seele' it is capable of an heroic ring as well as a velvety gentleness. His art is already marvellously assured, with everything fully cared for: an art at once strong and delicate. The brooding feeling of the last song is sensitively caught, and as we move on to the *Dichterliebe* songs the range of colouration is even more striking (the instantaneous change of the singer's whole being, for instance, from the first song to the second). His treatment is expansive and generous, so that one has no sense of hurry, as there often was on 78s. In 'Ich hab' im Traum geweinet' we hear his voice and style as they had developed in 1935: a slight ageing, but a most lovely mellowness, and a complete emotional commitment, colouring the tone darkly but not souring or draining it in the modern manner. In the early operatic recordings we hear some of the famous mezza voce effects, which could be breathtakingly lovely. But the essential firm basis of his singing is also striking, as in the true legato of the *Kuhreigen* aria. Nothing is without character; the Italian tenor's aria in *Rosenkavalier* (transposed down a semitone) is entirely in character and not offered as 'pure' singing, while in Mozart there is always a strong presence of character, nothing tepid or impersonal. The mastery of phrasing and the breath control that so impressed Schwarzkopf at the end of his career are strikingly evident in the *Don Giovanni* aria of 1923. The sensuous quality that made him so romantic a singer in spite of his appearance finds its ideal medium in *Die tote Stadt*, the duet being the only one he recorded with the radiant Lotte Lehmann. A romantic Walther von Stolzing is another rarity, the *Meistersinger* solos exercising the vocal charm and elegance which are hardly ever theirs in performance yet must be if the drama is to be convincing. These date from the middle of his career, while the *Freischütz* aria comes from one of his very last recording sessions, and shows how the essential texture of his voice remained uncoarsened to the end, while the attack, the dramatic vigour that never sacrifices musical tone, is still exemplary.

In all of these records, and in the operetta songs, we are aware of an essentially fertile artist. Music always drew a response from him and he in turn always drew from the music something newly perceived and newly felt. As we are coming to realise more and more with Chaliapin, the greatness lies in the combination of an intensely creative, individual art with the well-schooled use of a naturally beautiful instrument. Like Chaliapin, too, he stands the test of time, emerging strengthened and confirmed.

185

18. Mattia Battistini

Battistini had that most gratifying kind of career, where popular adulation is matched by critical respect and where each phase of a long life before the public has its due complement of achievement and reward. One disappointment only seems to have befallen him. In 1928 at the age of 72 he hoped to celebrate his golden jubilee as a singer by appearing once more in *La favorita,* the opera of his debut fifty years earlier. Sadly, he was by then a sick man, and that one triumph was denied him. There are not many singers for whom it would lie within the bounds of possibility; still fewer who so long afterwards retain such a special place in the regard of posterity and the annals of their art.

The five decades of his career flowed smoothly, middle and old age seeming to come upon him so gracefully and gradually that it is hardly appropriate to speak of 'phases' or to divide the half-century into periods at all. Success came instantly and his reputation enjoyed a steady growth in Europe and South America throughout the first fifteen years. Then there followed a new development, one common to many great opera singers of the age but in this instance of particular significance: he first visited Russia and, with many appearances in Poland, became a firm favourite so that virtually a new career opened up in Eastern and Central Europe. It ended only with the outbreak of the First World War, and with its conclusion one can say that the third and last period began. Battistini's career might well have faded out during the war, by which time he was sixty years old and, by the normal laws governing a singer's life, ripe for retirement. Marvellously, his technique and physical stamina supported the diminishing but still impressive vocal resources, so that eventually he made his final operatic appearances in opera in 1925 and sang for the last time in public at Graz in October 1927.

There must also have been a point by which the good and eminent singer became recognised as the great artist; and that point (happily again for symmetry) probably occurred just about half-way through his career around the turn of the century. His earlier appearances in England (in 1883 and 1887) had gained him praise but no special notice; when he returned in 1905 and 1906 it was as one of the supremely distinguished living singers. At his post-war concerts from 1922 to 1924

42. Mattia Battistini

he was something of a legend, the crowned king of baritones, proverbially acclaimed as the glory of his country, and a living monument to what was already being characterised as 'the golden age of opera'.

He was born at Contigliano, near Rome, on 27 February 1856. His father was a doctor and he himself studied medicine for a time, changing shortly to law. His biographer, Francesco Palmegiani, was the grandson of the lawyer whom he studied under and he recalls that it was the daughter of the house, 'una bravissima musicista e una espertissima pianista', who was immediately responsible for the further change of direction. To her accompaniments the young Battistini 'began to interpret with the ardour and enthusiasm of a neophyte'. At the start, apparently, he was singing as a tenor, and it was Venceslao Persichini (later Titta Ruffo's teacher) who placed his voice in the baritone register. At the Royal Philharmonic Academy of Rome he sang among the principal choristers in a performance of Mendelssohn's *St Paul* and then in *The Seasons*, described by Palmegiani as 'uno dei più grandiosi oratori di Haydn'. In 1878 he was given his first solo work, in the Cathedral at Rieti, where the Director of Music had written a setting of 'O salutaris Hostia', which Battistini affectionately kept in his repertoire throughout his life. Towards the end of that same year – 11 December is the date commonly given but later researches suggest 9 November – there came his stage debut in *La favorita* at the Teatro Argentina in Rome. It was followed almost immediately by an appearance in *Il trovatore*, and early in the new year in *La forza del destino* and *Rigoletto* at Ferrara. Four major roles in as many months by a newcomer to the stage, who a year earlier had not sung in public at all: this is not our idea of the classic method of preparation, the years spent on scales and exercises, that are supposed to lay the foundations of a durable career. It is some comfort to find that nothing has yet been discovered of further public appearances over the next twelve months.

The debut itself was a spectacular one. The Company had been in trouble with its baritones, two having come and gone because they had not pleased the public. *La favorita* had been announced: the Leonora was an eminent mezzo, Isabella Galletti, the conductor Luigi Mancinelli, so this was to be no scratch performance. But it lacked a baritone till the impresario remembered having met young Battistini, who was then duly sent for. He sang 'A tanto amor' to the maestro and the prima donna. She told him not to be nervous but to sing out and then joined him in the duet. Everyone was delighted, and the public, instead of dismissing the new baritone to follow his predecessors into oblivion, applauded so enthusiastically that Galletti, more generous than some of her kind, took hold of the youngster in the wings, assured him that the cries were all for him and propelled him towards the stage. No wonder the occasion remained with him in memory and that the old man had so set his heart on commemorating it in what should have been his jubilee year.

La favorita remained a favourite in his repertoire – he sang it as late as 1922 at Monte Carlo – and in some of his last recording sessions he remade the two principal arias, 'Vien, Leonora' and 'A tanto amor' which had been so ecstatically acclaimed at his debut. In his *Voci parallele*, Giacomo Lauri-Volpi, famous tenor and prolific writer, describes a performance he himself saw as a young man, when Battistini entered in the second scene and sang his opening phrases like one inspired. 'But,' writes Lauri-Volpi 'in the cadenza, on the words "il cor", he took a big breath, spinning it out in the long "i" sound, repeating a whole series of "i"s, to the front, to the left and then the right of the stage, and towards the various sections of the house. And the public would not let him stop, because of their joy in this bold virtuosity, the last relic of vocal athleticism in doubtful taste.' He comments that this was the weak side of the great singer; and no doubt it was the kind of thing that caused Battistini to be regarded very much as of 'the old school'. The stage-manner has its counterpart in the vocal style as heard on record, and of course one can raise objections. The other point of view, expressed by Desmond Shawe-Taylor (*Opera*, May 1957), might also be taken into consideration: 'There is a conscious arrogance, a grandeur, a theatrical swagger, about these performances which many people dislike: but the more I listen to him and to other baritones, the more I feel that Italian opera of this period not only can take such treatment, but usually demands it.' He adds that a correspondent who heard Battistini several times in 1910 remarked that he was by no means exceptional among his contemporaries in such matters and that 'compared with other Italian singers, he was extremely restrained'.

Operas added to his repertoire in the next dozen years included several that are well represented among his records: *L'africana*, *Amleto*, *Il barbiere di Siviglia*, *I puritani*, *Ernani*, *La traviata*, *Don Carlos*, *Un ballo in maschera* and in 1889 *Otello*. To read of some others, such as *Les Huguenots*, *Aida* and perhaps most of all *Simon Boccanegra* is to regret deeply that nothing from these operas survives on record. His Wagnerian roles were Telramund in *Lohengrin* (among the London operas of both his early visits as well as being in his first season at La Scala in 1888) and Wolfram in *Tannhäuser* which remained in his repertoire till 1916. There were also numerous operas either completely forgotten today or remembered mainly by virtue of the few recordings made by Battistini and his contemporaries: Donizetti's *Maria di Rohan* and *Il Guarany* (Gomez), for instance. *Don Giovanni*, which was to be one of the operas most closely associated with him, did not come into his repertoire until 1894 at St Petersburg.

The St Petersburg debut had taken place a year previously. His first role there was Hamlet, which he played to the Ophelia of Marcella Sembrich (with whom he was to appear several times more, in *Barbiere*, *Traviata* and *Rigoletto*). In Moscow at the Bolshoi he sang in *Faust* with Darclée (the first Tosca) and, the following year, in *Otello* with Tamagno (whom he would therefore have had to try to match in volume in the Oath Duet!). That autumn brought his first visit to Warsaw, very important to him over the years and the scene, incidentally, of his first performance in the role of Werther, which Massenet adapted specially for him. He also sang there with some of the relatively little-known artists who appear with him on records – the soprano Emilia Corsi, for instance, and the bass Aristodemo Sillich. There were fabulous international casts assembled for the opera in St Petersburg and Moscow. Arnoldson, Kruscelnicka and Boronat were among the sopranos who sang fairly regularly with Battistini, and in some seasons Tetrazzini and Boninsegna; while apart from Tamagno (in *Andrea Chénier* and *Trovatore* as well as *Otello*) the young Caruso joined the Company in the winter of 1899. During Battistini's time there he learnt quite an extensive Russian repertoire, including *Russlan and Ludmilla*, *The Queen of Spades*, *Eugene Onegin* (which became one of his great roles) and Rubinstein's *Demon* (which he also sang in Russian). He gave his last performances in the capital early in 1914, going on to tour through Kharkov, Kiev and Odessa. His final appearance in Warsaw was in 1911 when his less familiar roles included Scarpia in *Tosca* and Mephistopheles in *The Damnation of Faust*.

This period of tremendous popularity in Eastern Europe probably constituted the golden years. The moment of their initiation may well have been the particular day when he inherited from Antonio Cotogni the role of Don Giovanni. A pupil of Cotogni's was Beniamino Gigli who tells in his autobiography how the mantle of premier baritone was transferred. Cotogni, he says, 'called on Battistini unannounced one morning at eight o'clock. Battistini was somewhat taken aback. "Young man", said Cotogni, without preamble, "you must lose no time in preparing yourself to take over the role of Don Giovanni" '. He went over certain traditions which the audience would want to see observed and Battistini sang the role for the first time that very night. 'Cotogni embraced him in full view of the audience and then spoke a few words of farewell. He left for Rome the following day and never sang in opera again.'

From then on Battistini was not only Don but King. A Polish contributor to an early number of the magazine *The Record Collector*

(September 1952) recalls the immense prestige that Battistini enjoyed and also the magnificence of his lifestyle at the time, as he travelled throughout Europe with his 'thirty large and beautiful trunks with the large letters M.B., containing his costumes'. As for the honour in which he was held in high places, there is a well-known story told by Fred Gaisberg of Battistini's intervention on behalf of a political prisoner. He presented to the Grand Duke who held this man the sword he wore in the role of King Carlos in *Ernani*, reminding him of Carlos's words 'Perdono a tutti'. The man, under sentence of death, was released.

His performances in Russia and Warsaw are the subject of an interesting and intimate discussion in the memoirs of Sergeii Levik, himself a singer and, as he explains, originally unimpressed with Battistini in the role of William Tell. Only certain notes and phrases, caressed and endowed with nobility, seemed to him to rescue the early part of the opera. This voice, he felt, was more tenor than baritone and it scarcely matched up to the sonority of the Polish basses. Then in the next act came the revelation: here was an artist who knew how to conduct himself on stage with dignity, who knew how to stand still (and that was rare enough), and whose voice was an expressive instrument at the service of a higher objective, an emotional truth, which made Levik think not of other famous Italians but of Chaliapin. Not (he is careful to make the distinction) that Battistini could be described as a singing-actor who *became* the part, as Chaliapin did; rather, he was the character's spokesman, whose eloquence lay in his song, in the warmth of timbre and the expressiveness of cantabile. He was not an artist who assumed a new identity with each different role; nor was he one of those whom you would watch even when they were not singing. But when he sang he captured the audience by pure song, which in turn led, as through poetry, to a shared and profound emotional experience.

No such vivid account reaches us concerning Battistini's operatic appearances in London. In 1883 the talk was all of Patti and in 1887 (at Drury Lane) there was such a plethora of opera and so much excitement about the de Reszkes that few other singers received much individual critical attention. Plenty of enthusiastic adjectives concerning his return in 1905 could be collected, but nothing that really tells us very much. Not even *Eugene Onegin* in 1906 excited any detailed comment. The word evidently went around that here was something special. John McCormack came along, waving a newspaper at his wife just as they were off to Milan: 'Battistini in Tchaikovsky's *Eugene Onegin*! We simply must hear that. It's one of the great performances.' They caught the boat instead, but missing Battistini's Onegin remained a standing reproach for years, such was its reputation. Still the papers said little (for one thing they didn't think much of the opera itself). Battistini 'did an

191

excellent job' was the best the *Musical Times* could find to say, while *Punch*, which accompanied its 'review' (called *Tit-for-Tatiana*) with a cartoon and amused itself at the expense of the story, found a resemblance between the singer and Mr Henry Chaplin, their favourite sporting politician. To P.G. Hurst the *Traviata* of 1905 remained one of the great operatic experiences of a lifetime, with Battistini 'actually overshadowing Caruso and Melba'. Herman Klein, too (who claimed some credit for bringing him over here in the first place), found his performances the work of a great, accomplished and matured master. But it is not really till the 1920s and the astonishing series of recitals which he gave between 1922 and 1924 that we find English critics writing about Battistini with anything more than warm generalities.

His return in two concerts at the Queen's Hall was advertised as presenting to the public 'the greatest living exponent of bel canto'. On the Wednesday afternoon, May 3, his programme included arias from *La favorita, Maria de Rohan, Ernani, Dinorah, Roi de Lahore* and the Prologue to *Pagliacci*. On the evening of Friday the 12th he sang from *Puritani, Traviata, Ballo in maschera, Herodiade* and Saint-Saëns' *Henry VIII*. There were songs by Carissimi, Paisiello, Gluck and Beethoven ('Adelaide', which many remembered as the gem of gems). The press appears not to have been invited and such references as were made in the papers were oblique ones like this from the *Morning Post* commenting on another concert given in the same week: of the two baritones currently singing in London, the first (unnamed) 'displayed a traditional art in its perfection. Signor Titta Ruffo last night revealed a younger art with its imperfections.'

The next year, 1923, again brought two summer concerts on 12 and 18 May, and this time a good deal was written. The *Morning Post* took up the vexed question of bel canto, enlightening its readers with the definition: 'the proper use of the voice in singing'. 'Signor Battistini', the critic thought, 'has perfect mastery of it, and whatever he does he never fails to impart the real true vocal grace – the smooth, even, steady tone, the ability to cause it to rise and fall, messa di voce, and the perfect clearness of diction'. Wolfram's 'Gazing around' solo from *Tannhäuser* opened this programme, which also included some Mozart ('Deh, vieni alla finestra' and 'Non più andrai'), 'Eri tu' (sung twice, with 'a wonderful crescendo on the top F'), arias from *Andrea Chénier* and *Eugene Onegin*, 'Largo al factotum' and the Prologue to *Pagliacci* again: a vigorous programme, one might think, for a man half his age. The top notes were marvellous, said the critic, 'but it was his wonderful "spun" tone, the vocal "gesture" and the ever-present expressiveness that carried the day'. At the second concert the masterly breath-control and lightness of touch won special praise; the ability, too, to obtain dramatic effect: 'He gets it by those quick flashes of delicacy of tone-colour which are … all the more penetrating in that they retain the "bel canto" '. The adapted 'Pourquoi me réveiller' from *Werther* presented 'a striking example of the force of restrained singing and of vitality in repose'. The *Daily Mail* recorded one failure, Bach's 'Bist du bei mir', and noted that some phrases of the *Tannhäuser* solo lay too low for him; otherwise 'he is a model and a marvel of our age'. The *Musical Times* found him 'still the most eloquent of the arbiters of song'. They loved his 'gentlemanly dignity', his command of moods. 'His "Largo al factotum" bubbled with fun and was amazingly glib – no hint of extravagance. The *Pagliacci* Prologue itself was decent and courtly, even. "Deh vieni" breathed knightly grace.' The conscious mind, they felt, was 'happily at ease', while 'a complicated subconscious mechanism was busy doing all the right things for him'. His essential greatness 'lies in his perfect sense of style', and 'still defying time', he 'ravished our ears'.

The 1924 concerts provoked a sharp comment or two from the *Observer*. 'At 67 he gets a hard, dead tone in certain songs. In other things, marvellous … His audience (largely his own countrymen, I fear) applauded most when he sang worst.' *The Times*, reporting on his opening with 'Nemico della patria', felt 'at once that we were having the best of singing'. This time there were duets from *Don Giovanni* and *Barbiere di Siviglia* with a Madame Salteni-Mochi, and encores included Falstaff's 'Quand' ero paggio' (interesting because it was a role he would never sing on stage). He gave the second concert at the Albert Hall, and this appears to have been doubly impressive. The *Daily Telegraph* critic wrote: 'In these vast spaces the magnificent volume of his tone seemed even more imposing than it had been at Queen's Hall a few days ago, while in point of subtlety of inflection his work was once more unsurpassedly fine'. He summed up: 'In its youthful ardour and accuracy of tone, and the adaptation of it to the contours of a phrase, Signor Battistini's singing is as memorable an experience as the concert room of today has to give.' That was Sunday, May 25, and Battistini's last appearance in England.

The *Observer's* critic was a year out: Battistini was then 68. Later that year and again the following winter he sang at the Vienna Opera in (all told) five operas of Verdi, including a *Traviata* with Selma Kurz and Richard Tauber. In December 1925 he appeared in *Traviata*, *Ballo in maschera* and, of all things, *Tosca* at Budapest. More concert work followed, with the final concert on 17 October 1927. Then the preparation for the great jubilee and the growing awareness that it was not to be. He died at Colle Baccaro, near Rieti, on 7 November 1928.

Hearing his records now, especially in sequence from first to last, is a moving experience. I fancy that for some listeners it may also be a bewildering one. The art is marvellous, yes: the firm placing, the unshakable control, the shapely phrasing, the emotional commitment. The voice, too, is of surpassing beauty within its main working area, roughly the span of a sixth from the A flat up to F. Even so, from time to time, as one listens the brow puckers, the eyebrows rise, and one looks questioningly again at that wretched term 'bel canto'. 'The proper use of the voice' was the *Morning Post*'s none too bright definition.

Accepting it for the moment, and recalling that Battistini was billed on his return to London in 1922 as 'the greatest living exponent of bel canto', what are we to make of that habit of suddenly pressing a loud high note so that it changes tone and is knocked off the centre of its pitch? Then there are those places where we look for what we might conceive of as the bel canto style in music which often gets a hammering, only to find that Battistini hits just as hard as his noisy Italian successors and often not much more gracefully than our own contemporaries. Suppose too that we want to extend the definition a little to include some consideration of the quality of voice: is it really consistent with the ideal of 'bel canto' that the voice should lose colour and resonance as it goes down into lower notes that are normally reckoned to be part of the baritone's effective range? There are other matters of style and even of pronunciation which I think are likely to surprise a modern listener and to affect the conviction that this is indeed the prime exhibition of 'bel canto' in the form which it might be expected to take.

Far better, for the true appreciation of Battistini and the enjoyment of his records, is it to blow away these labels (bel canto, golden age of singing and so forth) and the preconceptions that go with them, and start not with the legend but with the fact. And one fact, I would say, is that Battistini may delight in one phrase and dismay in another – but that he never bores. His singing is never merely pedestrian, but is always animated by the detailed care of the artist and the strong feeling of the man. His records are quite as remarkable for their expressiveness as they are for what we might designate as 'pure singing'. From this point of view, they have more in common with the recordings of Tito Gobbi than with those of Giuseppe de Luca.

About Battistini there is often an astonishing recklessness. He does not spurn the fortissimo or the marcato, and this is as true of him at 68 as in what must have been more or less the period of his prime when those first records were made in 1902. Now, oddly, I think it is this sense of living dangerously in his singing that leads us back to 'bel canto' in the *Morning Post*'s phrase, 'the proper use of the voice': the point being that Battistini could not possibly have sung as he did and survived (vocally) as he did if the basic method had not been sound through and through. He can give and risk everything in a strenuous phrase, but the way of taking the notes, which seems to the listener to bring an exciting 'attack' to bear, is so accurately adjusted to the rest of the system that it will not harm the voice. The breath and the voice are also in perfect adjustment so that there is never any suggestion of a breathy admixture in the tone, but that all is converted into pure sound, while the breathing mechanism never in all those years goes flabby so as to produce even the faintest loosening of vibrations. After all those energetic performances through the decades, 'wobble' never remotely comes into question.

Among the very last recordings, in 1924, is that joyous banality, proud in its Spanish swagger, 'Senza tetto' from *Il Guarany*. It lies in the best part of the voice and it has something of the ebullience that Battistini loved to capture in song: but what a miracle it is, for here the voice of the sixty-eight-year-old has all the resonance of youth, and the vibrancy is of unflawed evenness, the spontaneous boldness of spirit never being betrayed by an ageing body or a faltering technique. Only a few years back, in 1921, he gave another astonishing exhibition of surviving mastery on a grand scale in the aria from Donizetti's *Maria de Rudenz*. The refinements of shading and shaping, the unimpeded flexibility and brilliant cadenza provide triumphantly eloquent evidence to all subsequent generations of a kingly singer in whom the bold exercise of power is instinctive. This was surely one side of the art that had audiences on their feet in his recitals at this advanced age; indeed, with the piano accompaniment on this record, it is very easy to imagine oneself as present on one of those privileged occasions.

Another side is exquisitely represented in the legendary pair of recordings made for the Fonotecnica Company in Milan around 1920. His way with Tosti's 'Ideale' we know already from that lovely group of song recordings made in the summer of 1911. Even so, here it is still more poetic and lingering, while the additional space around the voice (the acoustic of a large room, not a box of a studio) enables us to listen as though 'in the flesh'. The 'Caro mio ben' is still more precious, with its beautiful pianissimo opening and reprise, its fine crescendo in the middle section, its stylish joining of phrases: one of the gems of the whole collection. Reverting then to the 1911 songs, these too surely bring us very close to the true Battistini, and to the singer in his prime. That incomparably clear, free middle register heard at the start of 'Non m'ama più' is a joy in itself; but the pleasure lies not only in the sound of the voice, for it is a very complete art that is brought into play here, wonderfully varied and expressive, for instance, in 'Mia sposa sarà la mia bandiera' which can sound a dull nonentity of a song when less imaginatively handled. It really is in these things – rather than in Mozart or Gluck's 'O del mio dolce ardor' which Compton Mackenzie nominated as the best of Battistini's records – that we have the singer as most personally and irreplaceably his true self. It is so even in the Warsaw 1902s. There are fine things among the operatic arias, but the real joy in singing, and the real closeness to the artist, comes with Denza's 'Occhi di fata' and, best of all, Tosti's 'Ancora'.

The 1906 opera list – most especially that magical 'Vieni meco' from *Ernani* – is also part of the priceless legacy: priceless, that is, as a human achievement, which means an imperfect one.

If we follow his records chronologically, we first meet Battistini in his version of Don Giovanni's Drinking Song, and we take leave of him (as the last of the records issued with a regular catalogue number) in the Serenade: the latter a flawed performance, the former frankly deplorable. Some of the records that come in between have no particular claim on us. Some we may reject: veneration of these legendary singers of long ago breeds forgetfulness of the fact that they were all modern once and were, quite rightly, subject to criticism even as our own contemporaries are.

There remains a greatness. It instructs still; it entertains still. More than that, and in a more deeply human way, it *warms*. Compton Mackenzie once wrote an essay that was headed 'Battistini' but which appeared to say nothing about him whatsoever except that listening to him was like drinking good old burgundy and that, however antique the records and however old-fashioned the music, 'we hear Battistini and the sun is shining warmly through a tattered curtain'. Perhaps after all he said what matters most.

Part III

Critics at the Opera
1919-1939

19. 'Figaro' of *Musical Opinion*

Back numbers of *Musical Opinion* make interesting reading. The magazine covered a wide range of subjects in its articles and reports, and in opera it did particularly well. That was partly due to a tradition of spirited, detailed commentary founded by their critic 'Waldvogel' (pen-names were much in fashion in those days). He was the regular writer on opera in the early years of the century up to 1916, and it was a 'Waldvogel' who again took over the opera page in 1937. In the meantime, for twenty years, the regular 'World of Opera' article was written by 'Figaro'. He was an excellent critic, experienced, independent and shrewd, broad in his interests and sympathies. He wrote entertainingly without trivialising his subject, and he achieved that difficult task of establishing a personal tone of voice without undue intrusion of personality. During his time, *Musical Opinion* provided a critical commentary on opera in Great Britain second to none.

His memory went back a long way. By 1916 he had seen 91 different operas. The singers who to him were 'the modern generation' (as opposed to Patti, the de Reszkes, Tamagno and so forth) were Destinn, Melba, Caruso, Scotti. And he had heard Fernando De Lucia, who last sang in London (at the Waldorf Theatre) in 1905. Yet he was no backward-looking old-timer. He was always keen to welcome good new operas (*Wozzeck*, broadcast in 1934, came excitingly as evidence to all 'that opera really is an art-form and alive'). He was always ready to praise new singers. The season of 1936, which proved to be his last, saw the debut of Kirsten Flagstad, 'who,' he wrote, 'at once took rank in the long line of royal singers heard at Covent Garden.' And – willing to be committed to a definite statement – he added: 'She is a great singer.' The dangers of the closed mind, the weary sighing and wincing of the connoisseur, the numbing power of the past to spoil the pleasure of the present, were all well-known to him. His review of the first post-war international season began with a warning on that very subject:

Edward Fitzgerald swearing that no singer ever was or could be like his famous Pasta; the grizzled Covent Garden 'dug-up' damping down our enthusiasm for A and B by dilating on the incomparable qualities of the

Madame Melba

43. Nellie Melba as Violetta in *La Traviata*

long-defunct Y or Z; the old colonel in the club swearing that an army composed of regiments such as he commanded in '86 would have won the war outright in the course of a weekend; or the old clubman holding forth that since the days of WG cricket has gone to the 'demnition bow-wows'. What is it all but age's pathetic attempt to cover up in 'swank' its incapacity for appreciation? Age holds the whip-hand and knows it.

It did not follow, of course, that the past was a dead letter. The standards in the pre-war seasons were very much in the mind of the man who now in the summer of 1919 took his seat as a professional critic.

200

And it may be of interest to note that what he missed in comparison with the old days was not in the first place the great voices or the excellence of individual performances but the excellence of ensemble. Of the first night of the new season which, with Beecham conducting, brought Melba back to the house and introduced the Lancashire-born tenor Tom Burke, he wrote:

> *Bohème* artistically was a poor thing. Instead of perfectly harmonised ensemble we had on exhibition a star who has among her many arts that of beguiling us into the belief that she is not 'starred', a new tenor obviously in trouble because of the triple handicaps of the newness, the social bigness of the occasion, and the strain of trying to live up to the expectations raised by those preliminary 'puff pars', a quartet whose methods and humours were of a somewhat elderly order, and an orchestra that made a symphony of musical high-jinks ... The dominant note was a ponderous squareness.

He had a good deal to say about Melba herself. He found the quality of her voice better than he had known it before: 'The same evenness and roundness of tone throughout and effortlessness of production, a shade more volume, and something approximating to warmth, though as ever dramatically expressive of nothing but naivety.' But he returned to his theme of the need for satisfying team-work by the singers in *Bohème*, and this, he said, did eventually emerge:

> Ensemble came into its own at a later performance, made memorable by Martinelli's return. His now ripened beauty of voice and mellowed fervour of youth had a perfect foil in Gilly's superbly sung Marcello ... Sheridan (was) a singer of grace and charm with an engagingly fresh and supple voice ... but hardly displayed conviction ... But the fact that the generally high level of singing was not centred in one or even two made for a vocal, which meant more than a histrionic, ensemble; the enthusiasm of the audience was spontaneous and real.

The following year, in 1920, he concluded his survey with the summary that the season had been the most disappointing in memory, and again his mind went back to the years before the war when 'Covent Garden used to give you the finest singing the world could produce, plus ensemble that could not be bettered'. Maintaining that the 'star' system did not necessarily produce poor teamwork, he instanced the production, in 1909 it must have been, of *Il barbiere di Siviglia*: 'I cannot recall a better ensemble than a particular performance ... in which we had Tetrazzini, Anselmi, Sammarco, Marcoux and Gilibert.'

The emphasis on ensemble was salutary in its time. What could be of

44. Maria Ivogün as Gilda in *Rigoletto*

benefit to present-day criticism, with its emphasis on stage-production, is Figaro's responsiveness to the work of individual singers. This was not always favourable, but he was thoughtful, and reading him usually brings one nearer to a feeling of gaining direct experience of the singer concerned. Reverting to Melba a few months later after the season had ended, he comments on some remarks made by Ernest Newman:

> Mr Newman is plainly not too enamoured of Melba, and again, unlike other critics, has the courage to say so. Hers is indeed a wonderful voice – but it begins and ends with the pure and expressionless production of tone. As the first basic quintessence of singing she is supreme – but there it stops ... By isolating its owner, an isolation that is not assuaged by subtle art in acting, it (her voice) emphasises the sterile monopoly of the 'star' ... To hear Melba in one opera is to hear her in all. Yet that quality of cool purity in her voice is a musical feast in itself ... it is a voice that would be incomparable in such a part as Mélisande.

45. Maria Ivogün as Konstanze in *Entführung aus dem Serail*

The opera of the future, he felt, lay much more with singers like Destinn (or Destinnova as she preferred to be known in those years). He remarked that he knew no artist to equal 'her poignancy of expression or match her capacity to obtain the maximum effect without sacrificing beauty of tone or outraging the melodic line'. The singer who came nearest to her in this, 'in my limited experience', he says, was the tenor De Lucia. He draws upon his stock of exclamation marks to do justice to her pianissimo, her breath control, phrasing, effortlessness and 'capacity to vary her colours without sacrificing roundness of tone'.

No other soprano drew from him any comparable enthusiasm till the arrival in 1924 of Maria Ivogün. He marvelled at her Zerbinetta in *Ariadne auf Naxos* and loved her Gilda in *Rigoletto*:

There was something more than Gilda in the quiet superfine impersonation of Maria Ivogün, an Ariel of the opera world, an

203

46. Giacomo Lauri-Volpi as
Cavaradossi in *Tosca*

emanation, a woman of fire and air ... The voice is not large but unlike
most coloraturas it is capable of great varieties of expression ... and the
singer's quiet intensity of acting ... is a thing to wonder at.

As the years passed he welcomed Elisabeth Rethberg, Rosa Ponselle,
Lotte Lehmann, Frida Leider – though in all of these there were
interesting reservations. Among the tenors, Fernand Ansseau was a
favourite; to Gigli he was a rather late and reluctant convert; and
Lauri-Volpi was at first an object of amusement rather than anything
else. He writes vividly of Lauri-Volpi's debut in 1925:

The performance of *Andrea Chénier* resolved itself into little more than
the conquest of London by Lauri-Volpi. One had at times to rub one's
eyes. After the aria in the first act, during which he sang with volcanic
power, but out of tune and shrill on his high notes, the burst of applause
was such that Mugnone, the conductor, gave up his attempts to get the
orchestra going again. Thereupon, Lauri-Volpi, who had meanwhile
crept behind a pillar at the back of the stage where he was coyly hiding,
came smiling forth and flung his hands (and heart) at the gallery. This was
the note of the evening. After each act, there was vociferous applause –
Mugnone was dragged on ostensibly to take his bow as conductor but in
effect to add to the glory of Lauri-Volpi by shaking his hand effusively,
patting him on the back, and even (as one account says, though from my

position I missed this thrill) kissing him … There could be no counting the number of recalls at the end, or Lauri-Volpi's gestures of thanks to the upper part of the house.

He goes on to write about the tenor's voice, with the interesting comment that it had a baritonal quality, a memorable richness in some of the chest notes (in fact he felt Lauri-Volpi produced the best baritone notes of the evening and Franci the best tenor ones), but that the high notes lacked any of the finer graces, and that the most one could say about the voice as a whole was that it 'may well become great if he can contrive to discipline it'. In later years, it should be added, when Figaro heard him in Paris and again in London it appears that he had done just that.

Figaro did not overlook the British singers or British opera. He followed the affairs of the British National Opera Company, the Carl Rosa, Sadler's Wells and others, with the same interest as he gave to the 'Grand' seasons at Covent Garden. In November 1933 he wrote a paragraph which must have given warm encouragement where it was needed:

At the Wells, they worship the job, which means they subordinate themselves to the composer … and that is why one had such a thrill at the performance of *Otello* this year when the chorus struck the true, dramatic

47. Sadler's Wells: *Die Meistersinger*, Act III, 1936

205

note at the outset without hesitation and sustained it to the end. The principals also were in splendid form, and a friend whom I first met at Covent Garden thirty years ago agreed that that performance was one of the most pleasurable he had ever witnessed – and in that opera we had seen any number of 'stars' in the past, including Melba, Scotti, Sammarco, Slezak, Zenatello, Melchior. The Wells performance was not a stellar affair, and yet it thrilled.

In his very last article, in January 1937, he reviewed the British Music Drama Season, finding Albert Coates's *Pickwick* 'a great occasion' and giving special praise to Harold Williams's Boris. The last opera he saw, very probably, was the Sadler's Wells *Mastersingers*, and it is pleasant to record that the last singer who earned the warmth of his experienced enthusiasm was Joan Cross: 'not only the best English Butterfly but probably the best since the great days of Destinn.'

It was in the next issue of *Musical Opinion* that readers learned of Figaro's death and also of his real name. He was A.P. Hatton; he had been writing since 1920; and he claimed to have heard every opera produced in this country during the previous thirty years.[1] The disclosure of his identity sends one back to the early volumes, before 1916 when his 'Figaro' column began, and there one finds a number of articles written under his own name. They are worth turning up partly out of personal interest and partly for the light they shed on the thought and tastes of those times.

The first articles I have traced are on 'Modern Opera' (April and May 1913). He clearly hopes that the future lies with what he calls 'the happy marriage of realism with lyricism'. 'Modern' composers whom he sees as writing with some prospect of enduring success are Puccini, Charpentier, Humperdinck and Wolf-Ferrari. Though he thinks *Der Rosenkavalier* the best of Strauss's operas, he likes it less than *The Secret of Susanna*, and *Salome* and *Elektra* he likes not at all ('his attempts at dramatic interest are quite childishly crude and unconvincing'). It is with this type of work that he hopes the future does not lie:

> Once upon a time a grand opera was merely a concert in fancy dress for the gratification of trick singers – and now it is fast becoming an elaborate stage-managed symphony for the gratification of trick composers.

He also had misgivings about the directions in which writing for the voice seemed to be going. Having quoted with some approval the novelist Charles Reade's attack on 'coloratura' singing, the demise of

---

[1] Among deaths recorded in the General Register Office early in 1937, Andrew Lamb found that of Arthur P. Hatton of London, aged 55.

which seems not to grieve him, he foresees a new menace just coming into existence:

> There is however ground for the suspicion that some of the ultra-modern music-dramas make neither for the dignity and advancement of the singer nor of her art ... Muscular rather than vocal attributes are required of her: a terrible revenge for the days when the singers led composers by the nose.

And of some 'modern' writing for the voice he remarks: 'Plain spoken dialogue would in many cases be infinitely preferable.' I cannot swear that such a notion has never entered my own head.

He touches a few sensitive spots too when discussing the principles and practice of music criticism. The subjectivity of most writing about voices is well illustrated (having found 'veiled beauty', 'sublimated clarinet-tone' and 'the fascinating ring of shining, penetrating steel' used by different critics about the same singer). He also has a good passage on another, more insidious danger:

> the hypnotic attraction of Names and the self-flattering savour of being one of the Elect of the world who understand and applaud ... Or an assumption of superior critical knowledge to the sheep-like crowd may excuse the crushing deletion of the great one's name from your favour.

And, as I suppose we all know, any number of personal factors may affect the judgment at any particular time:

> When the critic most strenuously blames the music it may be only he that is out of key.

I mentioned matters of personal interest. There are several, for here (one can tell from his breadth of reference and vocabulary) is a man for whom music had an organic relationship with life as a whole. Yet biographical details are rare: one wishes there were more. In earlier years he had met 'Swazis in the wild' (they could teach something to composers of rag-time). And he had had at some time a nervous breakdown – for which the cure that a whole army of doctors and specialists could not find was effected by a performance of Gluck's *Iphigenia in Tauris*! But one does not need more biographical facts to recognise this critic as a human being. I recall that his first article as Figaro was partly about the cheese-paring attitude in the theatre which was responsible for disgraceful seating ('could anyone, for example, conceive anything more vile and inharmonious than the galleries of

Drury Lane and the Shaftesbury Theatre, or the "slips" of Covent Garden?'). And it may be that in these days, when cutting is deemed just about the worst of sins in the opera house, another of Figaro's remarks might sometimes restore a sense of proportion:

> The great composer [he is thinking of Wagner] declares that to cut down his work is to sacrifice art – but there is no greater art than to suit human needs. When he writes for the immortals, he may scorn claims on supper.

20.   'Our Man' of *The Times*

In the reading rooms of the larger public libraries visitors will occasionally look across with mild curiosity at the person studying, apparently, neither a book nor a newspaper, but a box. It is well that the curiosity should be mild: the box might almost be Pandora's for the fearful fascination it exercises, and the person is in all probability an addict. What he has in front of him is a month of *The Times* on microfilm. He came in to look up, shall we say, the death on 16 June 1930 of Elmer Sperry, inventor of the gyroscopic compass, and found that on that same day mixed bathing was first permitted in the Serpentine. That was two hours ago. Since then he has remained in that month and in that library, which he had every intention of leaving after the ten minutes it took to find an obituary notice. This time next week he will be back again for more.

In the same way, one goes to look up some piece of music criticism or make a few notes on a particular event, and before long is hopelessly caught up by the dictators and the crises, noting that the Cost of Living Index was up by 56 per cent in 1938 on July 1914. Absurd irrelevance, you might say. But I am not sure that one of the most valuable things about the musical criticism in *The Times* is that it is put into context: one gets inevitably and with perhaps incomparable immediacy a sense of period.

This is so sometimes with the criticism itself. Covent Garden then was not Covent Garden now. Opening nights in the interwar years had a different kind of interest:

> There was a brilliant scene when the first note of the National Anthem brought the whole audience to their feet. Prince Henry occupied the royal box, and with him were Lord and Lady Shaftesbury and Sir Frederick Ponsonby. Princess Helen Victoria was in the stalls.

That was in 1925, before a *Rosenkavalier* with Lotte Lehmann, Delia Reinhardt, Elisabeth Schumann and Richard Mayr, Bruno Walter conducting. It took a practised eye to assess the 'brilliance'. That year it

1952.

48. Lotte Lehmann as the Marschallin in *Der Rosenkavalier*

was evidently greater than in the previous season, which had opened with *Das Rheingold*:

> Diamonds were never in vogue for the *Ring* performances, and here and there a gleaming headdress in box or stalls did not necessarily indicate precious stones.

'Paste', as somebody said of *The Jewels of the Madonna*. But the scene in boxes and stalls was described in this way right down to 1939, when there was an account in minute detail of the dress of Queen Mary and of all the lesser ladies such as Lady Bonham-Carter 'who wore black satin with a short coat of daisy patterned satin'. And what do we say to all this now? I think that a part of us reflects that we really are rather a dowdy sight these days; while the rest probably snorts 'good riddance!' *The Times* itself did not permit anything so ill-bred as a snort, but a certain asperity is perceptible even so. *Die Zauberflöte*, presented on the opening night in 1938,

> seemed a daring choice of an opera ... for it is a natural tendency of audiences who have faced the camera and know that they will be inevitably described as 'brilliant' next morning to compete with the stage for attention, and *Die Zauberflöte* is too delicate a thing to admit of any divided attention.

The audiences in those interwar seasons had, especially in the gallery, an enviable freshness, humour and feeling of excitement. *The Times* was not entirely uninfected by the euphoria which a new season would bring with it. At that *Rosenkavalier* of 1925, for instance, the theatre is described as

> filled as to stalls and boxes with a gay company, and as to gallery and slips with a vociferous one (every seat was filled and every one hot and happy). It seemed to show that London means to make the best of its opportunity, a short one, and ready to forego our dinners to be in our places by 7.15.

The loyalty of these audiences was put to some severe tests in those days. *The Times* praised all concerned with *Tristan und Isolde* in 1935 (in spite of its being one of those occasions when Beecham 'takes to beating on his score, a practice which we hope will not become a habit with him'). 'But', demanded the critic, 'what is the management of Covent Garden about? Are we never again to hear Wagner's third acts to their conclusion?' The performance, it seems, had started at 6.30, and Act III had not begun till near 11.

Even so, this was not the principal cause for complaint: the behaviour of the audience not infrequently *was*. A notorious occasion was the opening night in 1934, for which *Fidelio* (Lehmann, Franz Völker, Alexander Kipnis) was considered to be a bold choice:

> The audience may have been *socially* brilliant but not artistically, and the conductor had to shout 'Stop talking' while the Overture was in progress. As far as we could hear from a place at the back of the stalls, the Overture was beautifully played while the peripatetic stall-holders, unconcerned with the music, sought their seats guided by the electric torches of the attendants, flashed to and fro as in a cinema. The first thing the new management must do is to educate its audience, and perhaps it would have been better to wait a little before casting Beethoven before them.

Presumably when reading *The Times* at the trough next morning the

49. The Royal Opera House, Covent Garden, in the 1930s

peripatetic offenders would be unlikely to turn to the arts page; or perhaps 'a knavish speech sleeps in a foolish ear'. Anyway, here was the critic of 'The Thunderer' sounding an alarm for culture. Beecham

212

50. Queen Mary visits the Royal Opera House in the 1930s

himself made a statement concerning further enormities such as 'barbarous applause at the end of the *adagio* opening of *Leonora* 3' quoted in the next day's issue (2 May 1934):

213

I am told that the audience was stupefied by what I did. They were astonished at being asked to stop talking. I am glad, and what I said had the desired effect. I certainly used the phrase 'Stop talking' and later 'Shut up, you' ... If it occurs again I shall stop and address the house. Yes, I shall do that. I shall ask if they are savages or the fine flower of the audience of the greatest city of the world. That is what they are considered to be.

Perhaps the Covent Garden audience never recovered from their stupefaction on this occasion, because next year the critic had to chide them for quite a different failure:

Madame Conchita Supervia may exercise all her arts and run divisions through the whole compass of her voice without fear or hope that her flaccid listeners will obliterate one note of even the most perfunctory orchestral coda ... The sextet ... received just one clap from a single pair of hands in recognition of its excellence ... The Teutonic discipline has rendered operagoers phlegmatic.

This was at the first performance of *La cenerentola* in May 1935. Supervia, said the critic, made 'a captivating thing of it, if only the audience would allow itself to be captivated'.

Turning from the auditorium to the stage, the critic found much more to approve of, though it was comparatively rare for the staging itself to occupy him for long. In 1937 (May 14) at the first night of *Otello* 'effective grouping of the crowds at the entry of the Venetian ambassador ... reminded one of the opulent canvas of Paolo Veronese', and in the same season the production of *Rheingold* was said to have 'improved out of recognition'. In 1933 *The Times* noted an improvement in the staging of *Die Walküre*: 'A good deal has been done at Covent Garden in spite of necessary use of scenery and props which date from the era of Richter to make the pictorial effect of the stage accord with the high level of musical interpretation.' Again 'stage grouping' was noted, and (rare occurrence) the effect was 'accomplished chiefly by lighting'. Still, there were times, particularly in the earlier years, when it was better simply to shut the eyes tight and listen (which is what the critic recommended during the scene changes in *Rheingold*). Wagnerian performances would also afford opportunity for a little urbane humour. In 1934, for example, the critic at *Siegfried* noted that 'the dragon walked on four legs and looked like a rhinoceros ... At any rate it did credit to the Tarnhelm'. At a performance of *Tristan und Isolde* in 1933 the singing of Maria Olczewska was said to be exquisite:

but when Brangaene enters for the last time it should not be necessary for

214

her to push to one side a rock, presumably weighing about a ton, in order to take up her chosen position beside her mistress.

Staging claimed relatively little critical attention in the interwar years, and no doubt the critics of that time would have been mildly astonished if they could read those modern reviews where comment on the production allows a few sentences to be spared somewhere towards the end for the musical side of the performance. It does not follow that they cared little about the way the singers acted. In fact this clearly weighed heavily in their judgment, and I personally am sometimes disappointed to find how little the *Times* critics had to say in any detail about the singing itself. The great Wagnerians, for instance, were judged to quite an extent on the dramatic side of their art. The account they give of Leider's Isolde in 1925, for instance, has some comments on the singing and the voice, but what seems to have impressed most was the power of the acting:

She makes the Irish princess not a mere woman of ordinary scale, but a great tragic figure, and at moments her acting reaches an almost terrible intensity ... It is her command of gesture, including facial expression, which makes her performance so remarkable. She discards nearly all the conventional movements; yet we feel that nearly always what she does is right, and not merely dictated by the fact that it is different from what others have done. Indeed, her hands, which are the chief instruments of her acting, seem to follow every movement of the music and to be a visible expression of it like those of a dancer.

In Italian opera, too, the critic is clearly delighted when he can report genuine distinction in the acting. He found it, for instance, in the Otello of Renato Zanelli who in 1930

built up the character by gesture, facial expression and by increasingly fullblooded acting of high dramatic quality. His voice is warm and ample, his presence is commanding, his conception of the character is all of a piece, and his delineation is magnificent.

At Martinelli's return in 1937

he proved himself a first-rate actor, and his Cavaradossi was a young painter in love, and not, what he too often is, a tenor with no thought for anything but his own part.

Like others, the *Times* critics were slow to approve of Gigli, but by 1939 he too was being praised for his 'subtlety in acting' in the role of

215

51. Beniamino Gigli and
Maria Caniglia in *La
traviata*

Cavaradossi, and 'the little scene with Angelotti', for instance, could not
have been better done.

It was no doubt partly this interest in the dramatic element that led
The Times to join in the general disparagement of early nineteenth-
century opera. Even *La traviata* was considered poor stuff (or 'old paste')
and it needed all the arts of Rosa Ponselle to 'make us forget the
anticlimax of the later acts'. Verdi was by no means in favour as he is
today ('there is a good deal of the mediocre and perfunctory in the
earlier parts' of *Don Carlos*). As for Donizetti, not even Toti Dal Monte
could reconcile *The Times* to *Lucia di Lammermoor*. The performance at
which the prima donna of La Scala made her London debut in 1925
drew as grouchy a review as any. The baritone Ernesto Badini had a
tiresome vibrato, and Dino Borgioli, the Edgardo, was called 'a
newcomer with a monotonous quality of tone and no dramatic
personality'. 'But,' the review continued, in mock-heroic vein:

> all these things pale in importance before the eagerly awaited Mad Scene.
> Madame Toti Dal Monte had answered the earlier questions
> satisfactorily when, with perfect sanity and self-command, with a

216

52. Royal Opera House programme: Chaliapin in *Boris Godunov*

217

deliberation enforced by long pauses between each phrase of the cadenza she reached the climax of her display, and pirouetted vocally for our delight. Throughout the evening she seemed more concerned to assure us of her competence than anything else. The high notes above B flat are a little hard, but that ensures brilliance of attack. Below that pitch, smoothness, ease and a certain coolness of quality (particularly pleasant on a summer night) are her musical assets. There is also the charm of her soft diatonic scales, which come into cantabile melodies like little ripples on the surface of otherwise calm waters. One could enjoy her accomplishment thoroughly, even while feeling that all her skill is directed towards rather small ends and while wondering whether her beautiful voice has any personal quality by which one must remember it afterwards. The audience does well to shower their applause on her for without her their evening's entertainment would have been barren indeed.

The whole article may strike a modern reader as strange. If the reviewer cared so little for the occasion as a whole and could give only such qualified praise to Dal Monte's part in it, why did he accord so much status to the event? But of course it is a matter of 'the times', and the great Lucias of the past were still such dazzling names in the musical world that it was felt their probable successor must be treated in some way, even if a sceptical way, as a noteworthy phenomenon.

Dal Monte never reappeared at Covent Garden, but she was to be heard in concert – a fact I never knew till one of those addictive sessions with *The Times* that I referred to earlier. There is often an absorbing interest to opera-goers in the concert appearances of the great opera singers, and *The Times* was very good on its reports here. The reappearance of Dal Monte, for instance, was at a concert in May 1935 (she also sang in London and Birmingham shortly after the Second World War) given at the Queen's Hall for Queen Charlotte's Maternity Hospital, and with her in the concert was John McCormack. They did not, as far as we gather from *The Times*, sing duets (what an opportunity missed), but Dal Monte sang arias from *Sonnambula* and *Lucia di Lammermoor* ('faultlessly executed *fioriture* which showed off the purity of her voice ... It floats in the air, full, clear and flexible' – and then come the criticisms) and McCormack gave a group of Handel arias including 'a fine and spacious example rescued from the forgotten opera *Lotario*'. Then follows what must register as one of the most ungrateful sentences ever written:

But why did he appropriate the soprano aria 'O sleep' from *Semele* since its phrases do not sound right on a tenor voice?

Nobody who knows McCormack's recording of it, with its miraculous run and tight, elegant trill, will be lost for an answer.

Many famous singers gave concerts but not operatic performances in those years – Battistini, Ruffo, Galli-Curci, Schipa, Tetrazzini, Calvé, Koshetz, Slezak, for example. Battistini's concert of May 1924, we learn, began with 'Nemico della patria' of all things (he was then 68) and among the encores was 'Quand'ero paggio':

> We felt at once we were hearing the best of singing ... the long levels of rich sound begun without effort and stopping only too soon. The tone comes on to the note at once; there is no conscious attack; it is there. The tone and the word are one thing.

In the same months, just a week later, came Chaliapin, an exponent of what they called 'The Hymn Book Method': 'We waited in vain last night at the Albert Hall for him to choose something from the 101 songs in his repertoire which would be really worthy of him, until with a dramatic gesture and a rough tone he completely shattered Schubert's "Ständchen".' When he sang 'La calunnia', however, 'we felt once more in the presence of the Boris and Ivan of 1914'.

When the great Calvé sang the 'Habanera' at a concert in 1920 they did not quite feel themselves in the presence of the Carmen of 1893. Her voice, they reported, had five good notes and some pleasant ones. What she did with these limited resources, however, was beyond the scope of 'today's singers':

> They are all so busy steering a passage between the Scylla of voice-production and the Charybdis of interpretation that they never get out onto the open sea of pure song and let their sails fill with a lusty breeze.

One may suspect that such sentences are less rich in meaning than in vocabulary. Old Burgess in *Candida* would certainly recognise them as 'a 'igh-class bit o' litrichor'. And there is another of Shaw's characters, Charles Lomax in *Major Barbara*, whose views on the subject perhaps deserve to be quoted:

> There is a certain amount of tosh about *The Times*; but at least its language is reputable.

219

21. Ernest Newman of the *Sunday Times*

↶ The world of opera ↷

MR ERNEST NEWMAN
the leading musical critic of the day, has joined the staff of the *Sunday Times* and will contribute his first article to the paper next Sunday. Mr Newman's critical contributions to the *Manchester Guardian* and other papers have aroused the interest of the musical world by their brilliant insight and acumen and by their fine literary quality. He has also made valuable contributions to musical literature, notably by his *Study of Wagner* and *Wagner as Man and Artist*, and he is at present engaged on a *History of Modern Music.*

Such was the text of the announcement in the *Sunday Times* of 29 February 1920; large print, thick type and prominent display were employed to give added significance to the portent. The *Sunday Times* was proud of its *coup*, though they could hardly have foreseen that the great man, already over fifty, would be with them for very nearly forty years to come. He wrote his first article for the paper on March 7, and the new broom swished every bit as vigorously as had been expected.

Newman's predecessor was one H.B. Dickin, a mild, benevolent critic, who liked practically everything but drew the line at Mascagni's *Iris*. Readers of the *Sunday Times* must have become accustomed to hearing that an artist who had been 'very good' last week was now 'even better' and next week would turn out to be 'better than ever'. They were in for a change. Newman started his famous column 'The World of Music', in which he discussed at length, and without fear or favour, some topic of current interest, normally arising out of the week's reviews, the majority of which he wrote himself. He was, of course, a weighty scholar, but he wrote as a journalist, and proud of it:

So few authors have brains enough or literary gift enough to keep their end up in journalism that I am tempted to define 'journalism' as 'a term of contempt applied by writers who are not read to writers who are'.

He himself was read because he was interesting. Even the musical establishment, whom he regularly infuriated, had to read him: the *Musical Times* might well have run a regular 'What is Mr Newman saying now?' column, for they were constantly impelled to take him to task for one enormity or another. The sentence about journalism appears in an article (26 June 1932) on Mr Bernard Shaw as Musical Critic and one can at once see that Shaw and Newman were in many ways kindred spirits. Often one might have assumed Newman to be acting on the Shavian principle of 'deciding with the utmost seriousness what you think and then saying it with the utmost levity'. In that article he paid tribute particularly to the opera criticism of Shaw, whose *Music in London*, recently reprinted, was then new to him:

> He wrote about these matters in a style that, for pace, for directness, for point, for wit and humour, for variety of colour, makes the best that is being written by the musical critics of today look third-rate.

Newman also envied Shaw the freedom of speech and fearlessness in the face of possible libel action that they enjoyed in those days. Comparing the musical world then and in his own time, he wrote:

> While the evils and absurdities remain the same, the apparatus for dealing with them has changed for the worse. They call for plainer speaking than is possible in these degenerate days.

Indeed, if our own days were not in that respect still more 'degenerate' (mealy-mouthed or polite, according to one's point of view), some might be tempted to apply the comparison made between his own contemporaries and Shaw to himself and ours.

Opera was always among his prime interests. The first 'World of Music' article was headed 'Actors and Actresses in Opera', and it arose out of some thoughts prompted by Frank Mullings's performance in *Tannhäuser*.

> Mr Mullings's genius the other evening gave us a Tannhäuser that was quite incredible but intensely interesting. Wagner's Tannhäuser is either an ass or a prig. No one but an ass could prefer Elisabeth to Venus or the solemn bores and noodles of the Wartburg to the ballet of the Venusberg. No one but a prig could pretend that he did. Mr Mullings makes Tannhäuser a man of such fine intellect that we can only wonder how he could even have lived a year with the Landgrave and the rest of the pious dullards without despising them from the bottom of his heart.

This, the specific application of his general thoughts to the week's music, came late in the article, its main theme being the stereotypes among women's roles in opera and the comparative difficulty of the men's. It illustrated straight away the kind of attitude Newman was to bring to his opera reviewing. He could be irreverent or downright deadly, but he was not afraid of the word genius and would award it gladly when he saw fit. He would even award it to an opera singer (and a tenor at that), but only to one in whom he could see intelligence and the ability to act a role as well as sing it. Throughout his career, Newman returned again and again to the need for balance in the musical and dramatic constituents of opera, and it was rare for more than a few weeks to pass without his leading article concerning itself with some aspect of operatic art – and not necessarily the Wagnerian.

In reviewing, the essential focus of his concern was naturally upon Covent Garden, and it soon became clear that in his view 'concern' would be an understatement. Quite frequently Covent Garden was his despair. The basis on which it existed (one 'Grand' season and one 'British' in the year, both of them short) meant, as far as he could see, that the word 'considering' ('very good considering') had to be an understood appendage to any praise that might possibly be given to any evening's opera taken as a whole. There might be fine individual performances, and Covent Garden might indeed be better than the Metropolitan ('I know no place where the stage style is so bad as at the Metropolitan, where, seemingly, the "stars" are allowed to do what they like', 29 May 1927). But generally the conditions were hopeless. Newman's remark about the Metropolitan was sparked off by the appearance of Nanny Larsen-Todsen as Brünnhilde: 'She comes from the Metropolitan Opera, New York, and shows it'. He then continued:

> I suppose we must put up with this kind of thing occasionally if we persist
> in running opera as we do in London, engaging singers from all parts of
> the earth and flinging them together without any attempt at a genuine
> production, for which, indeed, there is no real time.

The trouble was that performances at Covent Garden did not show the effects of inadequate rehearsal just 'occasionally' but habitually. Even after a *Ring* cycle in 1927, in which the resources of the opera house had been at their best, Newman could only write that it was 'as good as we can expect under London conditions'. The orchestra played with decent tone, but 'as everyone knows, it is under-rehearsed', and the conductor could hardly do more than make sure the notes were right:

> The finer shades of playing and the imaginative following by the
> instrumentalists of every stage of the drama are out of the question. We

222

can cordially repeat the formula of praise and say that no other orchestral players in the world would do so well under such difficult conditions, at the same time wishing from the bottom of our hearts that the conditions were different. All that can be done with the hasty assembly of spare parts that we call an opera orchestra in this country has been done by the genius and magnetism of Bruno Walter, and for the most part the men have responded admirably, though it must be evident to the most casual ear that some of the individual material is well below the first-rate.

What was to be done about it? Here, as Newman saw clearly, conditions in the opera house were at the mercy of conditions outside it. A larger and more regular public for opera would make a great difference. But how to get it? He felt pessimistic about the prospects, arguing (4 July 1937) that 'our public has no real interest in opera in the larger sense of the term, and perhaps never will have: opera simply isn't in its blood'. A genuine national opera seemed the remotest of possibilities, especially with the Covent Garden public in mind: 'Its range of interests is narrow, and English opera, or foreign opera in English, does not seem to come within that range.' The best policy, he concluded, must be to keep at least this nucleus of an opera public together, by raising standards of performance in the limited repertoire which that public would accept. It was useless to offer works that were off the beaten track if they could not be performed well (as, for instance, with the totally inadequate *Don Pasquale* and *Prince Igor* that season). Instead, the management should concentrate on productions of the standard works; but they should *be* productions:

> This will mean two things – placing the productions in the hands of some high authority in these matters and giving him the absolute power, and bringing all the principals to the theatre long enough before the season opens for them to be moulded into the shape he desires.

It is interesting that in the search for solutions he rejected the remedy of government subsidy. He did so on the old-fashioned principle that there is too much spending of other people's money. The proper way, he thought, was to support Sir Thomas Beecham's proposal for an Imperial League of Opera, though he also knew the scheme had no chance. Under the heading 'The Future of Opera', subtitled 'Aut Beecham aut nullus' (24 February 1929), he argued that the relatively small response to Beecham's appeal showed 'that as yet only a small proportion of the public wants opera; and the fifty who do not want it may reasonably jib at the prospect of being taxed for the one who does'. Opera lovers, he concluded, must help themselves. Later, in 1931, he celebrated the new year with a challenge delivered in the public press to Colonel Blois,

53. Kerstin Thorborg as Kundry in *Parsifal*

managing director of Covent Garden, insisting that as the Syndicate had now accepted a state subsidy all of their dealings were of public concern. Accordingly he would not accept Blois's invitation to meet him privately:

> If the replies are not to be made public subsequently, I am not interested in hearing them. If they are to be made public, Colonel Blois can gratify public curiosity direct. And a public reply will here be a legitimate matter for further public comment.

In the September of that year he also pointed out that the subsidy changed the position of the critic. Formerly he had gone to the opera as a guest, and was prepared accordingly to make allowances when judging the performance. Now he was doing a public duty and was bound to protest as he saw fit. And protest he did. The 'English' season had brought a debased *Bartered Bride*, a dire *Valkyrie* ('something at any rate of the truth must be told') and a vulgarised *Fledermaus*:

> This sort of thing, to speak quite plainly, is not nearly good enough for the leading lyric theatre of the British Empire. These performances have once more brought the operatic question to a head … [It will not do] to go on monkeying with the operatic problem as we have been doing for the last few years.

If the solution to 'the operatic problem' was to involve a 'high authority' in charge of productions, with time and power to 'mould' the principal singers, then it follows that Newman was no friend to the 'star system' of the days when opera had been a relatively going concern. He was not; yet he fully recognised the importance of the singers and the necessity for them really and truly to sing. He reverted to this repeatedly, and it was a well-known theme of his that a basic trouble with modern singers was that most of them could not sing. In 1937 (pretty well the bottom of the pit for Newman) he wrote:

> Few will deny, I suppose, that the standard of singing is lower now than it has been for something like two centuries … I am dealing now purely and simply with singing in the sense of the production of exceptionally beautiful tone; and in that sense I take it everyone will agree with me that the day of the great voices is about over. (September 5: 'The Business of Singing – Can Science Help?')

He was also very clear in his view that an operatic singer was a great one only if the artist combined the great voice with a greatly expressive art. In the interwar years, among the international casts heard at Covent Garden, he found greatness pre-eminently in Ponselle and Chaliapin.

Others whom he admired included Ivogün, Lehmann, Leider (with qualifications), Lemnitz, Pampanini, Olczewska, Thorborg, Ansseau, Zanelli, Janssen, Hüsch, Schorr, Bockelmann. The list is by no means complete, and in fact, severe and crabby as he often appeared, his praise could be ungrudgingly given where he thought it due, and it then carried weight. The kind of performance which could turn his lemon water to wine was that of both principal women in the 1938 *Elektra*. His article was headed 'Acting and Singing, Problems of Opera':

> A case like the Clytemnestra of Kerstin Thorborg is unique in German opera. Here, as in the case of the roles in which Chaliapin was at his best, it is difficult to say where singing, acting, costume and make-up severally begin or end, so organically are they fused into one ... One has the terrible feeling, as one watches her, that it is only a few wires that hold the corrupt body and soul together ... [This] is realised by Madame Thorborg not only in all her postures and movements but in every one of her verbal and musical inflections. The character is all of a piece.

Rosa Pauly's Elektra he found similarly wonderful, and he marvelled at her performance in the recognition scene, where

> lo and behold, this voice, the one preoccupation of which seemed to be to beat down the huge orchestra, gives us a long stretch of singing of a delicacy and a purity and a sensitivity that one could never have anticipated from it. This is truly great singing of the kind to which one again instantly calls upon one's memory of Chaliapin to supply the parallel.

Of Chaliapin himself Newman has left some of the most vivid impressions we have. First and foremost he sees him as a great singer (that is, in the production of musical sound) even in his later years: 'He is in the fullest sense of the word a singer ... he can produce satisfying musical tone with his mouth in any position, pronouncing any vowel, any consonant, expression or shade of thought or feeling. He can sneer, or hiss, or cackle, or fume, and still the tone remains inexplicably musical.' He was also an actor whose characterisations were marvellously whole and individual, unforgettably individual in the death scenes:

> When the man Boris dies, a throne dies with him; when Don Quixote died the other evening, it was not merely the gaunt body that crashed to the earth when the hold of the tired old arms upon the tree relaxed, but a defeated soul from which the under-proppings of life's delusions had been suddenly and finally withdrawn. (28 June 1931).

226

'Chaliapin at fifty-eight', he added, 'can sing all the Italians off the stage.'

∽ War on Italy ∾

Italy, said a living wit, used to be the land of *bel canto*; it is now the land of *mal aria*.

Newman evidently thought that was a good one for he quoted it more than once. Francis Toye, the music critic of the *Morning Post*, once found himself in trouble for suggesting that Newman had 'teutonic predilections'; in correction of that error and others, a 'World of Music' piece (31 January 1937) entitled 'Some fallacies of Mr Francis Toye and others' ended with a paragraph on 'Mr Toye as mythmaker' and the dire promise to 'deal with this matter in a following article'. Myth or not, the impression had its origins. The suspicion of 'teutonic predilections' in their music critic cannot have utterly failed to cross the minds of Newman's readers, especially as they came to realise that there was one season of the musical year particularly inimical to his customary cheerfulness in the face of adversity. This was at the point when the Germans packed their bags to leave Covent Garden and the Italians opened theirs.

> The switchover from German to Italian opera has been accompanied by all the little sillinesses and vulgarities we have become accustomed to on these occasions – each aria being frantically applauded (the applause always beginning in a certain upper portion of the house), encores being demanded, the tenor bowing his approval of the audience's verdict, sometimes making a gracious gesture of assent to the conductor and beginning all over again, and all the rest of the time-honoured absurdity. (June 1938)

Under such circumstances, said Newman, it would be too much to expect any acting worthy of the name, and on this particular occasion (Gigli in *Tosca*) there was nothing much to be said for the singing either. It was the reiteration of a familiar theme. He had stated it plainly in 1927:

> Most periods of transition are painful, but I know few transitions so painful as that from the German opera to the Italian season each year at Covent Garden: the average Italian singing is technically so bad and intellectually so witless that in comparison the weaker members of the German company that has just left us seem stars of at any rate the second magnitude. (5 June 1927)

54. Aureliano Pertile as Radamès in *Aida*

If the point needed enforcing, there were some performances of *Il trovatore* just then that came to hand very happily. There on the stage were Aureliano Pertile and Armando Borgioli, while in the auditorium people were laughing ('disrespectful hilarity'). But when the Leonora sang, or the Azucena, 'no one thought of laughing ... though some of the former's music is as comically old-fashioned as any of Manrico's.' The point was that they, Frida Leider and Maria Olczewska respectively, had been brought up in the German schools and houses, and they 'brought

228

to bear upon this antiquated Italian dramatic style a force and a refinement of intelligence that are the results of long familiarity with much greater music'.

Those comments occur in an article headed 'Mr Pertile's Methods', and it is worth staying with the subject for a while as he clearly regards Pertile as symptomatic of the Italian 'mal aria'. A few nights before this, Newman had almost enjoyed *Aida* (Sigrid Onegin 'a *superb* Amneris, finely directing that magnificent natural vehemence of hers to the ends of the character'). Pertile then had seemed 'by far the best Italian tenor we have had here since the war'. The *Trovatore*, however, brought 'offences against taste and style with which he grieved his listeners'. Saving himself for his big moments, 'he cultivated an Olympian indifference to most of what went on when he himself was not in action; even his mother's lurid story of the burning of the child did not bring a line of anxiety or commiseration into his placid countenance'. When his time came for singing he sang as though essentially to impart the good news that he was a tenor with an admirable voice and remarkable ringing top notes. 'Away with dramatic propriety and the subtleties of psychology: the centre of the stage for him every time.' Other points about the singer in other seasons include these:

A fussy, unsympathetic Rodolfo; his voice is almost of the finest order, but his singing is marred by a persistent vibrato. (*Bohème* 1928)

A rantin' rovin' Robin who brought the house down with his shouts, sobs and convulsions. (*Pagliacci* 1928)

A good specimen of the Italian tenor, with more power than polish, more showmanship than style. (*Tosca* 1929)

Some finely shaded singing. (*Bohème* 1929)

Too bourgeois ... should be younger, more graceful, more charming, more sensitive. (*Manon Lescaut* 1929)

His voice when he does not abuse the vast power of it is about as good a specimen of the typical Italian as one could wish to hear ... one or two shattering demonstrations of the Italian prodigal Soho-ing his wild notes. (*Tosca* 1931)

Inherent absurdity increased by the ranting methods of Mr Pertile as Alvaro. (*Forza del destino* 1931)

We have to remember that this was the principal tenor of La Scala, a singer greatly admired by Toscanini and praised by Serafin as an artist of exceptional sincerity. Was Newman simply being testy on principle, or through some temperamental inability to enter into the Italian spirit of the thing? Or was he indeed using his ears and applying proper musical standards? We have evidence about Pertile's singing in the gramophone records he made during these years, and it has to be said that they exhibit many of the faults Newman names together with some he does not. They also show that there was more to Pertile than Newman conveys: an imaginative, personal way with music that would often bring an almost breathtaking delicacy to a phrase in the midst of quivering, barnstorming excess. That must have been what Newman noted as the 'finely shaded singing' of one of the *Bohème* performances. One can only wish he had used his pen to describe that fine shading as vividly as he depicts the 'Olympian indifference' on stage.

One sometimes feels that Newman would use anything that came to hand. When old Battistini appeared at the Albert Hall in June 1924 he wrote that the concert was 'the best possible preparation for the Italian season – except perhaps that Battistini sets a standard which few of the Italian singers we shall hear this season can hope to reach'. Under the circumstances, that sentence was true moderation. Earlier that year he had been reading Herman Klein's book on singing and found himself in complete agreement with its general proposition that singing was an art in decline, 'even in the land of singing – perhaps, indeed, more there than anywhere else'. It is odd to find him among the ranks of the golden-agers. In an article comparing the state of affairs at Covent Garden in 1899 and 1939 he unrolls a list of glittering names from the past and adds:

> Run a rake through the opera houses of Europe and America today and how many singers will you be left with fit to be mentioned in the same breath with the best, or even with most of these? (14 May 1939)

The paragraph is headed 'There were singers in those days'. One remembers that Shaw, to whom Newman was so much more akin, headed his article on the subject 'We sing much better than our grandparents'. Newman felt strongly that if Italy had once given the lead in matters of 'sheer singing', that lead had now passed to Germany. 'No one who has anything worth calling an ear would contend that the best of Italian singing today can compare with the best German singing' (29 May 1927). He reported in an ecstasy of irony the story that a few years back an Italian member of the company at Covent Garden had gone up to 'the most exquisite of the Germans after a particularly fine performance and said "Why Madame X-, you sing just like an Italian". The innocent fellow apparently meant it as a compliment.'

The years go by, then, and only occasionally can Newman report good singing in the Italian operas, let alone a satisfying all-round performance. Rosetta Pampanini makes a pleasant exception:

The finest artist that Italy has sent us since the war. She has a lovely voice of the genuine dramatic timbre and bigness, yet it is capable of the finest nuance. (*Madama Butterfly* 1928)

An almost perfect singer and an actress of unusual subtlety. (*Bohème* 1929)

He admired the baritone Cesare Formichi when he first appeared (less as the years went by), he found some complimentary (among some critical) things to say about Stabile, and he fully relished the work of Ezio Pinza. But generally it is a dreary story. When some less familiar Italian opera was added to the repertory Newman usually considered it rubbish: *Andrea Chénier* 'exudes ... all the tricks and all the banalities of Italian opera at its worst'; *Manon Lescaut* exhibits 'sentimentality at its thickest and greasiest', *La Gioconda* is 'despicable', its music 'mostly beneath contempt'. The performances sometimes goaded him into a cold fury:

There is of course no law to compel singers to be in exactly the same place at the same time as the orchestra, but there still lingers, among some listeners, an old-fashioned prejudice in favour of the procedure. (*Bohème* 1935)

And to make matters worse the audience seemed to be thoroughly enjoying themselves:

On Monday night the Italians gave us as deplorable a performance of *La Bohème* as I can remember; yet the applause showed that a large number of people were under the delusion that here was operatic singing of the finest kind. (*Bohème* 1931)

In 1937, Italian opera seemed to reach rock bottom. It was the year of Martinelli's return, and Newman was respectful but clearly found him *passé* as a singer. The opening night *Otello*, apart from the playing of the orchestra under Beecham, had little 'worthy either of the work or of the occasion'. *Don Pasquale* (which he considered a masterpiece) was 'little more than an exasperation and a pain from first to last'. Italy's leading Aida and the Amneris (Cigna and Stignani) were no more than 'efficient workwomen of the ordinary Italian opera type'. *Turandot* (Turner's power and Martinelli's subtleties apart) was just about 'up to average', with Ping, Pang and Pong 'an unmelodious trio', while 'old Timur's sufferings of seventy years' hardly accounted for his 'peculiar tones'.

We watched with bated breath the attempt of the executioner to stick into the stubborn soil of Covent Garden the pole on which was impaled the head of that luckless Prince of Persia ... At the fourth attempt, the executioner, probably reflecting that his union did not permit him to work overtime, just gave the thing up and walked away; the gruesome relic turned one last appealing look on us and then sank slowly to earth behind the rampart.

As for *Falstaff*:

The statement, current during the intervals, that the orchestra and the singers were never together may be dismissed as a calumnious exaggeration; I myself counted more than one occasion when they were.

At the end of it all, he summed up:

The season that has just ended has been, I think, the longest since the war, and by general consent – outside the theatre, if perhaps not inside it – one of the least satisfactory ... If Italy really has no better singers at present than some of those who have tried our patience this summer, then the art of singing in that country is truly in a desperate state. (4 July 1937)

If Italian opera brought him any real joy in those years, any comparable, that is, to his joy in Wagner and the best of the Wagner nights at Covent Garden, it probably arose out of two things – the discovery of a masterpiece in a new opera, *Turandot*, and the performances, in the seasons from 1929 to 1931, of Rosa Ponselle.

Newman is at his best on *Turandot*. He gave the opera time, let it work within him, and then committed himself whole-heartedly. He wrote several pieces on it, the strongest probably being an article in 1931. At the original performances, he says, 'the wise ones went around murmuring *Chu Chin Chow*'. But:

It is still slowly dawning on people that *Turandot* is Puccini's finest work, and that in his last years the composer was undergoing something of the same process of spiritual development that marks the last works of a Beethoven, a Wagner or a Verdi from all the works of theirs that have gone before ... It is the compassionateness of *Turandot* that gives that work its hold. It is pity again that lies at the base of the remarkable creation of Ping, Pang and Pong (which are) ... perhaps the subtlest of Puccini's creations.

232

There follows an interesting comparison between the character of Turandot as presented by Eva Turner ('with the power of her great voice and the vehemence of her temperament she gave us the impression of some implacable, irresistible power of nature') and that of Maria Nemeth, who showed 'the essential woman', so that at the end of the whole performance it was as though 'a profound psychological problem had been solved'. Given operas and artists that he could respect, Newman was so often their most rewarding critic: he had the sharpest ears, the liveliest brain and, when it came to it, the strongest feelings.

These qualities combined to provide a royal welcome for Ponselle. One might have expected him to do quite the opposite: after all, she came from the Metropolitan, which must have been a black mark from the start. Her arrival caused the sort of expectancy and general bally-hoo that could easily have antagonised him, and if that did not seal her doom then her proposed repertory might well have done so. But no. For one thing, he was actually looking forward to hearing *Norma* (as he had been looking forward to *Les Huguenots* in 1927). He writes ironically of the audience's reactions to the first two acts of the opera, and then:

> But most of those who endured to the end had a curious experience; they discovered that there was really something in the old work after all, besides the superb Miss Ponselle. They found a steady crescendo of dramatic interest to the final note.

As for 'the superb Miss Ponselle', he had evidently decided that here at last was a truly great singer:

> Not only is her voice one of great beauty but she has the art of making it convey every nuance of the mind without it ever for a moment losing its pure singing quality. It is a curious voice in some ways, with contralto timbre in its lowest register, yet a real high soprano up above. She is not only a mistress of coloratura technique in the abstract but has the rare gift of being able to make coloratura dramatic and psychological. Sung as she sings it, we begin to have an inkling of what it was in the old coloratura that made it, for our ancestors, not a mere vain vocal display but the carrier of all sorts of shades of dramatic meaning. (2 June 1929)

The following seasons brought Ponselle's *Traviata*, and here too Newman saw the play of a fine mind, as surely as he heard 'heavenly modulations of tone' and a vocal technique that was 'flawless'.

What it suggests is that when the old crosspatch sat smouldering and snorting in his stall during all those dreadful *Toscas* and *Bohèmes*, it was not that he was aligning himself with the spirit of Wagner to make war

233

upon Italian opera and its singers. It was that he had a clear conception of how it should sound and cared enough about it to rage at the distortions. His writing up to 1929 is that of one who has no expectations of paradise. The Ponselle years provided him with a glimpse of it. After 1931 he writes with the angry awareness of paradise lost.

ཚོ Wagner ଔ

In the days of my youth, which were those of Newman's great old age, a *New Statesman* clerihew competition delightfully brought out the following:

> Ernest Newman
> Said next week would be Schumann
> But when next week came
> It was Wagner just the same.

From the start, readers of the *Sunday Times* knew that, whatever else, they would be kept well up to date in matters Wagnerian. What may come as something of a surprise to those who knew him only in his late years or through the kind of reputation enshrined in the clerihew is the breadth of his work: in his first weeks, for instance, an article on actors and actresses in opera was followed by one on the symphonies of Sibelius, then Bach, then English song, and so forth. But certainly it was to Wagner that he returned most regularly. 'New Light on Wagner?', 'The Wagner Bombshell', 'Wagner and the Singer', 'New Wagner Material', there seemed no end to it, and as far as Newman was concerned there could be none and therein lay the glory. Sometimes his headings took a more unexpected turn. There was 'Wagner and Frank Harris', for example: no doubt having something to do with an earlier article on 'Wagner the Amorist'. In this he dealt with a protesting correspondent called Spalding who had suggested 'in shocked tones' that he (Newman) could never have read the Wagner-Wesendonk correspondence. The reply included an invitation and, incidentally, a snapshot:

> My Wagner collection (it occupies about twenty feet of shelf-space in my study) is cordially at the service of Mr Spalding if he wishes to pursue further researches into the fascinating subject.

This was in 1924: one wonders what shelf-space the collection required by the time the great Wagnerian studies came at last to an end for the ninety-year-old student in 1959.

It is fortunate that the great critic, and author of *Wagner Nights*, had some great Wagner nights to attend. Of course he grumbled, sometimes furiously, but in these interwar years the flames of Valhalla and the sunlight of midsummer Nuremberg really did shine. Newman was not given to what is loosely called 'appreciative' criticism or to expressing his private ecstasies in the public prints. Yet these sardonic, touchy reviews not infrequently told of real and deep satisfaction. Perhaps the high point of a long life's experience came with such performances as one of *Parsifal* in 1937, the enjoyment possibly intensified by what he reckoned to be the wretchedness of so much else in that season:

> It was not only the best that Covent Garden has ever given us but as good on the whole as anything one could hear in Europe today. The orchestra under Fritz Reiner's sure and sensitive guidance played superbly.

In 1935 it was Beecham and *Tristan und Isolde* that worked the spell, broke through all the normal critical reservations, and demanded commitment to total, once-in-a-lifetime enthusiasm. Having praised most of the singers (Leider, Melchior, Janssen, Kipnis) in the highest terms, he concludes:

> The great things, however, were the playing of the orchestra and Sir Thomas Beecham's reading of the score. In no other work in the whole history of art, I imagine, does the human mind function continuously at such high tension, yet at a tension always under supreme direction and control, as in *Tristan*. On Tuesday we had the maximum of tension with the perfection of control ... As it was, the orchestral part of the performance will remain in my memory as the greatest thing in all my long experience of opera: there is not another conductor in the world who could have equalled it.

That cast-list of itself is sufficient reminder of what Wagner nights could mean in Newman's time. It is hardly surprising that they gave some satisfaction; nor (knowing him) that Newman's satisfaction was usually mixed. He resigned himself, for instance, to the acceptance as of a simple fact of life that he was never going to hear a completely adequate *Tristan* or *Ring* because the roles of Siegfried and Tristan were beyond the accomplishment of any living tenor. Today, newly impressed by reissued recordings, we are likely to protest that surely, living as he did in the years of Lauritz Melchior's prime, Newman should have been regularly thanking providence for blessing him with the one incomparable Heldentenor of the century, but Newman did not see it that way at all, though he did come to have considerable regard for Melchior's work at its best.

It may be interesting to follow his commentaries here because it is a notable example of the way in which records and live performances can evidently create differing impressions of an artist's merit. Melchior appeared first at Covent Garden in 1924, but Newman begins to size him up in 1926. He allows that Melchior had 'the good quality of being always audible' and that 'his vitality was of itself a joy to us', but he still fell short of true distinction:

> Melchior's voice is unusually robust and at times exceedingly agreeable, though its main characteristic seems to me power rather than sensuous beauty; he does not, that is to say, make a lovely phrase all the more lovely by the sheer quality of his voice; we get the melodic line drawn with undeniable force and taking its due place in the orchestral ensemble, but it brings no honey with it. Anyone who has heard Lotte Lehmann or Olczewska sing twenty bars will understand the quality I mean – the delicacy of a musical thought not simply as a statement of musical fact, so to speak, but as a fact the mere contemplation of which moves the singer of it to ecstasy. Melchior has no subtleties, as far as I can see, in his singing.

The odd thing here is that the very qualities (the 'honey', the delicacy and indeed the ecstasy) that Newman finds lacking are precisely those that seem to us now, listening to his recordings, to set the seal upon Melchior's supremacy. In the following year we find that Melchior at first 'makes no great appeal to me either as actor or as singer', but then 'in the second act [of *Parsifal*] he astonished us all by the quality of his performance':

> He is hampered by an inexpressive exterior and a certain thickness of gesture in everything he does, so that I could never believe in his Parsifal when I looked at him ... But if we just listened to him and let the rest of his work go by we were struck by the sincerity and expressiveness of his singing.

With gramophone records, of course, we do 'just listen', and that might explain some of the discrepancy. In 1929 Melchior took another step forward, with a Siegfried in which 'one forgot his bulk in the genuine poetry of his reading of the part', involving in some lines a half-conversational tone which never deprived them 'of their essential musical quality' (in this review, incidentally, Newman anticipated Anna Russell, observing that Brünnhilde is Siegfried's step-aunt). In 1930 we hear of Melchior's 'old brilliance at the full power of his voice and the old lack of colour at half-voice'. But then in 1931 there comes a performance after which 'all previous estimates of Lauritz Melchior will have to be revised'. He was now effective throughout the full dynamic range and there was 'more poetic discretion than of old' in his fortissimo:

> As an actor he has improved beyond recognition, even in the short interval since last summer when I heard him at Bayreuth. His Tristan on Tuesday was not only dignified; it had a curious spiritual quality about it even in its moments of greatest frenzy. (3 May 1931).

That, we may feel, is more like it. Yet as the 1930s go by we find Newman approving and criticising Melchior's work in much the same proportions as he did in the 1920s, and that Tristan of 1931 remains, in Newman's record of events, the peak of his achievements.

The presence in those days of names – Leider, Melchior, Schorr and so forth – that are still, and perhaps even increasingly, honoured today did not, it appears, guarantee that even their part of the evening's performance was going to be treasurable. Leider's Brünnhilde might be 'of the utmost beauty and dignity', but she was 'badly wigged and badly gowned' (1924). Her Kundry left Newman 'quite unmoved', for her voice lacked seductiveness and her figure lacked wildness so that she seemed 'quite domestic'. Of Schorr's Wotan in *Die Walküre* Newman wrote that it was 'at any rate powerful, dignified and exceedingly well sung' but that 'his reading of the part lacked the fine intellectuality of Mr Bockelmann's'. An interesting sidelight is shed, however, by some remarks Newman made after visiting Bayreuth later that year, when in 'perfect acoustics' he again heard Schorr:

> Here in Bayreuth not only does his great voice sound greater than it does in London, but the increased volume brings with it not the usual coarseness of 'amplification' but an extraordinary fineness of texture.

The record collector can take some reassurance from that as to the historical validity of what he is hearing, for it is exactly this 'extraordinary fineness of texture' that draws him back to Schorr's records as to no other singer of comparable type.

Perhaps we should just briefly look now at Newman's assessment of other Wagnerian singers in the period. Among the sopranos were Gertrude Kappel ('better to listen with the eyes shut'), Elisabeth Ohms ('the most intensely and movingly human Brünnhilde I can remember', 1928), Lotte Lehmann ('electrically alive', 1931), Elisabeth Rethberg ('only an artist of her intelligence could or would have known how to use the voice' to portray the development from act to act of Elsa in *Lohengrin*, 1935), Flagstad ('power and ring and crystal brightness but

55. Fritz Wolff as Loge
in *Das Rheingold*

... I could not see in this placid figure the demon-possessed and fate-driven Senta of Wagner's imagination', 1937). The mezzos generally acquitted themselves as well as any: Olczewska ('In whatever she does she makes us feel that for the moment the whole drama centres in her', 1926), Onegin ('so commanding, physically and temperamentally, that we felt an impression of personal vehemence', 1929), Kerstin Thorborg ('All in all I would rank her as the greatest Wagnerian actress of the present day', 1937).

The tenors do worse in aggregate than individually ('after seeing some of them I have left the theatre for good at the end of the first act feeling that they could hardly bear comparison with Vesta Tilley or Hetty King as male impersonators!'). There were Walter Hyde's 'simple and poignant' Parsifal (1924), Walter Widdop's reliable competence (fortified from the start by having made his Covent Garden debut as

Siegfried 'after rehearsal in a London drawing-room set up as Mime's cave') and Heddle Nash's David, whose only fault was that he sang better than his master. Though Rudolf Laubenthal's Siegfried was 'vocally and dramatically what the boxing trainers call muscle-bound' (1926), his Tristan was 'sound and steady' (if somewhat 'bleached'). Fritz Wolff was 'the nearest thing to Wagner's Walther that I have ever seen' (1929). Max Hirzel had the distinction of making the small notes as well defined as the long ones (1935), and Torsten Ralf's bearing never lacked 'a sort of ligneous dignity' (1938). So there were some crumbs of comfort. A standard for the rest of the baritones was set by Herbert Janssen (but Newman comments that in *Tristan* he was 'manifestly miscast … This exceptionally fine artist, who excels in delicate shades of singing and acting, has neither the weight nor the roughness of voice for so blunt and rather crude an old dog as Kurwenal', 1929). The bass-baritones were led by Schorr and Rudolf Bockelmann; the individuality of Wilhelm Rode impressed him favourably ('something of Chaliapin's power of making speech and song reinforce each other', 1928); but not so, in the same year, Emil Schipper, with whom 'you had to rely on your memory for the words'. The 'giant'-basses all seem to have passed muster, with Kipnis and Andresen in the front rank even though 'these gentlemen were giants in the lateral rather than the vertical sense' (1929).

As for the three great conductors who were most closely associated with the Royal Opera House in these years, Beecham and Bruno Walter earned Newman's enthusiastic support, whereas Furtwängler seemed to him interesting rather than satisfying. Furtwängler 'does allow singers to bring out words and meanings', but under him *Rheingold* in particular would become dull because of the low level of tone ('almost as though chamber music, and *Rheingold* is not chamber music'). Under all these conductors the players did, at their best, the utmost that could be expected of them under their conditions of assembly and rehearsal, but sometimes, as in the 1930 *Götterdämmerung* with Leider, Olczewska, Melchior and Janssen in the cast, they were 'almost unbelievably bad, and again and again we had the feeling that it was only the powerful personality and consummate technical skill of Bruno Walter that was keeping things together at all'.

Production occupied less of his attention, probably because there was not much of it to attend to. 'The scenery is as shabby as ever, and the lighting full of the old pleasant vagaries that blandly defy the laws of science', he reported in 1931. When he visited Bayreuth he duly noted the beginnings of modern trends in production, but he considered them essentially 'evasions': 'Wagner thought in terms of representation … and to abolish or even diminish the representational is to destroy the unity of eye and ear at which he aimed'. On the stage at Covent Garden there was some genuinely good acting to be seen, and this mattered to Newman a great deal. But on the whole his feelings are expressed in a sentence of 15 March 1927: 'Over the stage one draws a respectful veil'. At least such conditions allowed him to concentrate on the score. 'And what a score!' he exclaimed after a performance of *Tristan* just a week earlier in that year. 'The more I know my Wagner,' he added, coming to a fair-and-square statement of creed, 'the more convinced I am that this is the most wonderful artist-mind that the earth has ever seen.'

22.   Klein and 'Beckmesser' of the *Gramophone*

‎୬‎   Herman Klein   ‎ଓ‎

Compton Mackenzie founded the *Gramophone* magazine in April 1923 and planned, as he said, 'with each new number ... to eliminate a little more of myself'. He had a small band of regular contributors and there were articles by well-known people of varied background such as Mark Hamburg, Frank Swinnerton, Edmund Fellowes and Francis Brett Young, with 'Verse to the Editor of the *Gramophone*' by Oliver St John Gogarty and 'Epigramophones' by Hilaire Belloc. Even so, some readers seemed to believe that the Editor wrote all the reviews himself, and it must have been a matter of some relief to him when he could announce, in May 1924, that he had obtained the services of a real expert. It was a matter of pride too, for 'Mr Herman Klein, who, if anyone, is *the* authority on bel canto' was also what the newspapers would call a living legend.

He was as old as the hills, and when younger men lifted up their eyes unto him in the corridors of Covent Garden and heard him say of a singer 'Behold he was very good', then that word was gospel. He had been there, it was felt, at the beginning. Speak of *Aida*, he had attended the Covent Garden première in 1876; mention *Pagliacci*, he had discussed the Prologue with Leoncavallo in 1893. In that same year a rehearsal for the first performance of *Samson et Dalila* was conducted in his studio with the composer present, and he again sat by the master's side in a box at Covent Garden in June 1913. He witnessed the first performance in England of *Carmen* in the company of his teacher, Manuel Garcia: that was in 1878. He travelled to Manchester in 1897 to see the new *La Bohème*, returning by train to London with the depressed Puccini sharing his carriage. When the Weber Centenary came round in 1926, Klein could recall not only performances of *Oberon* with Tietjens and Trebelli, but also conversations with Sir Julius Benedict, Weber's prize pupil. It was even said that he had spoken with people who had spoken with Beethoven.

Of more immediate relevance to the Editor of the *Gramophone* and his readers, this Methuselah of music criticism was still in full possession of

241

his faculties, was a meticulous writer and a tireless listener, and had had practical experience in the record business as adviser to American Columbia in 1906. And of more immediate relevance to the present series of articles, his brief was not merely to review the operatic records as they appeared, but also to write a monthly piece called "The Gramophone and the Singer.' This allowed him to choose a topic of current interest, and it soon became a regular feature of the articles that they should comment on the Covent Garden seasons and on the operatic scene in general. Thus when Melba made her Farewell in 1926, the *Gramophone* was represented by a critic who could remember her debut in 1888, and, turning from the sublime to the merely delightful, when each new Gilbert and Sullivan season opened at the Savoy they would know that their man had attended all the historic first nights from *The Sorcerer* onwards and had enjoyed many a chat with his old friend Sir Arthur. Thus we also have from him reviews of the seasons from 1925 to 1933, and a good deal of hard thinking about the future of opera in this country during those years when opera was on such a precarious footing that we in the present, seen from those times, must look like inheritors of the promised land.

His special interest in the Covent Garden seasons was the singing, and as a reviewer for the *Gramophone* he made a point of comparing the impression made by singers 'in the flesh' and on records. 1925 brought three gramophone celebrities to this country for the first time – Toti Dal Monte, Maria Jeritza and Elisabeth Rethberg. Klein commented: 'Experience has now proved that it is the exception rather than the rule for singers to live up to their gramophone reputations.' His account of Dal Monte's Lucia di Lammermoor goes as follows:

She has a pure soprano voice of fairly extended compass, with clear but occasionally hard head notes and sings like an Italian born and bred. In the 'Regnava nel silenzio', we heard a smooth legato, a delicate cantilena, a crisp, pearly scale (not so perfect in chromatic as in diatonic passages), and brilliance alike in the staccato and the shake. The air brought down the house, but somehow the Sextet failed to do so, perhaps for lack of a big climax in the voices to match that of the brass and the big drum. Here, if anywhere, Lucia should wake up to the awful cruelty of her brother's deception, and depict the anger and despair that precede her insanity. But Toti Dal Monte took the situation, so to speak, 'lying down', sang prettily and never attained an exciting moment. On the other hand, her Mad Scene was from first to last an elaborate conception, slow and deliberate in execution, replete with clever and often touching vocalisation, if not with brilliant flights as tours de force that could exactly be termed thrilling. She acted it well – indeed, acted well throughout – and

56. Maria Jeritza as
Tosca

altogether proved herself a highly accomplished stage artist. That, and
not a great singer, is what I must describe her as being.

I think I must also quote at length his account of Jeritza in *Tosca*. He is
not half as amusing as Ernest Newman, or ultimately, perhaps, as
persuasive in judgment as 'Figaro' of *Musical Opinion*; but it remains a
valuable report, the long life's experience enabling him to 'place' the
singer in historical perspective, and his conscientious approach as a
writer helping us to appreciate Jeritza's art in a way that her gramophone
records are quite unable to do:

The triumph of Maria Jeritza in *Tosca* on the following evening was due as
much to a winning personality and magnificent acting as to the effect of
her ringing, powerful tones and genuinely dramatic singing. Here, as I

fully expected, was an artist who could produce in the opera house a far deeper impression than that created by her gramophone achievements, therein differing from Toti Dal Monte, who resembles Galli-Curci (and most other coloratura singers, I imagine) in that her records attain a higher level of vocal perfection than when she is facing an audience. But what a Tosca! What a combination of all the qualities, human and artistic, that go to the making of that many-sided creature! Jeritza is not exactly like any one of her great predecessors in this role. She unites, though, some of the strongest characteristics that distinguished each, and she brings them into sharp contrast with the adroitness and skill of a mistress of her art. Thus by turn she gives you the feline touches of Sarah Bernhardt, the feminine devotion of Ternina, the tempestuous passion of Destinn, the shrinking fear of Emma Eames. Tenderness alternates with jealousy in the church scene; anxiety, alarm and resentment with burning rage, despair, gloating, satisfied vengeance in the terrific duet with Scarpia. Then, after the prolonged physical struggle, whilst she is lying full length on the ground, her face distorted and her wonderful hair all dishevelled, she half murmurs, half weeps the bitter plaint of 'Vissi d'arte' with an intensity of emotion such as no Tosca off the stage has ever yet dared to put into a gramophone record. It was not in this air that she 'forced' her tone, as has been suggested; but if she did so at all it was at certain moments in the tremendous episode when it was far more pardonable to overstress the *fortissimo* than do the reverse. At such a climax it seems wonderful how a singer with a temperament like Jeritza's can keep control of her forces as she does; for she makes you feel that the vocalist is not being studied in the least – that all physical power is being reserved to meet the demands of the actress. Altogether, then, her Tosca is an intensely striking and superb performance.

Later he used the phrase 'sheer genius', and I cannot recall that that ever came out of stock again to be used of any other new singer, unless it were Lehmann or Ponselle. He did not, for instance, apply it to Elisabeth Rethberg who had just appeared in her famous role of Aida not long after her excellent Brunswick recording of the solos had come to Klein for review. Rethberg's voice he found perfectly lovely and of exemplary steadiness, but it was not, he thought, the right voice for Aida: 'It sounded too light, too thin in volume, lacking in the richness and power that had satisfied one in the gramophone records.'

He reverts again to the theme of comparison between the recording and 'the flesh'. Her performance, he says, 'added one more proof to my growing conviction that the gramophone record, however perfect and pleasure-giving in itself, must not always be regarded as a reliable indication of the effect that the singer will produce either in the piece or the part inside the opera house'.

On the whole, Klein was a generous critic. He could so easily have used his great experience to make artists and public feel small. He never gave one the sense that he considered himself to be living in 'a day of small things, daily growing smaller', as his American counterpart, W.J. Henderson, born within a few months of him, wrote after a performance of *Die Walküre* with Melchior and Schorr. He was never mean in his attitude to new singers in great roles. He considered Frida Leider 'the greatest Isolde on the stage today', again relating her performance in the theatre to that on records:

> The admirable capacity for reserve that one notices in her records was put in evidence by the delicate gradations of strength with which she managed her crescendos, while never ceasing, meanwhile, to realise the exact meaning of a dramatic situation.

Lehmann's Desdemona in the same year (1926) would remain 'a fragrant and delicious memory'; never before had he seen so completely satisfying a singer in the role ('and I have heard nearly all of them'). Her great strength lay not in the Willow Song but:

> It was in that most difficult scene of all, the elaborate ensemble that follows after the Moor has struck Desdemona before his whole court – it was in this trying episode that Lotte Lehmann did so magnificently both as singer and actress, that she rose to heights never attained before, at least in my experience.

By 1926 Fernand Ansseau had become 'one of the world's few really great tenors'. In 1927 Elisabeth Schumann 'remains the Sophie of one's dreams'. In 1928 Elisabeth Ohms appeared as the *Götterdämmerung* Brünnhilde and Klein could remember 'none since Milka Ternina who threw such tragic force and depth of pathos ... into her performance'. 1929 brought superlatives in the Wagner season to Klein's appreciation of Ivar Andresen (his King Mark 'has never been surpassed in my experience'), Melchior ('In the Forging Songs I thought him simply magnificent, while the exquisite poetry of the forest scene likewise lost nothing in his hands'), Bockelmann and Fritz Wolff. 1930 found Stabile 'the best Iago since Maurel'. 1931 provoked the word 'genius' once more, this time for Rosa Ponselle whom he admired so greatly – in Romani's *Fedra* ('Not since Sarah Bernhardt ...') In 1932, with Leider, Melchior and Olczewska in the cast, Beecham conducting, *Tristan und Isolde* had Klein searching his memory for a better and deciding that you would have to go back to Toscanini at the Metropolitan in 1907.[1] Then

---

[1] Toscanini conducted his first *Tristan* at the Metropolitan in 1909.

finally, in 1933, he was happy to see British singers doing well: Mary Jarred a 'splendid' Fricka, all set to be Kirkby Lunn's successor, and Muriel Brunskill and Dennis Noble both superior to their Italian counterparts in *Aida*.

There were of course singers whom he did not admire (Capsir, Wildbrunn, O'Sullivan, Dino Borgioli, Rimini were among them), but generally he reserved his more severe utterances for causes rather than individual artists. The mention just now of British singers represents his concern that their opportunities should prosper, and he felt that the musical establishment in England did not help very much. Eva Turner's triumph as Turandot in 1928 led him to reflect on the prevailing lack of vision shown by the establishment in her earlier years:

> Those who could recognise the exceptional quality and power of her voice (if only she would keep it pure and free from tremolo) might have perceived that she had in her the makings of a great dramatic soprano. Only did they? Did they say 'Let us invest some money in this gifted young woman, not only helping her to attain fame and fortune, but very likely obtaining for our opera house or our "Celebrity List" a star that will recoup our outlay over and over again'? No, they preferred to wait for the reports from Milan and Rome; and if those were all right they would be willing to spend any amount to procure the services of the clever Bristol girl.[2]

He felt that management was often limited in vision and indeed in common sense, and that many of their economies (from a reduction of rehearsal time to a cut in press tickets) were penny-wise and pound-foolish. On the other hand as far as repertory was concerned, 'the public got what they wanted', in other words Wagner and Puccini with a few other operas whose name and nature did not matter greatly as long as they featured a star singer. The fashionable world, he noted, was not really very musical. It would patronise Covent Garden on the big occasions, but not many of these people were to be seen, for instance, at the London Opera Festival of 1930 at the New Scala Theatre, where could be seen such rarities as Monteverdi's *Orpheus*, Handel's *Julius Caesar* and Mozart's *La finta giardiniera*. Eventually *Freischütz* and Beecham arrived to save the season financially:

> As soon as the 'follow-my-leader' crowd heard how well Weber's opera had been put on, and that the aristocratic highbrows had at the last moment taken up the show, there was quite a rush for seats, and the concluding performances drew crowded audiences.

[2] Dame Eva Turner was, of course, born in Oldham, Lancashire, and her family moved to Bristol when she was about ten years old.

He was worried by the failure of schemes by Isidore de Lara, Thomas Beecham and others to secure the future of opera. He felt convinced of the need for State Subsidy (which Newman, for instance, opposed). He was sure that great harm was being done to young voices both by the influence of gramophone records and by charlatans in the teaching profession. One of his last articles was on this very subject, 'The Right to be a Teacher of Singing', and concluded:

> Meanwhile I am extremely anxious to see our English vocal standard kept up, both as regards singing and teaching and not least of all, our standards of Press criticism maintained at the highest level.

That was in the February issue of 1934, and in the March he died, having remained active as a teacher, a writer and (apparently) a tennis player right up to the end; his last book, *The Golden Age of Opera*, had been published the previous year. Christopher Stone wrote a warm tribute in the April number of the *Gramophone*, leaving a vivid personal impression of a man who had maintained his own standards in all ways – in his handwriting, his speech, his dress, and his physical vigour as well as in matters of moral and mental principle. The next month Compton Mackenzie, who had once said that Klein 'had forgotten more about singing than I ever knew', wrote of his death as coming 'like the portent of a change'. Klein had kept up the great tradition of operatic criticism; the way things were going at present, said the Editor, there would very soon be no opera to criticise.

➣ 'Beckmesser' ➢

> I prefer not to write of *Louise*. Suffice it to say that it was given three times. After various postponements and exaggerated blurbs for some simple illusory effects *The Tales of Hoffmann* was exquisitely played by Sir Thomas Beecham and the London Philharmonic Orchestra and sung by a very international cast. Two of the principals sang in French that both the French and I could understand; most of the rest used a jargon that bore little recognisable resemblance to any known language. I did not hear the impromptu *Bohème*.

The style, they say, is the man. This man, we say as we read him, certainly had a style: assured, Olympian indeed; the amusement has a contemptuous edge to it, the contempt for mediocrity balanced by an unhesitating acclamation of excellence; the tone saved from pomposity (but only narrowly) by its exuberance, its frank relish for judgment, its pleasure in the pen. The accent, surely, is familiar.

247

The *Gramophone* magazine used to include in its pages an annual review of the international opera season at Covent Garden. No doubt this was partly because each year brought the opportunity of hearing 'in the flesh' celebrity singers who had previously been known only through their recordings, and readers were interested to learn how the records compared with the reality. Another reason for such a survey becoming a regular feature of the magazine was that they had just the man to write it. This was Herman Klein, who died in 1934, and being irreplaceable he was not replaced. In 1936 'Beckmesser' made his debut. In 1937 he retired, his place being taken the following year by Harold Rosenthal, at that time a young man already known to readers through his contributions to the correspondence columns, pointedly argued and alarmingly well-informed.

'Beckmesser's' term of office was short. Dressed in a little brief authority, he crosses the stage twice in two years and then is heard no more. He was, however, too remarkable a man to disappear quite like that. The *Gramophone* office tells me they do not know who he was. I think I do.

Whoever he was, he knew how to write: his is a practised and professional hand. If there was indeed something of Sixtus Beckmesser about him in the awarding of black marks, there was also a sense of humour which the marker of Nuremberg conspicuously lacked. Having observed that 'only in amateur theatrical performances and at Covent Garden do men throw their shadows on the sky', he writes:

> The crying need for a producer reached its first climax in the first *Walküre*, where Rethberg, Melchior and List made such nonsense of Wagner's dramatic intentions that an audience composed of people understanding German would have laughed themselves hoarse. The fun began as the door opened. Melchior bounded in so exuberantly that I believe he thought he had to sing Siegfried that night. Then, hearing in the orchestra sounds that were obviously *Walküre*, he changed his mind and manner, and took on some of Siegmund's weariness, Rethberg strolled in from an inner room, walked down to the footlights completely ignoring the prostrate Siegmund, had a look at Sir Thomas, and remarked to the audience 'Ein fremdes Mann, ihn muss ich fragen' ... The supper scene was sung with all three characters full face to the audience, and for the love duet this Siegmund and Sieglinde clambered on to a pile of cushions like a couple of long-married and weary hikers seeking the softest piece of grass on which to rest their weary limbs before they settled down to their sandwiches.

Of course, these productions must have been easy game for any writer with a sharp eye, a keen sense of the ridiculous, and a zest for criticism. Approval, enthusiasm, warmth are much more testing, and ultimately

'Beckmesser's' value to us today lies not so much in his censorious energy as in his communication of enjoyment, his perception and savouring of excellence. He heard some great singers in those years, and, reading him, one comes uncommonly close to their greatness.

Herbert Janssen, for instance, is an artist who continues to exercise a remarkable fascination through his recordings. His performances at Covent Garden from 1926 to 1939 nearly always drew from the critics a respectful phrase, with very rarely any adverse comment. Yet his distinction among the singers of his time has never, in my reading, been so vividly caught in words as it is in 'Beckmesser's' two surveys:

> Janssen's Kothner was the best individual figure on the stage ... The Isolde and Brünnhilde of Flagstad are patently one woman, and Bockelmann's Wotan is disturbingly like his Sachs, but there are no points of similarity between Janssen's genial Kothner, his suffering Amfortas, his stupid, frustrated Gunther, and his rugged, devoted Kurwenal. There is only one feature common to the characters Janssen

57. Herbert Janssen as Amfortas in *Parsifal*

creates – they invariably sing as well as, if not better than, anyone else on the stage. (*Meistersinger* on the opening night, 1936)

He still stands immeasurably superior to other German baritones, tenors and basses in vocal culture, and without sacrificing any beauty of tone he conveys even more vividly than before the drained weariness of a man racked by spiritual and physical suffering. (*Parsifal* 1937)

Janssen has everything except the low Gs and A flats. He managed these pedal notes with such skill that not one percent of the audience realised that they do not really exist in his voice. As in all his work, he stood apart from the rest of the company by reason of his exquisite singing and his complete absorption in the character. (*Fliegende Holländer* 1937)

The writer summed up Janssen's qualities in his 1936 review and stated categorically his critical placing of him: 'His voice is of ravishing quality, he is musically and technically a faultless singer, and a magnificent actor … Janssen, I make bold to say, is the greatest artist on the contemporary operatic stage.'

A neat turn of phrase helped him to characterise other artists in a few words. Ludwig Weber's was a 'great gunmetal voice', Margarete Klose's 'smooth and indolent'; Lawrence Tibbett's 'line of tone is straight and solid as a piston rod'; Lauri-Volpi's voice is undeniably splendid 'but until he has it fitted with the vocal equivalent of a synchro-mesh or pre-selective gear box he will not give much pleasure to the connoisseur'. He was an interested observer of the state of the parties among the fans:

The prospect of Flagstad as the Brünnhilde of the second cycle of *The Ring* introduced, for a large section of the audience, a strong element of the partisanship that paradoxically enough is most in evidence in what passes in this country under the name of 'sport'. The Leider 'fans' were determined to show their favourite during the first cycle that whatever the future might bring forth by way of Brünnhildes, their loyalty would never waver.

Then, amused as he might be by these peripheral entertainments, he treated both of the great sopranos with the kind of critical appreciation they deserved.

Leider's genius drew the attention away from the fact that her voice tires more quickly than of yore. Leider has sung Brünnhilde for a dozen years at Covent Garden. She makes the same movements at the same moments as she had always done. She sings each phrase – allowing for the difficulty she now has with the top of her voice – in exactly the same way; but familiarity breeds in this case only admiration for an artist whose powerful and vital work begins where that of other singers leaves off.

Of Flagstad, who in 1936 was making her first appearances at Covent Garden, he wrote one of the most convincing and well-balanced of all critical accounts. It carries conviction because he has been listening not so much with the detached curiosity of a critic as with the practical interest of the impresario:

> I shall never forget my first hearing of Flagstad in Covent Garden at the dress rehearsal of *Tristan* ... She sat completely at ease in the middle of the stage, as restfully as if she had been drinking tea at home, and poured out such a flood of tone as I have never heard from a woman's throat, a tone that rode over the orchestra like a vast modern liner on the ocean. Her debut on May 18 was a triumph greater than any I have ever witnessed. You will have gathered from the Press that Flagstad is the ideal Isolde. I am not yet convinced ... This is the voice of which I have dreamed; but my brain and previous experience of *Tristan* hold me unconvinced that Flagstad is very Isolde of very Isolde. Her performance is musically flawless down to the last demi-semi-quaver, it is phrased with a heaven-sent instinct for moulding a melodic line, it is sensitive and lovely to behold; but it is not Isolde. It is too pleasant, too even-tempered, too placid; if one listens with closed eyes one hears that the voice expresses little but variants on amiability. Her tone did not once suggest the raging tigress that is Isolde in the first act, and only rarely did it breathe the nervous, sensual ecstasy of the love duet.

Again, in this memorably phrased, carefully weighed piece of criticism, one catches the style which is the man. A certain almost Churchillian sense of history attends him as he sits in his stall ('a triumph greater than any I have ever witnessed'): a certain grandeur accompanies his perceptions ('the voice of which I have dreamed'). He attends rehearsals; he has, one might suspect, itching fingers – to take matters into his own hands. He brings international standards to bear and is contemptuous of the parochialism he feels around him: 'Those who have seen the Bayreuth production of *Lohengrin* will not lightly and silently suffer such dire evenings as those on which *Prince Igor* was given at Covent Garden in June' (1937). 'One of Covent Garden's outstanding needs is a producer of genius who can in a few days impress style, or rather styles, upon the heterogeneous array of singers he has to work with.'

His interest is not narrowly focused upon singers. He concerns himself with the conductors, and is fascinated by, but not entirely enthusiastic about Furtwängler, whose *Ring* was new to the house in 1937 and presented a marked contrast with his predecessors':

> After the powerful, dramatic and brilliant performances by Beecham, Walter's vivid and highly nervous readings, and Heger's massive and deliberate treatment, Furtwängler gives the impression of showing the mighty work through the wrong end of a telescope. The playing was always supple and exquisitely flexible, but flexible almost to an invertebrate degree ... He weaves as lovely a melodic line as any conductor of our time, but that line is not punctuated with vehement or dramatic accent. He is excessively considerate to the singers. Faced with a covey of soft-voiced Valkyries, he scaled down the Ride from its elemental grandeur until it seemed like a rally of excited girl guides.

These, however, were real performances; they merited judgment by the highest standards. On the whole, 'Beckmesser' concurs with the general view of the critics that the Italian evenings did not. When a Rethberg comes and sings Aida he responds ('I cannot believe that Destinn at her best sang better than Rethberg has done this year in *Aida* and *Rosenkavalier*'). Hearing Stignani for the first time he salutes her magnificent voice, its range and its 'surprising variety of colours'. But for the most part, the performances struck him as sadly inadequate: he thought it would take a very expert eye, for instance, to recognise in this 'charcoal' *Don Pasquale* 'the sparkling diamond of Donizetti's creation'. At least there was Eva Turner's Turandot to enjoy (it 'completely vanquished the London Philharmonic Orchestra and Puccini's scoring'). And it is good to read that 'the hero of the Italian performances' in 1937 was Giovanni Martinelli:

> Of all the celebrities who took part in Italian and French operas he alone made credible the stories that are told of the Golden Age of Singing. His voice is not what it once was, but it has still ring and golden glow unlike any other in the world (except perhaps Björling, whose records hold promise of a voice great beyond even the cavil of 'fans' who write stupid letters about the objects of their indiscriminate admiration), and he phrases music as if he had sung only with Toscanini. He sang in *Aida*, *Tosca*, *Turandot*, *Otello* and one performance of *Carmen*, and on every occasion lit the stage and warmed the auditorium with the essence of greatness. Even when the music called for more voice than he has to give, as in much of *Otello* and the second Act of *Turandot*, he held attention rivetted by the style and intelligence of his work.

In such writing, 'Beckmesser' takes us nearer, I would say, to the experience of being present at these performances than does any other critic. Newman, of course, is as observant, but in a more detached manner and frankly in a more grumpy mood. 'Beckmesser', critical as he is, is altogether more involved, more nearly a participator.

In the two years following he was to become more directly involved, if my identification of him is correct. In the same year as the *Gramophone* lost its 'Beckmesser', the *Manchester Guardian* lost its 'W.L.'. As Beecham's assistant at the Royal Opera House, Walter Legge was able to help bring to the remaining pre-war seasons some of the qualities of which, as 'W.L.', he had argued the need. If 'W.L.' and 'Beckmesser' were not one and the same person, they certainly agreed with each other remarkably well, and, what is probably more significant, they never (as far as I can trace) disagreed. At *Louise*, 'W.L.' found that 'absence has not made the heart grow fonder', and 'Beckmesser' preferred not to talk about it at all. At *Rosenkavalier*, 'W.L.' reported that 'the Marschallin was indisposed but Elisabeth Rethberg had kindly consented to wear her clothes and sing her music ... gloriously'; 'Beckmesser' agreed. As for Tiana Lemnitz as Octavian, one column said that 'there was not a false touch in the whole creation', the other that it was 'a masterpiece of male impersonation, humour and fine singing'. At *Les Contes d'Hoffmann* 'Beckmesser' commented on the exaggerated blurb 'for some simple illusory effect'; 'W.L.' observed that Noel Maskeleyne's 'skill was apparently such that not merely Dr Miracle but the whole opera surprisingly disappeared from the theatre last Thursday'. Both conceded that Beecham secured some exquisite playing. In 1937 they shared the same high opinion of Kerstin Thorborg and Herbert Janssen, and the same dismay about the Italian operas, such as *Don Pasquale* and *Falstaff*. In the latter, Beecham was 'a model of clarity and precision, but only one of the singers consistently phrased with him. The ensembles ... were inelegant point-to-point races'. One of our two critics, having disposed of Cesare Formichi's Iago as being sung 'with Sparafucile's inflections and Amonasro's demeanour', wrote: 'I do not believe that Shakespeare would have admired Formichi's Falstaff any more than I did.' The other granted that not all of the singers were downright bad:

> But as a work for the stage *Falstaff* stands or falls by the player to whom the title role is entrusted. It fell.

'Beckmesser' or 'W.L.'?

23. Kaikhosru Sorabji of the *New Age*

With temperate language and balanced judgment a critic may earn respect; there is no doubt, however, that a little pride and prejudice in among the sense and sensibility help to make him much more readable. Where Cardus charmed and Newman chid, Sorabji burned. What he scorned (and that was much) he scorched; where he admired, his enthusiasms flamed.

The *New Age* was an intelligent weekly, concerned primarily with national and international affairs but including in its pages book reviews and comments on the arts. Until 1923 a mild, unadventurous paragraph or two of music criticism was contributed by Helen Rootham. Then came a number of surveys of contemporary music much more challengingly written by Cecil Gray. A period of cautious commentary by a lady called Dorothy Short intervened briefly, prompting a letter, or perhaps more descriptively a tirade, in the correspondence columns. It ridiculed 'the idea that any meagre, narrow-chested, weedy creature, with a throat like a wrung chicken's neck, is fitted to become a singer if he possesses a pleasant, inoffensive little pipe of a voice'. It derided the claims and reputations commonly supported by music critics and expressed astonishment on behalf of 'those who have an understanding of what is great singing ... and whose standards are somewhat higher than those of the newspaper men'. It was signed 'Kaikhosru Sorabji', and within a month its author had taken over the music column.

He wasted no time, and laid into the British National Opera Company in his first article ('indifferent, ragged, unkempt performances and frequently execrable singing'), visiting celebrities in the next ('the flood of bad singers continues with unabated volume'), and Covent Garden's Wagner productions (terrible staging, and lighting 'that would have disgraced a fifth-rate music-hall') as soon as the opportunity arose. The public came in for its share of the abuse: an Italian baritone had offered 'the scandal and insults of singing such filth as Neapolitan gutter songs', but 'as the audience was a Royal Albert Hall Sunday afternoon one, it probably got what it deserved, for it greedily gobbled up the vomit and clamoured for more'. If there was a race musically more degenerate than the English it was the Americans:

The latest arrival is Mme Margaret Matzenauer, who possesses, to judge from the American periodicals devoted to the trade in music and musicians, a fabulous reputation in the States in addition to being a Metropolitan Opera House star. It is safe to say that, with the exception of Titta Ruffo (another singer with a Brobdingnagian reputation in America) I have never heard worse singing or worse musicianship from a so-called 'big' artist.

He goes on to specify the abominations, one of them 'an incredible outrage', another 'shamelessly and sickeningly' sentimental, and all, apparently, highly approved of by the deplorable Americans.

His own standards of singing had been formed during the earlier years of the century, when his gods were Destinn, Calvé, Tetrazzini, Kirkby Lunn, Caruso, Battistini. He was devoted to the baritone Dinh Gilly, whose lectures on singing given in London in 1927 and 1928 'blew away the mists of pseudo-scientific cant with which the technique of singing becomes more surrounded *pari passu* its decline'. They also

58. Louise Kirkby Lunn as Ortrud in *Lohengrin*

255

59. Toti Dal Monte

had the merit of stating 'emphatically and vehemently ... points about singing and singers at which I have been hammering for years'. When some of the survivors from the great past reappeared, Sorabji would be there. Kirkby Lunn, despite a bad cold and a worse fog, shone through 'with an artistry that is richer, wider and more subtle now than it has ever been'. That was at the end of 1925, a year which had opened with a recital by Blanche Marchesi, also afflicted with a cold but nonetheless providing 'interpretations so consummate, so subtle and delicately coloured, so finely and sensitively nuanced, that one is safe in saying that no other singer could approach them'. Even old Tetrazzini, as late as 1929, reappearing at the Albert Hall, seemed to sing with powers scarcely diminished: 'still the same gorgeous, clear, forward quality, the same marvellous brilliance and evenness, and that deliciously personal quality of naiveté, all the more fascinating and séduisant, coupled with the dazzling technical perfection and superb mastery of style.' She too demonstrated the greatness of the past and by implication the degeneracy of the present.

As for 'the present', it offered little hope for the future as far as singing was concerned: 'Here and there the art still survives [this was in 1938] in a hole and corner and precarious manner, but for all practical purposes it is dead.' From time to time the torch of the great tradition glimmered; very occasionally it flared. When Toti Dal Monte sang her Rosina at Covent Garden in 1925 the line from the past was shown to survive: 'Her fioritura has all that gem-like, clear-cut quality, that mathematical precision and above all the crystalline sparkle without which fioritura is just not fioritura. Her style is exquisite ... Her intonation is of flawless certainty ... The voice is of extreme luminousness, brilliance, of perfect evenness, and wonderfully poised, as only the Italians know how.' In Rome as Lucia in 1929 she was at her very finest:

> I was left breathless by the miracles of singing she achieved. Her voice, always beautiful, has now attained such a pitch of development that it must rank as one of the greatest of the great fioritura sopranos and incomparably the greatest of any soprano leggiera. The quality, at once of incredible brilliance and luminosity, has a warmth, a roundness and a fullness that must be heard to be believed ... The tremendous Mad Scene was not only the highest imaginable apex of pure and beautiful singing, but it was a wonderful piece of interpretation as well.

In 1936 Dal Monte returned to England to sing at the Queen's Hall. At that concert, compensating to some extent for the shortening of her upper range, she sang some lyrical solos with 'the most delightful delicacy of phrasing and style, showing herself to be still a survival of a greater and more glorious past'.

There were a few other Italians to be valued: Lina Pagliughi, Lauri-Volpi, Dino Borgioli, Ezio Pinza (and it is pleasing to see that the Spaniard Antonio Cortis was greeted as 'without question the best tenor we have had in years'). Most – and these included Ponselle (American by birth but of Italian origin and generally esteemed the glory of the Italian seasons), Gina Cigna, Gigli, Schipa and Stabile – seemed to be emphatically not of the great tradition. Nor was he necessarily prejudiced in favour of anyone who came from 'the greater and more glorious past', for when Zenatello reappeared in 1926 Sorabji

60. Antonio Cortis as Johnson in *La Fanciulla del West*

considered him 'nearly the Italian tenor of caricature, a bad actor and singer; he hardly ever once removed his eyes from the front of the house, into which everything was shouted in the worst Italian manner'. But the object of his utmost loathing among the singers of this period, and the embodiment of practically everything he regarded as most rotten in the state of singing was Aureliano Pertile. In 1928 he took himself to *Cavalleria rusticana* and *Pagliacci* and was appalled:

> The singing of the Italians was utterly execrable ... Almost all of them wobbled abominably, produced sounds of hideous and detestable quality, and had not a notion of a pure vocal line ... Of the Canio of Aureliano Pertile it is difficult to speak with patience, such an exhibition of vulgar hysteria, mad ranting, and utter lack of anything resembling style or beauty of singing would be (one hopes) difficult to surpass. This performer should learn that to try to do as Caruso did – Caruso with a marvellous voice, a prodigious technique, a genius for singing – when you have an indifferent voice and even worse technique is only to expose your deficiencies still more ... The generation and type of singer to which belonged the Italians of this performance do not understand – indeed, have no conception of the art of imposing emotional colour into the voice without violating the bounds of pure singing. Knowing nothing of this

258

last, they are compelled, in order to make such detestably crude, vulgar and cheap effects as they are able to, to have recourse to various unpleasant noises, coughing, shouting, gasping, growling, howling, groaning and so forth, because this is the simple and easy way; but it is not singing, and has no place in anything sung.

When he revisited Italy he was equally distressed by the decline of singing in the land of song, and again saw the popularity of Pertile as symptomatic. 'I am credibly informed that a certain tenor whose execrable methods – denounced when he sang last season at Covent Garden – is an enormous favourite here [Rome], as well as with La Scala audiences. Such a decline in standards is all the more tragic in that it has come about in what has been the cradle of the art of singing in Europe.'

The traditional Italian method he still thought the best. The famous Germans who appeared regularly at Covent Garden in those years won his favour, but he often had disaparaging things to say about the German school as such. Lehmann, Rethberg, Lemnitz, Janssen and Schorr were unreservedly praised. The great Isoldes in his book were Gertrude Kappel and Elisabeth Ohms. He thought Flagstad musicianly and gifted but monotonous. Of Leider he gives varied reports but writes a most enthusiastic account of her Marschallin:

...a most beautiful, indeed, a consummate performance. Here were all the grace, dignity and subtlety of the character, expressed with superb insight and a superlative artistry that made this performance the greatest I have ever seen of the role. The marvellous elegance and ease with which the singer passed from a deliciously poised and buoyant recitative to pure and beautiful cantilena – the fascinating bravura and the light conversational tone in the first scene with Baron Ochs – the exquisite urbanity of this brilliant study of a great lady of eighteenth-century Vienna – made one marvel with admiration at an artist like Leider who can pass from the great high tragic roles of Isolde and Brünnhilde in which she is so justly celebrated to this beautiful, fine and delicate etching.

Of Olczewska he was often lost in admiration, but even from the start, in 1924, he had diagnosed 'a small indication of faulty production' and by 1931 he found a marked deterioration and noted that the faults of method were 'now bringing their inevitable Nemesis'.

He disliked the modern French school intensely. Fanny Heldy, for instance, 'sings in the typical French way – that dreadful, tight, hard, *dans la masque* business pushed to extremes'. Bourdin's Pelléas 'making allowances for a too-typically French production was acceptably sung, indeed as well sung as could be with such a production'. Claire Croiza, in a concert in 1928, had 'pinched, hard tone on nasals, constantly varying tone and quality (but at the same time extreme lack of command of tone colour) and her faulty phrasing was a continual vexation of the spirit'. To an admirer (such as myself) of Croiza's art on records this comes as a surprise, and it is good to find reassurance in the appraisal of Vanni-Marcoux's Golaud in 1937 as 'the best piece of operatic stage work I have seen for a long time'.

On the subject of English singing he was divided. Much of it provoked a stream of his favourite adjectives, beginning with 'execrable'. But equally often he would make a point of comparing our own efforts favourably with those of the famous foreign singers who came a-visiting. Croiza's concert was a case in point: 'every one of the songs sung by Mme Croiza I have heard better sung by several English singers and enormously better by two or three.' At the dreadful *Cav.* and *Pag.* the one respectable piece of singing was done by Enid Cruikshank as Lola. Florence Austral (stretching a point to claim her for the native school) could knock spots off the lot of them. In a Queen's Hall recital of 1928, which he describes as a 'profoundly moving artistic experience', she sang 'Abscheulicher' and an aria from *Un ballo in maschera*, with songs by Brahms and Strauss, ending with Brünnhilde's Battle Cry, and in all of these, when the great foreign names came to mind, there came also the 'delighted astonishment' of realising that here, in each case, was something better. As for Eva Turner, Sorabji, rare as it is to find him joining in everybody else's chorus of praise, had no doubts about this one. She was 'supreme'. And when Maria Nemeth (called 'Nemetti') came in 1931 to try out her Turandot at Covent Garden she had 'the impossible task' of following not only one who had 'wonderfully realised … the icy coldness and cruelty of the character' but also one of the great voices of the world.

What, then, of English opera? Contemptuous of the BNOC, the Old Vic, the Carl Rosa and various attempts to produce London seasons in English at smaller theatres, he eventually paid a visit to Sadler's Wells. This was in 1938, and it made him think again. The performance of *Rigoletto* 'went with admirable brio, dash and sparkle and for general all-round excellence I have heard no Covent Garden International Grand Season performance during the past few years approaching, let alone surpassing it in these respects'. The solo singing and acting were also excellent, and, though he still found 'opera not to be in the English blood', he was sufficiently impressed by what he saw and heard to conclude that if this represented the general standard of Sadler's Wells, then 'I have completely to revise my opinions of this institution'. The admission does him credit. So does his recognition of sturdy merit

61. Sir Thomas Beecham

whenever he found it in English singing, and his burning affirmation of the genius, among conductors, of Beecham: 'the incomparable Beecham', who could almost 'transform the sound of the Covent Garden Orchestra overnight' so that it would, upon occasions, contribute worthily to performances, such as that of *Götterdämmerung* in 1931, that could take their places among the dozen great musical experiences of a lifetime. '*Does* this country,' Sorabji demanded, 'for all the talk about him, truly realise the quality of Beecham? *Does* it, for instance, realise that there exist at the present time two conductors of the class of Toscanini in the whole world, that one of them is Toscanini himself, and the other Beecham? I doubt it.'

However great the leading conductor and the leading singer of the age, and even with the newfound excellence of Sadler's Wells to take into account, a genuine tradition of English opera was still to be found. It needed, for instance, some English operatic compositions of merit. Here again Sorabji saw little hope. In his first article for the *New Age* in April 1924 he had looked forward to a better future with the reopening of Covent Garden. His wishes included a hope 'that there *are* some better living composers of opera than Mr Gustav Holst and Mr Rutland Boughton' (Holst was the blackest of bêtes noires). He found much of interest in Goossens's *Judith* but, as he said, 'to produce a new opera for only two performances doesn't make sense'. A similar fate befell *Don Juan de Mañara* in 1937. Despite what Sorabji calls 'a very distinguished performance' by Lawrence Tibbett, Goossens's 'fine, accomplished and individual opera' had no chance of establishing itself in the repertory and again had to be content with two performances relegated to the end of the season, when orchestra, audiences and critics had all but lost whatever freshness had once been theirs. It was notable too, he thought, 'that the upper part of the house, where we are always being told *ad nauseam* that the genuine music-lovers are to be found, was scantily filled'. One wonders what Sorabji might have thought of the English opera renaissance of the 1950s – but in that same article which discusses the Don Juan opera there is mention of 'a so-called Sinfonietta' by Benjamin Britten, who is admonished not to confuse rhythm with St Vitus's Dance.

During the 1930s Sorabji was writing principally not for the *New Age* (which seems to have been increasingly taken over by 'Social Credit'), but for the *New English Weekly*. During all of this period, of course, he was primarily a composer. Occasionally he would express in his column, and always with a genuine and touching warmth of feeling, his gratitude to performers and helpers. He also turned more towards record reviewing (he had always an appreciative interest in the gramophone), his reviews being among the most perceptive and least automatic in response of those written at that time. In fact, somewhere between the extremes of the passionately beating pendulum of his judgments, there existed a man of good sense and remarkable integrity. His critical skirmishes with the 'execrable taste' of the 'crapulous age' had nothing in them of that superior boredom which is the real deadliness of criticism, and his hatred of mediocrity was the necessary obverse of his love of excellence. He was an extraordinary man. And, perhaps most extraordinary of all to realise at this present moment of writing ... he still *is*.[1]

---

[1] This article was published in June 1985. Kaikhosru Shapurji Sorabji (born Leon Dudley) died on October 15 1988, aged 97.

24.   Dyneley Hussey of the *Spectator*

Benjamin Britten once alluded to Dyneley Hussey as the deaf ear of the *Listener*. This was in the later years of Hussey's life when shortly after the Second World War he retired to Cheltenham and reported for the BBC's *Listener* magazine, mostly on broadcasts of opera. Whatever the condition of his ears at this stage,[1] he had in his time been a good critic: it is his acute hearing that enables us in the present to listen to several of those famous performances of the interwar years which have a way of being constantly referred to but rarely described. He wrote with grace and was distinguished among his colleagues by the breadth of his culture, and particularly by his knowledge of painting which also qualified him as a lecturer at the National Gallery. For over 30 years he was one of *The Times*'s principal music critics, and some of his unsigned work may well be among the pieces quoted in Chapter 20. What I am opening now are the strong, crackly, sturdily bound pages of those weekly reviews that were at the centre of intellectual life at that time, and in which Hussey wrote thoughtful, well-informed music notes ranging over the whole field but showing a special interest in opera.

These were the days of 'the elegant middle', articles which either embroidered a theme in the belle-lettrist tradition or occupied themselves with matters of less severely responsible public concern than those to which the reviews were essentially devoted. Hussey's earliest piece for the *Saturday Review* was about the opening night of the Proms in 1922, when John Coates sang 'Celeste Aida'. The young critic took a little sidesweep at scoffing colleagues who 'have of late condemned this emotional appeal as inartistic'; he says he doesn't know what music is supposed to appeal to if not the emotions. This may not have been quite what the *Saturday Review* and its readers wanted to hear, and Hussey rested until 1923. He then emerged to commend Holst, *The Perfect Fool*, and the Covent Garden management, on whose part it was 'a brave, gay venture to set this new English work, in sum so unlike anything that has yet been seen on the operatic stage, in the forefront of the "grand"

---

[1] I believe he sometimes used a hearing-aid. Britten's words – not the kindest under the circumstances – were 'I wouldn't dream of buying the *Listener*: that ear is too withered' (*Opera*, March 1952).

season'. The wit and beauty of the score, he suggests, do not preclude 'serious intention, which alone will commend Mr Holst's new work to earnest minds'. 'Earnest' was a word with faintly comical overtones in the 1920s (trained by Lytton Strachey and others to be amused by all Victorian values), and Hussey was probably wearing his Athenaeum suit with mock solemnity. On the other hand, 'style' was not yet a dirty word, and he could fashion and be congratulated on such a sentence as 'Mr Goossens held the intricate threads at his delicate finger-tips and they never got tangled.'

There are several more pieces of this kind where he tries his voice out and eventually manages to place it with his own natural tone finding its proper resonance. The first time he really catches the reader's ear is in 1924 with an article headed 'A Great Isolde'. He begins by remarking on the strange experience of hearing in the same week two performances of *Tristan und Isolde*, 'one of which was as high above the standard of a good performance as the other was below it'. The bad one was conducted by Karl Alwin, the good by Bruno Walter, then in his first post-war season at Covent Garden. The name of the Isolde was Frida Leider, and it had aroused no expectation as she was a newcomer and her arrival had not been prepared by the customary 'puff-paragraphs' in the press. The evening, said Hussey, 'was a magic spell woven by the hands of the Isolde about the rapture of her face and the loveliness of her voice':

> Her beauty is of an unusual type, with something in it of the primitive that absolutely accords with the part of Isolde, though it emphasised the grosser make of her fellows. Her voice is pure in quality, and she uses it, as only great singers can, like an instrument for the registration of every subtle implication in the words and music ... But it was her use of gesture, in perfect combination with the voice, which made this Isolde a great tragic figure on the heroic scale and yet never allowed us to forget her humanity. Her grace of movement is extraordinary and, since I never saw Duse, quite unparalleled in my experience even of the drama proper. In the scene with her scarf at the beginning of Act II she gave us always beautiful rhythms flowing in a marvellous cross-current to the music ... How different was this swaying figure from the morse-code signallings of other Isoldes one has seen ... Her face was the continual interpreter of the innermost emotions ... And her hands – how shall I describe their exquisite eloquence? They too expressed every emotion. When Isolde was beaten in spirit they hung limp and dejected; at her decision the wrist becomes, of a sudden, steel.

The article (*Saturday Review*, 17 May 1924) deserves to be reprinted in full for it is, to my mind, one of the best pieces of reporting on the immediate impact of a great performance. Hussey faces head-on Percy Scholes's criticism that Leider was a 'tremolist' and her voice 'harsh':

> Where I was sitting her voice sounded sweet and round, except when dramatic expression demanded a hard tone, as in her commands to Brangaene; and there was never, to my ear, a tremolo in the ordinary, bad sense of the word. Sometimes the notes thrilled with emotion; but it was done purposely, just as Gerhardt will set her tone quivering upon one important word in a song.

He captures some of her gestures in the *Liebestod*, almost as though filming them, and finally he returns to her hands:

> Those hands will not be forgotten by us who were fortunate enough to behold them, and they will be known to incredulous grandchildren who shall watch, with what patience they may, their dim reflections in the tremulous mirror of an old man's eloquence.

No, we would not write quite like that today; and today it would be even harder to conceive of grandchildren who would ('shall'!) watch or pay the slightest attention to Gramps when he claws the air and maunders on about some old bat he saw singing somewhere half a century ago. Still, the man was moved; and in a sense he does speak to the grandchildren of 1924, for his article, re-read now in the present time, is anything but a '*dim* reflection' of this Isolde's greatness. Partly attested by gramophone records, her greatness has needed precisely this kind of immediate verbal response to bring it before us in the mind's eye and ear.

Hussey was also particularly good on two other great artists who appeared in London in those years – Chaliapin and Martinelli. He saw Chaliapin first in his time of unspoilt greatness just before the First World War, and writing an obituary appreciation in the *Spectator* (22 April 1938) he recalled his appearances in *Prince Igor* and *Ivan the Terrible*:

> Despite his stature, despite certain gestures, which had not then developed into mannerisms, Chaliapin was unrecognizable as Chaliapin on stage. Galitzky and the Khan were two different persons, not one actor playing two parts. Each was a creation rather than an interpretation ... It was not make-up alone – the sharp features, built up on a naturally round face, the crossed braces that reduced his girth and the stooping attitude – that transformed the stalwart Chaliapin into the shrunken Ivan. By some power of mesmerism he made us imagine the whole body shrivelled up into the semblance of an old man, to whom only the piercing flash of the eyes gave an aspect of power, ruthless in its cruelty.

Hussey then asks how it was that in later years, 'though he never lost the power to move', he dwindled into 'the male equivalent of a spoilt prima donna'. He himself had chronicled, for the *Saturday Review*, two of Chaliapin's appearances which made him write that sentence in 1938. In *Faust* (1928) Chaliapin's acting was 'no more than posturing', and even in *Boris Godunov* (1929), though a kind of greatness remained, 'his methods belong to a school of acting which passed away in this country when Sir Herbert Tree died'. Vocally he was 'but the ghost of his former self', with effects 'purchased at the too high price of faulty intonation and bad rhythm'. The reason for the buffooneries and other excesses was, in Hussey's view, the fact that Chaliapin had returned to London not with a company but as 'a star'. Without a disciplined team about him, he vented momentary exasperations with the simple energy that under better conditions animated the genuine, and then incomparable, creation of character. Hussey concluded:

> We may forget these unhappy ebullitions now and remember only that he was the greatest of operatic singers in our time, whose example has more than any other man's changed for the better the whole idea of good operatic performance.

Giovanni Martinelli was another singer remembered from pre-war times. After his return in 1919, at the height of his power as a singer, he remained absent from Covent Garden for 18 years, reappearing in the Coronation season of 1937. The impressive concept of 'an Otello of great nervous and intellectual energy' was weakened, as Hussey and others reported on the first night, by the need for more 'sheer power of voice and physique'. At times the tone sounded 'curiously dry and unsympathetic', yet he could 'ravish the ear with the beauty' of certain phrases. In 'Niun mi tema' he was intensely moving, yet 'the terrible irony, the ice in the tone that should make the blood run cold' was missing in Act III. 'An able performance, and beautifully sung', Hussey concluded: a verdict respectful rather than enthusiastic.

It was later in the season that Martinelli's distinction became evident to him, and then overwhelmingly so:

> If some recent criticisms of mine upon singing have seemed to some to be unduly severe, let them go to Covent Garden on an evening when Signor Martinelli is singing, preferably in *Aida* or *Tosca*. They will then hear a singer who is worthy of the great traditions of his country. Signor Martinelli is no longer a young man, and it is regrettable that it is entirely on the older generation of singers that we must rely for a real command of their art. If, therefore, you wish to know how Verdi and Puccini should be sung, and to experience the thrill – one of the greatest that music can give

you, for all that it is a physical rather than an intellectual excitement – of hearing a fine voice under perfect control poured forth with open-throated generosity, my advice is 'Carpete diem' and gather your roses before the petals fall ... It is many years since we have heard 'Celeste Aida' phrased as Signor Martinelli phrases it ... And if it is *Tosca* you choose to hear, listen to that lovely liquid follow-through on the vowels in the last phrase of 'Recondita armonia'. Where most tenors nowadays take a breath and, however skilfully they do it, make a hole in the phrase, Signor Martinelli carries it on in a beautiful sweeping line that makes one jump in one's seat for joy. The worst of it is that this singer only makes nearly every one else sound foolish.

At this point Hussey must have recollected something, for he added: 'Miss Turner is an exception'!

Although his articles on singers have a special value (particularly to those of us who like to supplement the gramophone records of early singers with the reactions of people who heard them in their lifetime), Hussey's concern for opera was broadly based and urgently directed towards the problems of his time. In those years opera seemed to be fighting for its life; or not so much fighting as gasping, flapping about, never quite sure when its next breath would be drawn. In the *Weekend Review* of 14 May 1932, Hussey wrote a piece called 'Twilight of Covent Garden'. The 'grand' season had diminished to a four-week Wagner Festival, and even that had been achieved against the odds. It opened with 'the most exhilarating performance of *Die Meistersinger* I have ever heard'. Beecham obtained from his players such a miracle of clarity, flexibility and subtlety that could only have resulted from extremely thorough preparation and exceptional alertness throughout. Lehmann, Schorr and Fritz Wolff in the leading roles, Gladys Parr ('she looked as if she had stepped out of a picture by Cranach and gave real character to the part') was the Magdalene and Richard Watson an excellent Kothner, both representing native talent. But the tragedy was that it could lead nowhere:

> It is like the bursting into leaf of a fallen tree, that lives a little while upon the stored-up sap of a century. Covent Garden is to all intents and purposes dead. Next season, or the one after, that beautiful auditorium, as fine as anything in the world for sound and for the display of fashion, will belong to history.

Hard for us to realise, but at that time there seemed 'no hope of saving it from demolition'. The 1933 season ended with a certainty that this must be the end. We can easily enough share Hussey's feeling that 'it was impossible to leave the theatre without a lingering and sorrowful glance round the auditorium, that the beauty of its symmetry incomparable alike to eye and ear might be indelibly impressed upon the memory'.

Yet again the place was saved. In fact it was renovated, with the installation of a modern lighting system, and 'it is even rumoured that lighting rehearsals have been held'. Hussey rejoiced, more warmly and frankly than most of his fellows among the critics. But what he also saw, as clearly as any of them, was that all the renovations and technical improvements that the twentieth century could provide would not of themselves make an opera house 'modern'.

The notion that opera houses were now museums took uncomfortably definite shape in his mind. The 1934 season at Covent Garden boasted innovations in repertory as well as stagecraft: for one thing, *Arabella* was to be heard for the first time. And the other new item? Not *Wozzeck* or *Cardillac*, not *Neues vom Tage* or even *Jonny spielt auf*, but *Schwanda the Bagpiper*. Hussey mentioned all these operas in his article of May 18, and was doubtful whether any of them, including *Schwanda*, would hold their place in the repertory. *Schwanda*, he noted, 'mightily pleased an audience which had with difficulty concealed its boredom with the majesty of *Fidelio*'. He thought it 'a pretentious hotch-potch of incongruous styles'. But: 'The truth is that "grand" opera is no longer being written except by composers who are still living in the past.' *Schwanda* was 'a typical instance of an attempt to put back the clock' and:

> The moral of its production here is that Covent Garden should stick to its last and, being the museum it is, set before us the masterpieces, great and little, of the past, until and unless 'grand' opera becomes once more a living force.

The modern trend and its deadly effects he saw typified in a new opera put on the previous month at Sadler's Wells. This was Lawrance Collingwood's *Macbeth*: the text set 'to a uniform declamation' with 'the whole musical interest' concentrated in the orchestra. 'The main musical interest', said Hussey, laying down the law for once, 'should lie in the vocal parts, and there is no great opera in which this condition is not fulfilled'. The composer, he thought, had not 'realised' that Shakespearean soliloquies 'are the exact equivalent of aria in opera'. However debatable that proposition, Hussey had indentified the characteristics which right up to our own time have alienated audiences from modern operas.

He nevertheless saw this *Macbeth* as 'a welcome addition to the meagre repertory of English operas at Sadler's Wells'. English opera had always been of interest to him, and his appreciative comments on Covent

Garden's première of *The Perfect Fool* in 1922 were matched in 1934 by his admiration of the production, at the Royal College of Music, of *A Village Romeo and Juliet*: 'student performances have done more for English opera than all the full-blown professionals put together'. Somewhere here, in the intimacy of a smaller house, a genuinely modern opera might flourish. The imaginative production, with its unusual visual beauty, had moved him. So too, in these later years, did the excellence of company-work that was to be found at Sadler's Wells: here, if anywhere, was the growth-point for opera. This part of Hussey's operatic criticism, in fact, pointed forward unerringly. His care for English opera and his appreciation of Sadler's Wells now take shape, almost in the image of an ear listening in the void for what was to burst upon the theatre in Rosebery Avenue, and then upon the world, on 7 June 1945. A sad irony, therefore, that the composer of *Peter Grimes* should have been the one to pronounce his opinion worthless, his ear withered.

25. Neville Cardus of the *Manchester Guardian*

✍ Opera on trial ✍

And perhaps it will be as well for the season's good health if no further talk is heard about the 'duty' of the English people to support opera. Who was ever known to go to the theatre for reasons of national conscience in matters of art? There is only one case for opera, and that is the case an average Viennese would put in enthusiastic terms: it is a pleasure. Simply that and nothing more. The nation will not descend to the dogs musically if opera does not take root here; all that will happen is that our theatre will lose a most delightful form of entertainment. And there, in a nutshell, is the argument for opera.

Breezy common sense, a breath of fresh air for readers of the *Manchester Guardian* on 1 March 1928. Joyless Cant shaken out of the front door like a frowsty old mat that has been down gathering dust all winter, and Unaffected Pleasure welcomed as a guest for the season, which was to be that of the British National Opera Company in Manchester for the next three weeks.

The column was initialled 'N.C.', where in early years it would have been 'S.L.'. Samuel Langford had been the City's chief music critic for over twenty years, an institution almost, and when he died in May 1927 there must have been some who shook their heads over the succession to the post of the 38-year-old Neville Cardus. Langford, after all, had studied with Reinecke at Leipzig; Cardus had come up by way of the *Daily Citizen*. He also wrote on cricket, and the English are great believers in the proposition that if an expert in one field is discovered to be expert in another as well, his expertise is thereupon automatically halved. On the other hand, they had read him for a good many years now and (even the head-shakers would have to reflect) he was eminently readable. You might object to his 'nutshells', his 'simply that and nothing more', but you would have been presented with a thinking-point, a talking-point too, and there was something of the talking-voice in Cardus's style, so that a reader found himself personally engaged, spoken to by a fellow human-being and impelled to respond.

270

The paragraph about opera as duty and opera as pleasure is typical. It was also timely, for opera was in a state of financial crisis (then as ever), with the BNOC itself under threat. Cardus knew that opera was now on trial, and that if it was to survive it must be because people enjoy it. He also saw that on the whole people enjoy things when they see enjoyment around them and that the appeals in the national press to 'save opera' were largely, as modern jargon has it, counter-productive. The greater the emphasis given to Victorian values such as 'duty', the more likely the children of the twentieth century would be to seek their pleasures elsewhere.

A few days before the opera season opened, Beecham conducted the London Symphony Orchestra in an operatic concert, at the end of which he told Manchester that it was 'sheer rot' that opera was obsolete. The conductor's habitual gusto was matched by the critic's. Even so, and for all his insistence on enjoyment, Cardus criticised strenuously, so that when the BNOC arrived and opened their season with *The Marriage of Figaro* he reacted with indignation against the cheapening of the proper pleasures and the coarsening of style which marred the performance. The opera was given with spoken dialogue, and Cardus agreed there was much to be said for that:

> but there is no case at all for admitting into Mozart's exquisite world the flavour of our twentieth-century music-hall; to hear Figaro speaking about 'promiscuous osculation' is to have one's teeth set on edge. This language comes nearer to George Robey than to Mozart and Beaumarchais – *Figaro* should be brought only so close to life for the shadow of mortality to fall on it, as it does, most poignantly, when the Countess sings at the beginning of Act II.

Mozart reappeared that season in *The Magic Flute*, where decorum was better kept on stage than in the auditorium, the clatter of matinee tea-cups accompanying the solemnities of the Temple music.

For the second of the great operatic comedies that season, *The Mastersingers of Nuremberg*, Cardus prepared his readers with a long essay, its thread again being the richness of the work as entertainment: 'It provokes the sense of natural amplitude, of a laughter broad as ten thousand beeves at pasture' (he loved his similes). In the event the beeves were decimated: 'For want of a full orchestra last night's performance was unable to do more than suggest the greatness of the work.' Barbirolli conducted, and in Cardus's view he and his players were able in the end to achieve an illusion of 'the superb girth of the music'. But the effect was of an 'occasional' drama, whereas its true nature was 'epic with an untroubled gait and the largest magnanimity'. Among the artists, Robert Radford, then very near the end of his long

62. Arthur Fear as Sachs in *Die Meistersinger*

career, 'carried himself in the way of an ancient greatness' as Pogner. Walter Widdop's Walther 'lacked customary fullness' and ' "You ended in another key" came perilously near to being true.' Cardus's interest, however, centred on the new Sachs, Arthur Fear:

Hans Sachs cannot, it need hardly be said, be portrayed by a young man. All the fine singing in the world will not carry us to the heart of the wise, kindly philosophy of Sachs; a lifetime of culture is needed as well. But Mr Fear's performance was good enough to tempt us to this prophecy; in a few years, given ordinary fortune, Mr Fear will make the part his own, as far as English singers go. Already his voice has rich nature in it; he uses it with dignity, and has so true a resonance that he can place all of Sachs's argumentation somewhere near the world of genial music. If breadth comes and goes in his art at the moment he need not trouble; years and experience will bring him mastery over a continuous style. His singing of the two monologues was very promising indeed; clearly his mind was seeing the significance of every subtle transition. We felt this particularly in the 'Wahn! Wahn!' when the monologue goes to its end through marvellous changes of key and achieves one of the noblest crescendos in all music at the words 'und nie ohn' ein'gen Wahn gelingen'. Mr Fear's

272

voice did not quite fill out this giant passage, but the spirit, the sense of style was there. His stage action is not yet capacious, but that too will come. The beauty of his voice at times was remarkable; we must all watch this young artist's future with interest, and see that he gets the proper encouragement.

Though Arthur Fear went on to sing at Covent Garden the following season and continued to have a successful career during the 1930s, he did not entirely fulfil the promise that Cardus saw in him. Gramophone records show how fine the vocal material was, and in modern times an international career might well begin to open up for a British singer who made that sort of impression and was so reported by an influential critic. To right the balance, however, it is probably also true that nowadays a singer is lucky to be given a sentence in a newspaper review; rare indeed to find as full and considered an account as this.

The season advanced with a good standard repertory and with singers whose names are still remembered in Britain today. A matinee of *The Barber of Seville* with Noël Eadie, Heddle Nash and Dennis Noble was followed in the evening by a *Carmen* where Widdop's Don José was described as well sung but stiffly acted, where Arthur Fear again displayed 'true resonance', and where Elsie Boardman presented 'a Carmen of refinement'. Cardus left his deputy to attend the *Bohème* (Noël Eadie and Francis Russell in the leading roles), while he wrote an introductory essay to *Manon* and after the performance gave an enthusiastic account of the Des Grieux of Heddle Nash, coupled with a kindly worded admonition:

> So youthful and pleasant is his voice that it is often very difficult to realise that he really is a tenor. It would be good to feel that he is ready to trust a natural resonance; he certainly has no need for an artificial vowel in order to get a full, forward tone.

As for the opera itself, which in performance must be 'sentimental without grossness', he felt that it was tainted by associations for which Massenet himself could hardly be held responsible: 'Many a Hollywood arrangement in high passion and moonshine has faded away to the strains of *Manon*. Massenet's feline tunes purr away in the kinema palaces of Little Puddleton and the City of London alike.' Cardus and his readers might have been chary of prophesying that *Manon* would still be purring after the kinemas of Little Puddleton had closed down and Hollywood itself faded away, but it was probably necessary for some such decontamination to take place before the Massenet revival that we have witnessed in recent years could have been as successful as it has.

273

63. Frank Mullings as
Canio in *Pagliacci*

In fact, for all his freshness of expression and sturdy independence of judgment, Cardus's tastes coincided fairly closely with the establishment view of opera at the time: that is, that a musician's world of opera was filled largely by Mozart and Wagner, with the late Verdi and some isolated pieces from various national schools (*The Golden Cockerel* was an example in this season's repertory), the Italian by no means predominating. Puccini was not greatly to his liking. He took himself to the Saturday matinee of *Madam Butterfly* under Barbirolli and heard what he considered to be the best orchestral playing of the week. He remarked how in earlier years Rosina Buckman had managed 'to make Butterfly poignant in a genuinely pathetic way' whereas Noël Eadie was 'a little too cosy'. He also reflected that 'had *Butterfly* ended with the sad, helpless watch at night through the window – then we could have enjoyed it without apologies as a little masterpiece in toy pathos. The second part of Act II exploits the melodramatic coarseness of the worst sort of so-called realistic Italian opera.' The second week brought *Gianni Schicchi*, and this, he admitted, was a different matter altogether, an Italian operatic comedy second only to *Falstaff*. Yet even in praising this he underlined his antipathy to Puccini in general:

> *Gianni* atones for many of Puccini's excesses in other and more 'successful' works. The little comedy contains more invention than nearly all the familiar stuffs of Puccini put together.

It was coupled, in this performance, with *Pagliacci*, of which he did not need to spell out his low opinion. The opera was redeemed, in his view, only by the exceptional performance of Frank Mullings as Canio:

> Mr Mullings acted Canio in *Pagliacci* far beyond the plane of conventional Italian opera of the blood and sand order. His singing is not exactly all honey, but how intensely he lives in the part! He almost persuades us that there is real tragedy about – that if the puppet Canio were pricked blood and not sawdust would come forth.

It was such operas as *Pagliacci* that Cardus would have had in mind as an example of the second-rate when at the end of the three-week season he wrote an article in defence of opera against those who considered it an inferior art form or just plain stupid: 'Opera is stupid just as a fugue is stupid whenever it is exploited by a second-rate mind.' For its cultivation by a first-rate mind he constantly returned, despite bouts of reluctance and irreverence, to Wagner. Luckily, the BNOC also did much of its best work in Wagner, and in productions such as their *Valkyrie* and *Parsifal* Cardus was as warm a critic as any company could wish to have. The *Parsifal* on the last Friday night was 'one of the finest the company have given us in this city. With a cast ... which was perhaps the strongest this country is able to provide, last night's performance had distinction at every point'. Cardus admired Walter Hyde's 'elegant simplicity, directing all his expression to ends which are constantly poetic'. He found the Kundry of Gladys Ancrum 'one of the most remarkable pieces of work in the annals of operas as we count and remember them in England'. As for the Gurnemanz: 'If some of the German singers were able to capture the secret of Mr Allin's benignity, there would be fewer complaints about insomnia at Bayreuth.' Earlier in the week, *The Twilight of the Gods* had drawn 'loud cheers for a plucky attempt', and Cardus reverted to his point about the necessity for a large orchestra to do justice to Wagner's musical world:

This world lives, moves and has its being in Wagner's orchestra, which broods over *The Ring's* narrative like fate itself, foreseeing all, the end in the beginning and the beginning in the end. You cannot have Wagner without his full orchestra: you might as well try to fill the canvas of a late Turner with water colour as try to fill the canvas of *The Twilight of the Gods* with an orchestra of moderate size.

In the long column that followed there is one other feature that deserves mention: a complimentary remark is made about the staging, and a producer is actually named – George King.

Perhaps the warmest of all Cardus's reviews that season was written on the performance of *The Valkyrie* in the second week. It began with a reference to a speech made to the audience by Frederic Austin, hinting that the BNOC was 'likely to perish' unless Beecham's scheme for an Imperial League of Opera met with support. Cardus comments:

> Well, the performance of *The Valkyrie* was the best of all possible appeals – a more convincing argument in favour of the Beecham scheme than all the words, words, words in the language. As the evening rose to its climax, we thought: if our artists can do so much as this in the face of hardship, what might they not achieve given encouragement and the proper means?

He had interesting things to say about the singers, including Horace Stevens's Wotan – 'a patriarchal Wotan, … Elijah-ish … nonetheless a noble piece of work' and about the conductor, the young Leslie Heward; and he ended with a heartfelt tribute to the company, making his prose resound with an almost Churchillian sense of history, and donning his cricketer's cap for the occasion:

> Whatever the fate of the scheme, the work of the BNOC must never be forgotten. They have toiled in the face of odds, batted splendidly on a bad wicket. We should be less than sportsmen if we did not applaud their energies and – whatever else happens to opera in this land – do our utmost to keep the company going in a decent prosperity.

In a final article, when the little season was over, he concluded: 'Opera is now on trial … In the Imperial League of Opera rests our hope – and our last chance.' It was a somewhat forlorn hope, and the BNOC, though it returned to Manchester for a one-week season the following year, was also doomed. Happily, Cardus, right about so much, was unduly pessimistic about the last chance.

✺ The wisest man ✺

Opera was not his first love; nor his second, nor yet his third. 'A most

64. Wilhelm Furtwängler

delightful form of entertainment', he called it, a pleasure from which the dreary advocacy of Duty should be resolutely driven. But he nevertheless availed himself of the pleasure somewhat sparingly. When the British National Opera Company visited Manchester, he would attend a good number of performances; in 1928 we saw him present at most of them, and when he went he found plenty to say. In other seasons, and with the visits of the Carl Rosa Company, he would often leave much to his colleagues; and he does not seem to have been in any hurry to assert proprietory rights over the Grand Opera seasons in London. He could be an impressively prolific journalist, but (it seems) by fits and starts. In the last week of the BNOC at Manchester in 1928 he wrote an article of over a thousand words on the company's achievements and another on *Parsifal*; there was a 700-word review of

277

The Twilight of the Gods, with 600 on *The Magic Flute*; also a Hallé concert taking up a column of about 900, after an introductory article on the programme (some 700); and he even found time for a substantial appreciation of a violin recital which filled up a spare afternoon. That was a busy week by anyone's standards. Yet over many long stretches the initials 'N.C.' prove elusive, and the opera reviews are by 'E.B.' or 'W.L.' in London, 'G.A.H.' in Manchester.

Wagner undoubtedly interested him most, though his whole being, mental and physical, sometimes cried out in protest. He took himself off to Covent Garden in 1938 for some of Furtwängler's *Ring*:

> Dr Furtwängler's sense of detail and balance of periods lessen the rhythmic drive of the orchestra. As a consequence, we feel, more than we ought to feel, the mechanism of Wagner's sequential bridge-passages. Also the motifs are introduced almost with a bow – and we are reminded of Debussy's taunt about the visiting card ... Last night I felt once or twice an impulse to rise in my seat and protest at the eternal recurrence of the 'leading' themes. The Wagnerian method of transformation of motif occasionally recalls the quick-change artists of the old music-halls – out at one door in whiskers and in at the next door with a Tarnhelm instead of a hat.

Lively writing, but not, some might object, that of a critic with his mind on the job. Is it possible to be responsive to Wagner and yet talk about whiskers and music-halls, or (in Furtwängler's *Rheingold*) of the goings and comings of leitmotifs 'as routine as the arrivals and departures in a railway guide'? Cardus would no doubt have been ready with an answer – which might have been that it was no use expecting pious gravity from a critic who at an impressionable age had sat next to Samuel Langford and heard him whisper in the Grail Scene: 'Amfortas is the wisest man here tonight; he's brought his bed with him.'

The paradox of Wagner nights was one of his own leitmotifs. Sometimes it seemed a kind of insanity, this gluttony for punishment, this voluntary, self-inflicted committal to five hours detention. In 1936 he observed the audience taking their places for *Parsifal* at the ungodly hour of 5.45.

> We all knew we were imprisoned there for hours, with only short moments of respite. At the first interval the multitude came out of the anaesthetic and escaped to the streets to get another reassuring glimpse of the normal universe. We uttered our protests against this unreasonable tyranny of Wagner, this inordinate length and prolixity. 'It is preposterous,' we told ourselves, 'and heavily Germanic, utterly lacking in poise and taste.'

But we all went back to our seats well in time for the other acts; we had no choice; our resentment grew as the music's monotony, its timeless ebb and flow, numbed personal sense and identity in us. 'Never again,' said a noble lord at the fall of the last curtain; 'it is too much.' He has been saying the same thing for many years, and will probably die saying it.

And so it was: critics and noble lords may protest, 'but the old rattlesnake casts its spell'.

Cardus could be wonderfully alert and perceptive when under the spell. His reviews often had as much to say about the opera as about the particular performance, but the thoughts arose out of the performance; he never reads like a critic who has his piece written beforehand with a space or two left for the adjectives. Genial and generous as his writing normally was, he does not strike one as an easy man for singers or conductors to satisfy, especially in Wagner. Beecham would annoy him because 'he seems to enjoy *The Ring* almost wholly from the orchestra's point of view; the vocalists must fit their syllables into his rhythmical conception'. Furtwängler's care for the singers and his understanding of the texts contrasted with this, but he 'risked a miniature effect'. Flagstad's debut brought joy to the ears: 'But Flagstad is not yet a great Isolde; her voice has the fixed, almost abstract quality of a musical instrument; it seems unable to take on the colour of the singer's mind or temperament.' Rudolf Bockelmann, too, he conceded, was 'a fine vocalist', but: 'I have never found satisfaction in his Wotan. He lacks philosophy, and as the Wanderer his worries were, I thought, physical rather than metaphysical.' Even Herbert Janssen leaves a partial dissatisfaction: his Amfortas was 'like everything this great artist attempts, poetically conceived, but his voice is notably kindly and humane; it cannot easily pierce us with the spear of Amfortas's pain'.

Singing ('pure' singing) came second, with Cardus, to insight and feeling, yet he cared for it too. In the same review where Bockelmann's Wotan is found wanting, Melchior is criticised for unwillingness to sing legato ('he must needs emphasise two or three words in each of his sentences'). By contrast, the Alberich and Mime of that performance gave him exceptional pleasure precisely because they showed themselves to be good singers: 'at any moment he [Erich Zimmermann as Mime] could have sung Siegfried to sleep with a cradle song by Brahms', and the Alberich, Adolf Vogel, 'probably sang Elijah in the Nibelheim Three Choirs Festival. It was a joy to hear at the beginning of Act II an Alberich who did not bark like a dog.'

After this, one might fear for the English companies who undertook the Wagner operas, but Cardus respected their hard work, their pluck and, to some extent, their success. The BNOC opened their 1929 season at Manchester with *Parsifal*, an unfortunate choice, he thought, yet 'a feat demanding … the valiant heart that has made the British Empire what it is!' Carl Rosa's *Siegfried* in the same year 'had a vaulting ambition which roused one's sporting interests'. The following year came *Rheingold*, and: 'It was astonishing that Mr Arthur Hammond, the conductor, was able to produce from his forces a tone that was in the slightest Wagnerian in sonority … The wonder was that the music-drama was given at all in conditions which would have set the heart of a Karl Muck quaking.'

Of the singers he wrote with mixed sympathy, admiration and irritability. On the whole, it was the 'inner truth' of an operatic role that he wanted the singer to make for. The soprano Rachel Morton seemed to him a case in point, where a voice of outstanding beauty failed to give full satisfaction, because what she provided was 'vocalism in the abstract,

65. Frank Mullings as Otello

wanting the breath of the living word'. Her Kundry was 'in a vocal sense often more beautiful than any yet heard in Manchester', but 'it is not a voice that feeds on the music ravenously and mocks its own appetite by a disregard of conventional vocal standards'. As Isolde she was 'too intent on voice production', whereas:

> The singer who would go through Isolde's music triumphantly must plunge into it like a brave swimmer into an endless sea. When she is here and there submerged – as she is bound to be – by a noble breaking of an orchestral wave, we must feel she is rejoicing in the passionate storm. And we must feel, when the wave has died down, that she is still swimming, ploughing onward heart and soul.

Rachel Morton's 'abstract vocalism' contrasted with the more imaginative commitment of Gladys Ancrum, whose Kundry had 'extraordinary instinct and power; in the garden scene she sang like one possessed, and fastened on to every significance in her music ravenously, dangerously'. In Cardus's book, 'the finest singing lives on the word, not on the vowel'.

When he turned from Wagner to Italian opera he was prepared to face reality and relax his standards. Of course he made an exception for *Otello* (though the Oath Duet seemed to him a 'banal piece of rhetoric'), and particularly when the name-part was sung by Frank Mullings:

> The evening was touched to greatness by Mr Mullings. He is at liberty to sing badly, to ask us to accept a succession of attitudes as acting. By sheer power of a sincere conception he moved us. At times his soft singing was beautiful; at others he ranted us out of all music, declaimed and shouted. He even committed the questionable act of going behind art to the crude emotional stuff. But he silenced every scruple as he built up in his own way a great figure of a fine, simple mind suffering dethronement.

Falstaff he thought three times worth *Otello* ('comedy is much more precious than tragedy, and much harder to achieve'). It was the Glyndebourne *Macbeth* of 1938 which persuaded him that the early Verdi could sometimes deviate into sense. He recalled seeing the opera in Vienna some years previously, and finding it 'crude, foolish, tawdry'.

> Glyndebourne transformed the work beyond belief. I have never seen anywhere a much better piece of all-round opera production than this, a production in which all the elements of opera were more easefully and imaginatively fused.

66. Sadler's Wells: *The Snow-Maiden*, 1933

He paid tribute to John Christie and Fritz Busch, the lighting, the work of the chorus, the intelligence of the soloists, concluding that: 'Salzburg seldom, if ever, did anything better than this, or more to the manner born'. He then hurried back to London for a Toscanini concert the next day.

Something of this all-round excellence – or if not excellence then at least reliability – was just coming, in those last years before the war, to be provided by Sadler's Wells. Nor was it such a far cry from Glyndebourne's outstanding *Macbeth* to the Wells's *Don Carlos* in the December of that year. The stage was not large enough, and the cast could not be headed by six great Verdi singers as they were not to be found, Cardus held, 'in England today' or in any other day. Nevertheless it was a production not to be missed, 'an astonishing piece of resourceful work on the part of the cast, the scene painters, the stage technicians and the orchestra'. Producer and designer were mentioned by name (rare), and the principals (Dusseau, Coates, Davies, Llewellyn, Stear) were praised for their respect for the company's sense of ensemble.

Three days before Christmas, Cardus 'fought through snow and slush', and then, as he says, 'found the theatre warm with the fantasy of Rimsky-Korsakov's little masterpiece'. This was *The Snow-Maiden*. He loved the work and admired the production:

282

The Sadler's Wells Company attend faithfully to the details, and the only thing lacking is the veil of poetry through which we should always see the action. But there is the happy accident which has endowed Miss Olive Dyer with the right diminutive pathos for Snegorochka; this is one of the most lovable pieces of work on the contemporary operatic stage.

In January there followed a *Valkyrie* (presented in English while 'to the bewilderment of our foreign visitors' Covent Garden was given over to pantomime). Again the Sadler's Wells Company could not provide everything, such as 'the full surge of Wagner's orchestra'. But there were advantages too:

> Seldom if ever have I heard so much of the dramatic text of the opera or been so much engrossed in the action. The scene between Wotan and Fricka was as interesting as a debate, simply because at Sadler's Wells an intimate whisper becomes a public statement. Hunding overwhelmed the tuba; Wotan strode through the fire-music unscathed as any Siegfried. At most Wagner performances we feel sorry for the singers; at this one it was the orchestra that had to work hard to save themselves from sinking and drowning, all hands.

He loved Joan Cross's Sieglinde, which 'survives comparison with more famous interpretations of the part given elsewhere'. This was not only so in her full-bodied singing but also in the naturalness of her acting. In fact all that side of the production met with Cardus's approval, except for an observation about Hunding's homecoming, such as old Langford might well have whispered to him long ago in Manchester: 'I have never seen a *Valkyrie* yet in which the poor old chap was given a decent meal when he came home late.'

British opera had indeed progressed a little since Cardus's apprentice days. He himself might have claimed some share in the achievement of securing recognition of the progress, for he gave it at least as much of his attention as the international seasons at Covent Garden. Recognition did not come readily either, for the notion that foreign goods are best, in opera if in nothing else, dies hard. Cardus was aware of this and deplored it, knowing no doubt that at times he had fallen into the way of it himself:

> It is the custom of criticism in London to discuss, consciously or unconsciously, the doings of Sadler's Wells from a patriotic angle; the artists are invariably praised in some such implied terms as 'This is as good as any Continental performance'. We feel at work the English inferiority complex in music whenever notices of opera at Sadler's Wells appear in the London papers. This attitude does less than justice to a

skilful band of singers, producers and musicians who themselves have set up standards which prompt criticism that can rise above 'loyal support'.

This wanted saying, and Cardus said it well. But then, so he did most things. Like Newman's, his criticism looked or pointed ahead. It saw, at Salzburg, at Glyndebourne, in the new Sadler's Wells and fitfully at Covent Garden, what opera could become: a team-art where music and drama were as one, where the beauty of 'pure' singing was fired by the power of 'the living word'. The critics who have been the subject of this short series of articles were men with a sense of humour, and they needed it. They could all be devastatingly sharp in their comments, for they wrote with style and relish and to a remarkable degree without fear or favour. If Newman was the most formidable, Cardus was the most human. And if Newman was the most clever man among them, perhaps Cardus was the wisest. Like Amfortas, he was quite capable of bringing his bed along with him; or at least of admitting that he sometimes felt like getting into it when Duty insisted he should be wakeful. But then, for him opera was not to be thought of as duty but as 'a most delightful entertainment'. In the last years of these decades he saw it beginning to develop, in practice and in England, into the kind of entertainment he had always wanted it to be. His words about the belittling effect of 'loyal support' of English opera were those of a wise man. Unhappily, they were written in the first week of 1939, when more than the future of English opera was at risk.

INDEX OF MUSIC

285

GENERAL INDEX

Dates (where known), voice-description and nationality are given against the names of singers only.